Computational Biology:
An Introduction

Computational Biology:
An Introduction

Edited by
Mitchell Spencer

www.larsen-keller.com

Computational Biology: An Introduction
Edited by Mitchell Spencer
ISBN: 978-1-63549-072-5 (Hardback)

© 2017 Larsen & Keller

☴ Larsen & Keller

Published by Larsen and Keller Education,
5 Penn Plaza,
19th Floor,
New York, NY 10001, USA

Cataloging-in-Publication Data

Computational biology : an introduction / edited by Mitchell Spencer.
   p. cm.
Includes bibliographical references and index.
ISBN 978-1-63549-072-5
1. Computational biology. 2. Biology--Data processing. 3. Bioinformatics.
I. Spencer, Mitchell.
QH324.2 .C66 2017
570.285--dc23

The publisher's policy is to use permanent paper from mills that operate a sustainable forestry policy. Furthermore, the publisher ensures that the text paper and cover boards used have met acceptable environmental accreditation standards.

Printed and bound in the United States of America.

For more information regarding Larsen and Keller Education and its products, please visit the publisher's website www.larsen-keller.com

Table of Contents

Preface

The study of various social, biological and behavioral systems using the techniques and theories of computational data analytics, mathematical modeling and other theoretical methods is called computational biology. Sometimes referred to as bioinformatics, the field allows for the storage and processing of biological data. The book unfolds the innovative aspects of computational biology, which will be crucial for the holistic understanding of the subject matter. It outlines the processes and applications of the field in detail. Most of the topics introduced in it cover new techniques and the applications of the subject area. This textbook is a complete source of knowledge on the present status of this important field.

To facilitate a deeper understanding of the contents of this book a short introduction of every chapter is written below:

Chapter 1- Computational biology includes modern technology and methods of study of biology. It includes subjects such as applied mathematics, animation, molecular biology and anatomy. This chapter will provide an integrated understanding of computational biology.

Chapter 2- The key concepts explained in this text are bifurcation theory, biological applications of bifurcation theory, hidden Markov model, flux balance analysis, gene prediction etc. The section strategically encompasses and incorporates the major components and key concepts of computation biology, providing a complete understanding.

Chapter 3- Modelling biological system is an important part of computational biology. It helps in the development of algorithms and data structures. Some of the aspects of modelling biological systems explained are protein structure prediction, simulated growth of plants and epidemic model. This text is an overview of the subject matter incorporating all the major aspects of modelling biological systems.

Chapter 4- The topics that have been discussed in this chapter are metabolic network modelling, multi-compartment model, Wagner's gene network model and Morris-Lecar model. Metabolic network reconstruction and stimulation is used as an understanding of molecular mechanisms of any organism whereas multi-compartment model is used in explaining materials that are conveyed among the sections of a system. This section elucidates the crucial theories of mathematical modelling of biology system.

Chapter 5- The computational analysis used to understand biology from the genome sequences is termed as computational genomics. Genome project and Mycoplasma laboratorium are one of the significant and important topics related to computational genomics. The following chapter unfolds its crucial aspects in a critical yet systematic manner.

Chapter 6- Computational neuroscience is the study of brain functions; it links fields such as neuroscience, cognitive science and psychology. Topics such as neural coding, neural binding and neuroinformatics have elucidated in the following section and helps the readers in developing an in-depth understanding of computational neuroscience and its relation to computational biology.

Chapter 7- Bioinformatics helps in the development of methods and tools for a better understanding of biology and biological data. Some of the features broadly explained in the text are sequence analysis, sequence assembly, sequence alignment, BLAST, multiple sequence alignment etc. This chapter is a compilation of the various aspects of bioinformatics that form an integral part of the broader subject matter.

Chapter 8- Biological networks are networks that relate to biological systems. Biological networks offer mathematical illustrations that are found in ecological or physiological studies. The following section is an overview of the subject matter incorporating all the major characteristics of biological networks.

I would like to share the credit of this book with my editorial team who worked tirelessly on this book. I owe the completion of this book to the never-ending support of my family, who supported me throughout the project.

Editor

Introduction to Computational Biology

Computational biology includes modern technology and methods of study of biology. It includes subjects such as applied mathematics, animation, molecular biology and anatomy. This chapter will provide an integrated understanding of computational biology.

Computational Biology

Computational biology involves the development and application of data-analytical and theoretical methods, mathematical modeling and computational simulation techniques to the study of biological, behavioral, and social systems. The field is broadly defined and includes foundations in computer science, applied mathematics, animation, statistics, biochemistry, chemistry, biophysics, molecular biology, genetics, genomics, ecology, evolution, anatomy, neuroscience, and visualization.

Computational biology is different from biological computation, which is a subfield of computer science and computer engineering using bioengineering and biology to build computers, but is similar to bioinformatics, which is an interdisciplinary science using computers to store and process biological data.

Introduction

Computational Biology, sometimes referred to as bioinformatics, is the science of using biological data to develop algorithms and relations among various biological systems. Prior to the advent of computational biology, biologists were unable to have access to large amounts of data. Researchers were able to develop analytical methods for interpreting biological information, but were unable to share them quickly among colleagues.

Bioinformatics began to develop in the early 1970s. It was considered the science of analyzing informatics processes of various biological systems. At this time, research in artificial intelligence was using network models of the human brain in order to generate new algorithms. This use of biological data to develop other fields pushed biological researchers to revisit the idea of using computers to evaluate and compare large data sets. By 1982, information was being shared amongst researchers through the use of punch cards. The amount of data being shared began to grow exponentially by the end of the 1980s. This required the development of new computational methods in order to quickly analyze and interpret relevant information.

Since the late 1990s, computational biology has become an important part of developing emerging technologies for the field of biology. The terms computational biology and evolutionary computation have a similar name, but are not to be confused. Unlike computational biology, evolutionary computation is not concerned with modeling and analyzing biological data. It instead creates algorithms based on the ideas of evolution across species. Sometimes referred to as genetic algorithms, the research of this field can be applied to computational biology. While evolutionary computation is not inherently a part of computational biology, Computational evolutionary biology is a subfield of it.

Computational biology has been used to help sequence the human genome, create accurate models of the human brain, and assist in modeling biological systems.

Subfields

Computational Biomodeling

Computational biomodeling is a field concerned with building computer models of biological systems. Computational biomodeling aims to develop and use visual simulations in order to assess the complexity of biological systems. This is accomplished through the use of specialized algorithms, and visualization software. These models allow for prediction of how systems will react under different environments. This is useful for determining if a system is robust. A robust biological system is one that "maintain their state and functions against external and internal perturbations", which is essential for a biological system to survive. Computational biomodeling generates a large archive of such data, allowing for analysis from multiple users. While current techniques focus on small biological systems, researchers are working on approaches that will allow for larger networks to be analyzed and modeled. A majority of researchers believe that this will be essential in developing modern medical approaches to creating new drugs and gene therapy. A useful modelling approach is to use Petri nets via tools such as esyN

Computational Genomics (Computational Genetics)

Computational genomics is a field within genomics which studies the genomes of cells and organisms. It is often referred to as Computational and Statistical Genetics. The Human Genome Project is one example of computational genomics. This project looks to sequence the entire human genome into a set of data. Once fully implemented, this could allow for doctors to analyze the genome of an individual patient. This opens the possibility of personalized medicine, prescribing treatments based on an individual's pre-existing genetic patterns. This project has created many similar programs. Researchers are looking to sequence the genomes of animals, plants, bacteria, and all other types of life.

One of the main ways that genomes are compared is by homology. Homology is the study of biological structures and nucleotide sequences in different organisms that come from a common ancestor. Research suggests that between 80 and 90% of genes in newly sequenced prokaryotic genomes can be identified this way.

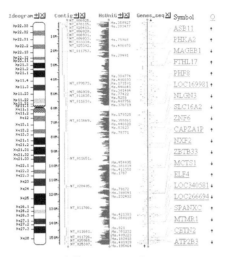

A partially sequenced genome.

This field is still in development. An untouched project in the development of computational genomics is the analysis of intergenic regions. Studies show that roughly 97% of the human genome consists of these regions. Researchers in computational genomics are working on understanding the functions of non-coding regions of the human genome through the development of computational and statistical methods and via large consortia projects such as ENCODE (The Encyclopedia of DNA Elements) and the Roadmap Epigenomics Project.

Computational Neuroscience

Computational neuroscience is the study of brain function in terms of the information processing properties of the structures that make up the nervous system. It is a subset of the field of neuroscience, and looks to analyze brain data to create practical applications. It looks to model the brain in order to examine specific types aspects of the neurological system. Various types of models of the brain include:

- Realistic Brain Models: These models look to represent every aspect of the brain, including as much detail at the cellular level as possible. Realistic models provide the most information about the brain, but also have the largest margin for error. More variables in a brain model create the possibility for more error to occur. These models do not account for parts of the cellular structure that scientists do not know about. Realistic brain models are the most computationally heavy and the most expensive to implement.

- Simplifying Brain Models: These models look to limit the scope of a model in order to assess a specific physical property of the neurological system. This allows for the intensive computational problems to be solved, and reduces the amount of potential error from a realistic brain model.

It is the work of computational neuroscientists to improve the algorithms and data structures currently used to increase the speed of such calculations.

Computational Pharmacology

Computational pharmacology (from a computational biology perspective) is "the study of the effects of genomic data to find links between specific genotypes and diseases and then screening drug data". The pharmaceutical industry requires a shift in methods to analyze drug data. Pharmacologists were able to use Microsoft Excel to compare chemical and genomic data related to the effectiveness of drugs. However, the industry has reached what is referred to as the Excel barricade. This arises from the limited number of cells accessible on a spreadsheet. This development led to the need for computational pharmacology. Scientists and researchers develop computational methods to analyze these massive data sets. This allows for an efficient comparison between the notable data points and allows for more accurate drugs to be developed.

Analysts project that if major medications fail due to patents, that computational biology will be necessary to replace current drugs on the market. Doctoral students in computational biology are being encouraged to pursue careers in industry rather than take Post-Doctoral positions. This is a direct result of major pharmaceutical companies needing more qualified analysts of the large data sets required for producing new drugs.

Computational Evolutionary Biology

Computational biology has assisted the field of evolutionary biology in many capacities. This includes:

- Using DNA data to reconstruct the tree of life with computational phylogenetics

- Fitting population genetics models (either forward time or backward time) to DNA data to make inferences about demographic or selective history

- Building population genetics models of evolutionary systems from first principles in order to predict what is likely to evolve.

Cancer Computational Biology

Cancer computational biology is a field that aims to determine the future mutations in cancer through an algorithmic approach to analyzing data. Research in this field has led to the use of high-throughput measurement. High throughput measurement allows for the gathering of millions of data points using robotics and other sensing devices. This data is collected from DNA, RNA, and other biological structures. Areas of focus include determining the characteristics of tumors, analyzing molecules that are deterministic in causing cancer, and understanding how the human genome relates to the causation of tumors and cancer.

Software and Tools

Computational Biologists use a wide range of software. These range from command line programs to graphical and web-based programs.

Open Source Software

Open source software provides a platform to develop computational biological methods. Specifically, open source means that anybody can access software developed in research. PLOS cites four main reasons for the use of open source software including:

- Reproducibility: This allows for researchers to use the exact methods used to calculate the relations between biological data.

- Faster Development: developers and researchers do not have to reinvent existing code for minor tasks. Instead they can use pre-existing programs to save time on the development and implementation of larger projects.

- Increased quality: Having input from multiple researchers studying the same topic provides a layer of assurance that errors will not be in the code.

- Long-term availability: Open source programs are not tied to any businesses or patents. This allows for them to be posted to multiple web pages and ensure that they are available in the future.

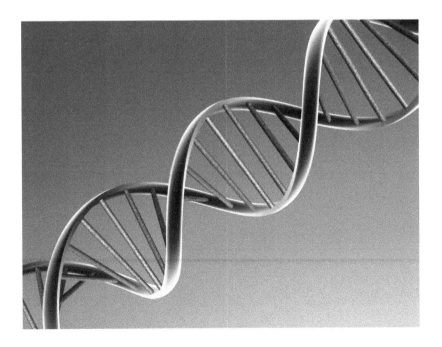

Related Fields

Computational biology, bioinformatics and mathematical biology are all interdisciplinary approaches to the life sciences that draw from quantitative disciplines such as mathematics and information science. The NIH describes computational/mathematical biology as the use of computational/mathematical approaches to address theoretical and experimental questions in biology and, by contrast, bioinformatics as the application of information science to understand complex life-sciences data.

Specifically, the NIH defines

Computational biology: The development and application of data-analytical and theoretical methods, mathematical modeling and computational simulation techniques to the study of biological, behavioral, and social systems.

Bioinformatics: Research, development, or application of computational tools and approaches for expanding the use of biological, medical, behavioral or health data, including those to acquire, store, organize, archive, analyze, or visualize such data.

While each field is distinct, there may be significant overlap at their interface.

Key Concepts of Computational Biology

The key concepts explained in this text are bifurcation theory, biological applications of bifurcation theory, hidden Markov model, flux balance analysis, gene prediction etc. The section strategically encompasses and incorporates the major components and key concepts of computation biology, providing a complete understanding.

Bifurcation Theory

Bifurcation theory is the mathematical study of changes in the qualitative or topological structure of a given family, such as the integral curves of a family of vector fields, and the solutions of a family of differential equations. Most commonly applied to the mathematical study of dynamical systems, a bifurcation occurs when a small smooth change made to the parameter values (the bifurcation parameters) of a system causes a sudden 'qualitative' or topological change in its behaviour. Bifurcations occur in both continuous systems (described by ODEs, DDEs or PDEs) and discrete systems (described by maps). The name "bifurcation" was first introduced by Henri Poincaré in 1885 in the first paper in mathematics showing such a behavior. Henri Poincaré also later named various types of stationary points and classified them.

Bifurcation Types

It is useful to divide bifurcations into two principal classes:

- Local bifurcations, which can be analysed entirely through changes in the local stability properties of equilibria, periodic orbits or other invariant sets as parameters cross through critical thresholds; and

- Global bifurcations, which often occur when larger invariant sets of the system 'collide' with each other, or with equilibria of the system. They cannot be detected purely by a stability analysis of the equilibria (fixed points).

Local Bifurcations

A local bifurcation occurs when a parameter change causes the stability of an equilibrium (or fixed point) to change. In continuous systems, this corresponds to the real part of an eigenvalue of an equilibrium passing through zero. In discrete systems (those described by maps rather than ODEs), this corresponds to a fixed point having a Floquet multiplier with modulus equal to one. In both cases, the equilibrium is *non-hyperbolic* at the bifurcation point. The topological changes in the phase portrait of the system can be confined to arbitrarily small neighbourhoods of the bifurcating fixed points by moving the bifurcation parameter close to the bifurcation point (hence 'local').

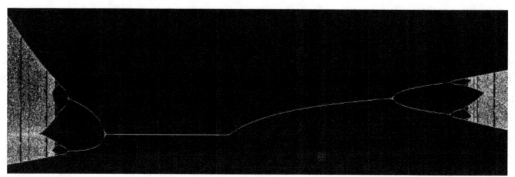

Period-halving bifurcations (L) leading to order, followed by period doubling bifurcations (R) leading to chaos.

More technically, consider the continuous dynamical system described by the ODE

$$\dot{x} = f(x,\lambda) \quad f : \mathbb{R}^n \times \mathbb{R} \to \mathbb{R}^n.$$

A local bifurcation occurs at (x_0, λ_0) if the Jacobian matrix df_{x_0, λ_0} has an eigenvalue with zero real part. If the eigenvalue is equal to zero, the bifurcation is a steady state bifurcation, but if the eigenvalue is non-zero but purely imaginary, this is a Hopf bifurcation.

For discrete dynamical systems, consider the system

$$x_{n+1} = f(x_n, \lambda).$$

Then a local bifurcation occurs at (x_0, λ_0) if the matrix df_{x_0, λ_0} has an eigenvalue with modulus equal to one. If the eigenvalue is equal to one, the bifurcation is either a saddle-node (often called fold bifurcation in maps), transcritical or pitchfork bifurcation. If the eigenvalue is equal to −1, it is a period-doubling (or flip) bifurcation, and otherwise, it is a Hopf bifurcation.

Examples of local bifurcations include:

- Saddle-node (fold) bifurcation

- Transcritical bifurcation

- Pitchfork bifurcation

- Period-doubling (flip) bifurcation

- Hopf bifurcation

- Neimark–Sacker (secondary Hopf) bifurcation

Global Bifurcations

Global bifurcations occur when 'larger' invariant sets, such as periodic orbits, collide with equilibria. This causes changes in the topology of the trajectories in the phase space which cannot be confined to a small neighbourhood, as is the case with local bifurcations. In fact, the changes in topology extend out to an arbitrarily large distance (hence 'global').

Examples of global bifurcations include:

- Homoclinic bifurcation in which a limit cycle collides with a saddle point.
- Heteroclinic bifurcation in which a limit cycle collides with two or more saddle points.
- Infinite-period bifurcation in which a stable node and saddle point simultaneously occur on a limit cycle.
- Blue sky catastrophe in which a limit cycle collides with a nonhyperbolic cycle.

Global bifurcations can also involve more complicated sets such as chaotic attractors (e.g. crises).

Codimension of a Bifurcation

The codimension of a bifurcation is the number of parameters which must be varied for the bifurcation to occur. This corresponds to the codimension of the parameter set for which the bifurcation occurs within the full space of parameters. Saddle-node bifurcations and Hopf bifurcations are the only generic local bifurcations which are really codimension-one (the others all having higher codimension). However, transcritical and pitchfork bifurcations are also often thought of as codimension-one, because the normal forms can be written with only one parameter.

An example of a well-studied codimension-two bifurcation is the Bogdanov–Takens bifurcation.

Applications in Semiclassical and Quantum Physics

Bifurcation theory has been applied to connect quantum systems to the dynamics of their classical analogues in atomic systems, molecular systems, and resonant tunneling diodes. Bifurcation theory has also been applied to the study of laser dynamics and a number of theoretical examples which are difficult to access experimentally such as the kicked top and coupled quantum wells. The dominant reason for the link between quantum systems and bifurcations in the classical equations of motion is that at bifurcations, the signature of classical orbits becomes large, as Martin Gutzwiller points out in his classic work on quantum chaos. Many kinds of bifurcations have been studied with regard to links between classical and quantum dynamics including saddle node bifurcations, Hopf bifurcations, umbilic bifurcations, period doubling bifurcations, re-connection bifurcations, tangent bifurcations, and cusp bifurcations.

Biological Applications of Bifurcation Theory

Biological applications of bifurcation theory provide a framework for understanding the behavior of biological networks modeled as dynamical systems. In the context of a biological system, bifurcation theory describes how small changes in an input parameter can cause a bifurcation or qualitative change in the behavior of the system. The ability to make dramatic change in system output is often essential to organism function, and bifurcations are therefore ubiquitous in biological networks such as the switches of the cell cycle.

Biological Networks and Dynamical Systems

Biological networks originate from evolution and therefore have less standardized components and potentially more complex interactions than many networks intentionally created by humans such as electrical networks. At the cellular level, components of a network can include a large variety of proteins, many of which differ between organisms. Network interactions occur when one or more proteins affect the function of another through transcription, translation, translocation, or phosphorylation. All these interactions either activate or inhibit the action of the target protein in some way. While humans build networks with some concern for efficiency and simplicity, biological networks are often adapted from others and exhibit redundancy and great complexity. Therefore, it is impossible to predict quantitative behavior of a biological network from knowledge of its organization. Similarly, it is impossible to describe its organization purely from its behavior, though behavior can indicate the presence of certain network motifs.

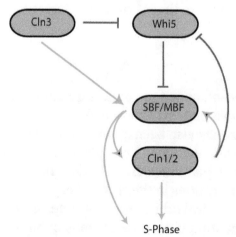

fig.1. Example of a biological network between genes and proteins that controls entry into S phase

However, with knowledge of network interactions and a set of parameters for the proteins and protein interactions (usually obtained through empirical research), it is often possible to construct a model of the network as a dynamical system. In general, for n proteins, the dynamical system takes the following form where x is typically protein concentration:

$$\dot{x}_1 = \frac{dx_1}{dt} = f_1(x_1, \ldots, x_n)$$

$$\dot{x}_i = \frac{dx_i}{dt} = f_i(x_1, \ldots, x_n)$$

$$\dot{x}_n = \frac{dx_n}{dt} = f_n(x_1, \ldots, x_n)$$

These systems are often very difficult to solve, so modeling of networks as a linear dynamical systems is easier. Linear systems contain no products between xs and are always solvable. They have the following form for all i:

$$f_i = a_{i1}x_1 + a_{i2}x_2 + \cdots + a_{in}x_n$$

Unfortunately, biological systems are often nonlinear and therefore need nonlinear models.

Input/Output Motifs

Despite the great potential complexity and diversity of biological networks, all first-order network behavior generalizes to one of four possible I/O motifs: hyperbolic or Michaelis–Menten, ultra-sensitive, bistable, and bistable irreversible (a bistability where negative and therefore biologically impossible input is needed to return from a state of high output).

Ultrasensitive, bistable, and irreversibly bistable networks all show qualitative change in network behavior around certain parameter values – these are their bifurcation points.

Bifurcations

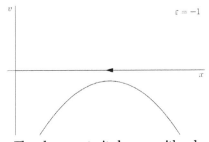

fig. 2. Saddle node bifurcation – The phase portrait changes with values of ε. As ε decreases, the fixed points come together and annihilate one another; As ε increases, the fixed points appear. dx/dt is denoted as v.

Nonlinear dynamical systems can be most easily understood with a one-dimensional example system where the change in some measurement of protein x's abundance depends only on itself:

$$\dot{x} = \frac{dx}{dt} = f(x)$$

Instead of solving the system analytically which can be difficult for many functions, it is often best to take a geometric approach and draw a phase portrait. A phase portrait is a qualitative sketch of the differential equation's behavior that shows equilibrium solutions or fixed points and the vector field on the real line.

Bifurcations describe changes in the stability or existence of fixed points as a control parameter in the system changes. As a very simple explanation of a bifurcation in a dynamical system, consider an object balanced on top of a vertical beam. The mass of the object can be thought of as the control parameter. As the mass of the object increases, the beam's deflection from vertical, which is x, the dynamic variable, remains relatively stable. But when the mass reaches a certain point – the bifurcation point – the beam will suddenly buckle. Changes in the control parameter eventually changed the qualitative behavior of the system.

For a more rigorous example, consider the dynamical system shown in figure 2

$$\dot{x} = -x^2 + \varepsilon$$

where ε is the control parameter. At first, when ε is greater than 0, the system has one stable fixed point and one unstable fixed point. As ε decreases the fixed points move together, briefly collide into a semi-stable fixed point at $\varepsilon = 0$, and then cease to exist when $\varepsilon < 0$.

In this case, because the behavior of the system changes significantly when the control parameter ε is 0, 0 is a bifurcation point. This example bifurcation is called the saddle-node bifurcation and its bifurcation diagram (this time for $\dot{x} = x^2 + \varepsilon$).

Other types of bifurcations are also important in dynamical systems, but the saddle node bifurcation is more important in biology. The reason for this is that biological systems are real and include small stochastic variations. For example, adding a very small term, $0 < h << 1$ to a pitchfork bifurcation yields a stable fixed point and a saddle node bifurcation (figure 4). Similarly, a small error term collapses a transcritical bifurcation to two saddle-node bifurcations.

Combined saddle node bifurcations in a system can generate multistability. Bistability (a special case of multistability) is an important property in many biological systems often produced by network architecture that contains positive feedback interactions and ultra-sensitive elements. Bistable systems are hysteretic, that is, their behavior depends on the history of the input. A hysteretic network can produce different output values for the same input value depending on its state (produce by the history of the input), a property crucial for switch-like control of cellular processes.

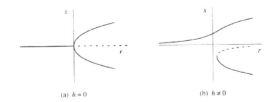

(a) $h = 0$ (b) $h \neq 0$

fig.3. Bifurcation diagram for a pitchfork bifurcation without imperfection (left) and with a small imperfection term (right).

Examples

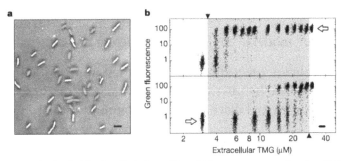

fig.4. GFP expression in individual cells induced by GAL promoter activation follows a bimodal distribution (left). GFP expression as a function of TMG (lactose analogue) concentration shows bistability with two bifurcation points

Networks with bifurcation in their dynamics control many important transitions in the cell cycle. The G1/S, G2/M, and Metaphase–Anaphase transitions all act as biochemical switches in the cell cycle.

In population ecology, the dynamics of food web interactions networks can exhibit Hopf bifurcations. For instance, in an aquatic system consisting of a primary producer, a mineral resource, and an herbivore, researchers found that patterns of equilibrium, cycling, and extinction of populations could be qualitatively described with a simple nonlinear model with a Hopf Bifurcation.

Galactose utilization in budding yeast (S. cerevisiae) is measurable through GFP expression induced by the GAL promoter as a function of changing galactose concentrations. The system exhibits bistable switching between induced and non-induced states.

Similarly, lactose utilization in E. coli as a function of thyo-methylgalactoside (a lactose analogue) concentration measured by a GFP-expressing lac promoter (figure 5) exhibits hysteresis and bistability.

Hidden Markov Model

A hidden Markov model (HMM) is a statistical Markov model in which the system being modeled is assumed to be a Markov process with unobserved (*hidden*) states. An HMM can be presented as the simplest dynamic Bayesian network. The mathematics behind the HMM were developed by L. E. Baum and coworkers. It is closely related to an earlier work on the optimal nonlinear filtering problem by Ruslan L. Stratonovich, who was the first to describe the forward-backward procedure.

In simpler Markov models (like a Markov chain), the state is directly visible to the observer, and therefore the state transition probabilities are the only parameters. In a *hidden* Markov model, the state is not directly visible, but the output, dependent on the state, is visible. Each state has a probability distribution over the possible output tokens. Therefore, the sequence of tokens generated by an HMM gives some information about the sequence of states. The adjective 'hidden' refers to the state sequence through which the model passes, not to the parameters of the model; the model is still referred to as a 'hidden' Markov model even if these parameters are known exactly.

Hidden Markov models are especially known for their application in temporal pattern recognition such as speech, handwriting, gesture recognition, part-of-speech tagging, musical score following, partial discharges and bioinformatics.

A hidden Markov model can be considered a generalization of a mixture model where the hidden variables (or latent variables), which control the mixture component to be selected for each observation, are related through a Markov process rather than independent of each other. Recently, hidden Markov models have been generalized to pairwise Markov models and triplet Markov models which allow consideration of more complex data structures and the modelling of nonstationary data.

Description in Terms of Urns

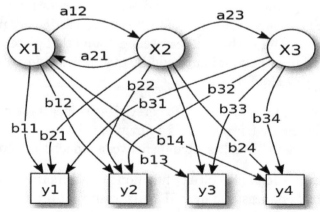

Figure 5. Probabilistic parameters of a hidden Markov model (example)

X — states
y — possible observations
a — state transition probabilities
b — output probabilities

In its discrete form, a hidden Markov process can be visualized as a generalization of the Urn problem with replacement (where each item from the urn is returned to the original urn before the next step). Consider this example: in a room that is not visible to an observer there is a genie. The room contains urns X1, X2, X3, ... each of which contains a known mix of balls, each ball labeled y1, y2, y3, ... The genie chooses an urn in that room and randomly draws a ball from that urn. It then puts the ball onto a conveyor belt, where the observer can observe the sequence of the balls but not the sequence of urns from which they were drawn. The genie has some procedure to choose urns; the choice of the urn for the n-th ball depends only upon a random number and the choice of the urn for the $(n - 1)$-th ball. The choice of urn does not directly depend on the urns chosen before this single previous urn; therefore, this is called a Markov process. It can be described by the upper part of Figure 1.

The Markov process itself cannot be observed, only the sequence of labeled balls, thus this arrangement is called a "hidden Markov process". This is illustrated by the lower part of the diagram shown in Figure 1, where one can see that balls y1, y2, y3, y4 can be drawn at each state. Even if the observer knows the composition of the urns and has just observed a sequence of three balls, *e.g.* y1, y2 and y3 on the conveyor belt, the observer still cannot be *sure* which urn (*i.e.*, at which state) the genie has drawn the third ball from. However, the observer can work out other information, such as the likelihood that the third ball came from each of the urns.

Architecture

The diagram below shows the general architecture of an instantiated HMM. Each oval shape represents a random variable that can adopt any of a number of values. The random variable $x(t)$ is the hidden state at time t (with the model from the above diagram, $x(t) \in \{ x_1, x_2, x_3 \}$). The random variable $y(t)$ is the observation at time t (with $y(t) \in \{ y_1, y_2, y_3, y_4 \}$). The arrows in the diagram (often called a trellis diagram) denote conditional dependencies.

From the diagram, it is clear that the conditional probability distribution of the hidden variable $x(t)$ at time t, given the values of the hidden variable x at all times, depends *only* on the value of the hidden variable $x(t - 1)$; the values at time $t - 2$ and before have no influence. This is called the Markov property. Similarly, the value of the observed variable $y(t)$ only depends on the value of the hidden variable $x(t)$ (both at time t).

In the standard type of hidden Markov model considered here, the state space of the hidden variables is discrete, while the observations themselves can either be discrete (typically generated from a categorical distribution) or continuous (typically from a Gaussian distribution). The parameters of a hidden Markov model are of two types, *transition probabilities* and *emission probabilities* (also known as *output probabilities*). The transition probabilities control the way the hidden state at time t is chosen given the hidden state at time $t-1$.

The hidden state space is assumed to consist of one of N possible values, modeled as a categorical distribution. This means that for each of the N possible states that a hidden variable at time t can be in, there is a transition probability from this state to each of the N possible states of the hidden variable at time $t+1$, for a total of N^2 transition probabilities. Note that the set of transition probabilities for transitions from any given state must sum to 1. Thus, the $N \times N$ matrix of transition probabilities is a Markov matrix. Because any one transition probability can be determined once the others are known, there are a total of $N(N-1)$ transition parameters.

In addition, for each of the N possible states, there is a set of emission probabilities governing the distribution of the observed variable at a particular time given the state of the hidden variable at that time. The size of this set depends on the nature of the observed variable. For example, if the observed variable is discrete with M possible values, governed by a categorical distribution, there will be $M-1$ separate parameters, for a total of $N(M-1)$ emission parameters over all hidden states. On the other hand, if the observed variable is an M-dimensional vector distributed according to an arbitrary multivariate Gaussian distribution, there will be M parameters controlling

the means and $\dfrac{M(M+1)}{2}$ parameters controlling the covariance matrix, for a total of

$$N\left(M + \frac{M(M+1)}{2}\right) = \frac{NM(M+3)}{2} = O(NM^2)$$ emission parameters. (In such a case,

unless the value of M is small, it may be more practical to restrict the nature of the covariances between individual elements of the observation vector, e.g. by assuming that the elements are independent of each other, or less restrictively, are independent of all but a fixed number of adjacent elements.)

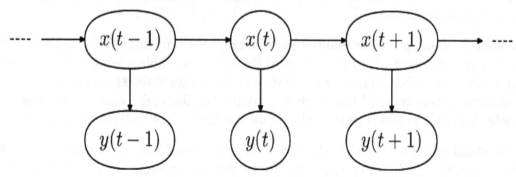

Inference

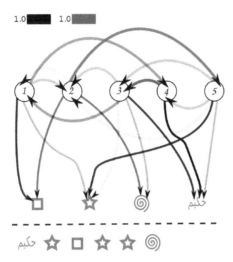

The state transition and output probabilities of an HMM are indicated by the line opacity in the upper part of the diagram. Given that we have observed the output sequence in the lower part of the diagram, we may be interested in the most likely sequence of states that could have produced it. Based on the arrows that are present in the diagram, the following state sequences are candidates:

5 3 2 5 3 2
4 3 2 5 3 2
3 1 2 5 3 2

We can find the most likely sequence by evaluating the joint probability of both the state sequence and the observations for each case (simply by multiplying the probability values, which here correspond to the opacities of the arrows involved). In general, this type of problem (i.e. finding the most likely explanation for an observation sequence) can be solved efficiently using the Viterbi algorithm.

Several inference problems are associated with hidden Markov models, as outlined below.

Probability of an Observed Sequence

The task is to compute in a best way, given the parameters of the model, the probability of a particular output sequence. This requires summation over all possible state sequences:

The probability of observing a sequence

$$Y = y(0), y(1), \ldots, y(L-1)$$

of length L is given by

$$P(Y) = \sum_X P(Y|X)P(X),$$

where the sum runs over all possible hidden-node sequences

$$X = x(0), x(1), \ldots, x(L-1).$$

Applying the principle of dynamic programming, this problem, too, can be handled efficiently using the forward algorithm.

Probability of the Latent Variables

A number of related tasks ask about the probability of one or more of the latent variables, given the model's parameters and a sequence of observations $y(1), \ldots, y(t)$.

Filtering

The task is to compute, given the model's parameters and a sequence of observations, the distribution over hidden states of the last latent variable at the end of the sequence, i.e. to compute $P(x(t)|y(1), \ldots, y(t))$. This task is normally used when the sequence of latent variables is thought of as the underlying states that a process moves through at a sequence of points of time, with corresponding observations at each point in time. Then, it is natural to ask about the state of the process at the end.

This problem can be handled efficiently using the forward algorithm.

Smoothing

This is similar to filtering but asks about the distribution of a latent variable somewhere in the middle of a sequence, i.e. to compute $P(x(k)|y(1), \ldots, y(t))$ for some $k < t$. From the perspective described above, this can be thought of as the probability distribution over hidden states for a point in time k in the past, relative to time t.

The forward-backward algorithm is an efficient method for computing the smoothed values for all hidden state variables.

Most Likely Explanation

The task, unlike the previous two, asks about the joint probability of the *entire* sequence of hidden states that generated a particular sequence of observations. This task is generally applicable when HMM's are applied to different sorts of problems from those for which the tasks of filtering and smoothing are applicable. An example is part-of-speech tagging, where the hidden states represent the underlying parts of speech corresponding to an observed sequence of words. In this case, what is of interest is the entire sequence of parts of speech, rather than simply the part of speech for a single word, as filtering or smoothing would compute.

This task requires finding a maximum over all possible state sequences, and can be solved efficiently by the Viterbi algorithm.

Statistical Significance

For some of the above problems, it may also be interesting to ask about statistical significance. What is the probability that a sequence drawn from some null distribution will have an HMM probability (in the case of the forward algorithm) or a maximum state sequence probability (in the case of the Viterbi algorithm) at least as large as that of a particular output sequence? When an HMM is used to evaluate the relevance of a hypothesis for a particular output sequence, the statistical significance indicates the false positive rate associated with failing to reject the hypothesis for the output sequence.

A Concrete Example

Consider two friends, Alice and Bob, who live far apart from each other and who talk together daily over the telephone about what they did that day. Bob is only interested in three activities: walking in the park, shopping, and cleaning his apartment. The choice of what to do is determined exclusively by the weather on a given day. Alice has no definite information about the weather where Bob lives, but she knows general trends. Based on what Bob tells her he did each day, Alice tries to guess what the weather must have been like.

Alice believes that the weather operates as a discrete Markov chain. There are two states, "Rainy" and "Sunny", but she cannot observe them directly, that is, they are *hidden* from her. On each day, there is a certain chance that Bob will perform one of the following activities, depending on the weather: "walk", "shop", or "clean". Since Bob tells Alice about his activities, those are the *observations*. The entire system is that of a hidden Markov model (HMM).

Alice knows the general weather trends in the area, and what Bob likes to do on average. In other words, the parameters of the HMM are known. They can be represented as follows in Python:

```
states = ('Rainy', 'Sunny')

observations = ('walk', 'shop', 'clean')

start_probability = {'Rainy': 0.6, 'Sunny': 0.4}

transition_probability = {
   'Rainy' : {'Rainy': 0.7, 'Sunny': 0.3},
```

```
    'Sunny' : {'Rainy': 0.4, 'Sunny': 0.6},
    }

emission_probability = {
    'Rainy' : {'walk': 0.1, 'shop': 0.4, 'clean': 0.5},
    'Sunny' : {'walk': 0.6, 'shop': 0.3, 'clean': 0.1},
    }
```

In this piece of code, start_probability represents Alice's belief about which state the HMM is in when Bob first calls her (all she knows is that it tends to be rainy on average). The particular probability distribution used here is not the equilibrium one, which is (given the transition probabilities) approximately {'Rainy': 0.57, 'Sunny': 0.43}. The transition_probability represents the change of the weather in the underlying Markov chain. In this example, there is only a 30% chance that tomorrow will be sunny if today is rainy. The emission_probability represents how likely Bob is to perform a certain activity on each day. If it is rainy, there is a 50% chance that he is cleaning his apartment; if it is sunny, there is a 60% chance that he is outside for a walk.

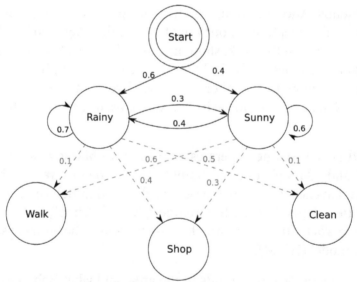

A similar example is further elaborated in the Viterbi algorithm page.

Learning

The parameter learning task in HMMs is to find, given an output sequence or a set of such sequences, the best set of state transition and emission probabilities. The task is usually to derive the maximum likelihood estimate of the parameters of the HMM given the set of output sequences. No tractable algorithm is known for solving this problem exactly, but a local maximum likelihood can be derived efficiently using the Baum–Welch algorithm or the Baldi–Chauvin algorithm. The Baum–Welch algorithm is a special case of the expectation-maximization algorithm.

Mathematical Description

General Description

A basic hidden Markov model can be described as follows:

N	=	number of states
T	=	number of observations
$\theta_{i=1\ldots N}$	=	emission parameter for an observation associated with state i
$\phi_{i=1\ldots N, j=1\ldots N}$	=	probability of transition from state i to state j
$\phi_{i=1\ldots N}$	=	N-dimensional vector, composed of $\phi_{i,1\ldots N}$; must sum to 1, the row of the matrix $\phi_{i=1\ldots N, j=1\ldots N}$
$x_{t=1\ldots T}$	=	(hidden) state at time t
$y_{t=1\ldots T}$	=	observation at time t
$F(y \mid \theta)$	=	probability distribution of an observation, parametrized on θ
$x_{t=2\ldots T}$	~	Categorical($\phi_{x_{t-1}}$)
$y_{t=1\ldots T}$	~	$F(\theta_{x_t})$

Note that, in the above model (and also the one below), the prior distribution of the initial state x_1 is not specified. Typical learning models correspond to assuming a discrete uniform distribution over possible states (i.e. no particular prior distribution is assumed).

In a Bayesian setting, all parameters are associated with random variables, as follows:

N, T	$=$	as above
$\theta_{i=1...N}, \phi_{i=1...N, j=1...N}, \phi_{i=1...N}$	$=$	as above
$x_{t=1...T}, y_{t=1...T}, F(y \mid \theta)$	$=$	as above
α	$=$	shared hyperparameter for emission parameters
β	$=$	shared hyperparameter for transition parameters
$H(\theta \mid \alpha)$	$=$	prior probability distribution of emission parameters, parametrized on α
$\theta_{i=1...N}$	$\sim$	$H(\alpha)$
$\phi_{i=1...N}$	$\sim$	$\text{Symmetric- Dirichlet}_N(\beta)$
$x_{t=2...T}$	$\sim$	$\text{Categorical}(\phi_{x_{t-1}})$
$y_{t=1...T}$	$\sim$	$F(\theta_{x_t})$

These characterizations use F and H to describe arbitrary distributions over observations and parameters, respectively. Typically H will be the conjugate prior of F. The two most common choices of F are Gaussian and categorical; see below.

Compared with a Simple Mixture Model

As mentioned above, the distribution of each observation in a hidden Markov model is a mixture density, with the states of the corresponding to mixture components. It is useful to compare the above characterizations for an HMM with the corresponding characterizations, of a mixture model, using the same notation.

A non-Bayesian mixture model:

N	$=$	number of mixture components
T	$=$	number of observations
$\theta_{i=1...N}$		parameter of distribution of observation associated with component i
$\phi_{i=1...N}$	$=$	mixture weight, i.e. prior probability of component i

ϕ	$=$	N-dimensional vector, composed of $\phi_{1...N}$; must sum to 1
$x_{t=1...T}$	$=$	component of observation t
$y_{t=1...T}$	$=$	observation t
$F(y\mid\ )$	$=$	probability distribution of an observation, parametrized on θ
$x_{t=1...T}$	$\sim$	Categorical(ϕ)
$y_{t=1...T}$	$\sim$	$F(\theta_{x_t})$

A Bayesian mixture model:

N,T	$=$	as above
$\theta_{i=1...N},\phi_{i=1...N},\phi$	$=$	as above
$x_{t=1...T},y_{t=1...T},F(y\mid\theta)$	$=$	as above
α	$=$	shared hyperparameter for component parameters
β	$=$	shared hyperparameter for mixture weights
$H(\theta\mid\alpha)$	$=$	prior probability distribution of component parameters, parametrized on α
$\theta_{i=1...N}$	$\sim$	$H(\alpha)$
ϕ	$\sim$	Symmetric-Dirichlet$_N(\beta)$
$x_{t=1...T}$	$\sim$	Categorical(ϕ)
$y_{t=1...T}$	$\sim$	$F(\theta_{x_t})$

Examples

The following mathematical descriptions are fully written out and explained, for ease of implementation.

A typical non-Bayesian HMM with Gaussian observations looks like this:

N	$=$	number of states
T	$=$	number of observations

$\phi_{i=1\ldots N, j=1\ldots N}$	$=$	probability of transition from state i to state j
$\phi_{i=1\ldots N}$	$=$	N – dimensional vector, composed of $\phi_{i,1\ldots N}$; must sum to 1
$\mu_{i=1\ldots N}$	$=$	mean of observations associated with state i
$\sigma^2_{i=1\ldots N}$	$=$	variance of observations associated with state i
$x_{t=1\ldots T}$	$=$	state of observation at time t
$y_{t=1\ldots T}$	$=$	observation at time t
$x_{t=2\ldots T}$	$\sim$	$\text{Categorical}(\phi_{x_{t-1}})$
$y_{t=1\ldots T}$	$\sim$	$\mathcal{N}(\mu_{x_t}, \sigma^2_{x_t})$

A typical Bayesian HMM with Gaussian observations looks like this:

N	$=$	number of states
T	$=$	number of observations
$\phi_{i=1\ldots N, j=1\ldots N}$	$=$	probability of transition from state i to state j
$\phi_{i=1\ldots N}$	$=$	N -dimensional vector, composed of $\phi_{i,1\ldots N}$; must sum to 1
$\mu_{i=1\ldots N}$	$=$	mean of observations associated with state i
$\sigma^2_{i=1\ldots N}$	$=$	variance of observations associated with state i
$x_{t=1\ldots T}$	$=$	state of observation at time t
$y_{t=1\ldots T}$	$=$	observation at time t
β	$=$	concentration hyperparameter controlling the density of the transition matrix
μ_0, λ	$=$	shared hyperparameters of the means for each state
ν, σ^2_0	$=$	shared hyperparameters of the variances for each state

$\phi_{i=1\ldots N}$	$\sim$	Symmetric-$\text{Dirichlet}_N(\beta)$
$x_{t=2\ldots T}$	$\sim$	$\text{Categorical}(\phi_{x_{t-1}})$
$\mu_{i=1\ldots N}$	$\sim$	$\mathcal{N}(\mu_0, \lambda\sigma_i^2)$
$\sigma_{i=1\ldots N}^2$	$\sim$	$\text{Inverse-Gamma}(\nu, \sigma_0^2)$
$y_{t=1\ldots T}$	$\sim$	$\mathcal{N}(\mu_{x_t}, \sigma_{x_t}^2)$

A typical non-Bayesian HMM with categorical observations looks like this:

N	$=$	number of states
T	$=$	number of observations
$\phi_{i=1\ldots N, j=1\ldots N}$	$=$	probability of transition from state i to state j
$\phi_{i=1\ldots N}$	$=$	N-dimensional vector, composed of $\phi_{i,1\ldots N}$; must sum to 1
V	$=$	dimension of categorical observations, e.g. size of word vocabulary
$\theta_{i=1\ldots N, j=1\ldots V}$	$=$	probability for state i of observing the jth item
$\theta_{i=1\ldots N}$	$=$	V-dimensional vector, composed of $\theta_{i,1\ldots V}$; must sum to 1
$x_{t=1\ldots T}$	$=$	state of observation at time t
$y_{t=1\ldots T}$	$=$	observation at time t
$x_{t=2\ldots T}$	$\sim$	$\text{Categorical}(\phi_{x_{t-1}})$
$y_{t=1\ldots T}$	$\sim$	$\text{Categorical}(\theta_{x_t})$

A typical Bayesian HMM with categorical observations looks like this:

N	$=$	number of states
T	$=$	number of observations

$\phi_{i=1...N, j=1...N}$	=	probability of transition from state i to state j
$\phi_{i=1...N}$	=	N-dimensional vector, composed of $\phi_{i,1...N}$; must sum to 1
V	=	dimension of categorical observations, e.g. size of word vocabulary
$\theta_{i=1...N, j=1...V}$	=	probability for state i of observing the jth item
$\theta_{i=1...N}$	=	V-dimensional vector, composed of $\theta_{i,1...V}$; must sum to 1
$x_{t=1...T}$	=	state of observation at time
$y_{t=1...T}$	=	observation at time t
α	=	shared concentration hyperparameter of θ for each state
β	=	concentration hyperparameter controlling the density of the transition matrix
$\phi_{i=1...N}$	~	Symmetric-Dirichlet$_N(\beta)$
$\theta_{1...V}$	~	Symmetric-Dirichlet$_V(\alpha)$
$x_{t=2...T}$	~	Categorical($\phi_{x_{t-1}}$)
$y_{t=1...T}$	~	Categorical(θ_{x_t})

Note that in the above Bayesian characterizations, β (a concentration parameter) controls the density of the transition matrix. That is, with a high value of β (significantly above 1), the probabilities controlling the transition out of a particular state will all be similar, meaning there will be a significant probability of transitioning to any of the other states. In other words, the path followed by the Markov chain of hidden states will be highly random. With a low value of β (significantly below 1), only a small number of the possible transitions out of a given state will have significant probability, meaning that the path followed by the hidden states will be somewhat predictable.

A Two-level Bayesian HMM

An alternative for the above two Bayesian examples would be to add another level of prior parameters for the transition matrix. That is, replace the lines

β	$=$	concentration hyperparameter controlling the density of the transition matrix
$\phi_{i=1...N}$	$\sim$	Symmetric- Dirichlet$_N(\beta)$

with the following:

γ	$=$	concentration hyperparameter controlling how many states are intrinsically likely
β	$=$	concentration hyperparameter controlling the density of the transition matrix
η	$=$	N-dimensional vector of probabilities, specifying the intrinsic probability of a given state
η	$\sim$	Symmetric- Dirichlet$_N(\gamma)$
$\phi_{i=1...N}$	$\sim$	Dirichlet$_N(\beta N \eta)$

What this means is the following:

1. η is a probability distribution over states, specifying which states are inherently likely. The greater the probability of a given state in this vector, the more likely is a transition to that state (regardless of the starting state).

2. γ controls the density of η Values significantly above 1 cause a dense vector where all states will have similar prior probabilities. Values significantly below 1 cause a sparse vector where only a few states are inherently likely (have prior probabilities significantly above 0).

3. β controls the density of the transition matrix, or more specifically, the density of the N different probability vectors $\phi_{i=1...N}$ specifying the probability of transitions out of state i to any other state.

Imagine that the value of β is significantly above 1. Then the different ϕ vectors will be dense, i.e. the probability mass will be spread out fairly evenly over all states. However, to the extent that this mass is unevenly spread, η controls which states are likely to get more mass than others.

Now, imagine instead that β is significantly below 1. This will make the ϕ vectors sparse, i.e. almost all the probability mass is distributed over a small number of states, and for the rest, a transition to that state will be very unlikely. Notice that there are different ϕ vectors for each starting state, and so even if all the vectors are sparse, different vectors may distribute the mass to different ending states. However, for all of the vectors, η controls which ending states are likely to get mass assigned to them. For example, if β

is 0.1, then each ϕ will be sparse and, for any given starting state i, the set of states $\mathbf{J}_i$ to which transitions are likely to occur will be very small, typically having only one or two members. Now, if the probabilities in η are all the same (or equivalently, one of the above models without η is used), then for different i, there will be different states in the corresponding $\mathbf{J}_i$, so that all states are equally likely to occur in any given $\mathbf{J}_i$. On the other hand, if the values in η are unbalanced, so that one state has a much higher probability than others, almost all $\mathbf{J}_i$ will contain this state; hence, regardless of the starting state, transitions will nearly always occur to this given state.

Hence, a two-level model such as just described allows independent control over (1) the overall density of the transition matrix, and (2) the density of states to which transitions are likely (i.e. the density of the prior distribution of states in any particular hidden variable x_i). In both cases this is done while still assuming ignorance over which particular states are more likely than others. If it is desired to inject this information into the model, the probability vector η can be directly specified; or, if there is less certainty about these relative probabilities, a non-symmetric Dirichlet distribution can be used as the prior distribution over η. That is, instead of using a symmetric Dirichlet distribution with the single parameter γ (or equivalently, a general Dirichlet with a vector all of whose values are equal to γ), use a general Dirichlet with values that are variously greater or less than γ, according to which state is more or less preferred.

Poisson Hidden Markov Model

Poisson hidden Markov models (PHMM) are special cases of hidden Markov models where a Poisson process has a rate which varies in association with changes between the different states of a Markov model. PHMMs are not necessarily Markovian processes themselves because the underlying Markov chain or Markov process cannot be observed and only the Poisson signal is observed.

Applications

HMMs can be applied in many fields where the goal is to recover a data sequence that is not immediately observable (but other data that depend on the sequence are). Applications include:

- Single Molecule Kinetic analysis
- Cryptanalysis
- Speech recognition
- Speech synthesis
- Part-of-speech tagging
- Document Separation in scanning solutions

- Machine translation

- Partial discharge

- Gene prediction

- Alignment of bio-sequences

- Time Series Analysis

- Activity recognition

- Protein folding

- Metamorphic Virus Detection

- DNA Motif Discovery

History

The forward and backward recursions used in HMM as well as computations of marginal smoothing probabilities were first described by Ruslan L. Stratonovich in 1960 (pages 160–162) and in the late 1950s in his papers in Russian. The Hidden Markov Models were later described in a series of statistical papers by Leonard E. Baum and other authors in the second half of the 1960s. One of the first applications of HMMs was speech recognition, starting in the mid-1970s.

In the second half of the 1980s, HMMs began to be applied to the analysis of biological sequences, in particular DNA. Since then, they have become ubiquitous in the field of bioinformatics.

Types

Hidden Markov models can model complex Markov processes where the states emit the observations according to some probability distribution. One such example is the Gaussian distribution, in such a Hidden Markov Model the states output are represented by a Gaussian distribution.

Moreover, it could represent even more complex behavior when the output of the states is represented as mixture of two or more Gaussians, in which case the probability of generating an observation is the product of the probability of first selecting one of the Gaussians and the probability of generating that observation from that Gaussian.

Extensions

In the hidden Markov models considered above, the state space of the hidden variables is discrete, while the observations themselves can either be discrete (typically generated from a categorical distribution) or continuous (typically from a Gaussian distribution). Hidden Markov models can also be generalized to allow continuous state spaces. Examples of such models are those where the Markov process over hidden variables is a linear dynamical system, with a linear relationship among related variables and where all hidden and observed variables follow a Gaussian distribution. In simple cases, such as the linear dynamical system just mentioned, exact inference is tractable (in this case, using the Kalman filter); however, in general, exact inference in HMMs with continuous latent variables is infeasible, and approximate methods must be used, such as the extended Kalman filter or the particle filter.

Hidden Markov models are generative models, in which the joint distribution of observations and hidden states, or equivalently both the prior distribution of hidden states (the *transition probabilities*) and conditional distribution of observations given states (the *emission probabilities*), is modeled. The above algorithms implicitly assume a uniform prior distribution over the transition probabilities. However, it is also possible to create hidden Markov models with other types of prior distributions. An obvious candidate, given the categorical distribution of the transition probabilities, is the Dirichlet distribution, which is the conjugate prior distribution of the categorical distribution. Typically, a symmetric Dirichlet distribution is chosen, reflecting ignorance about which states are inherently more likely than others. The single parameter of this distribution (termed the *concentration parameter*) controls the relative density or sparseness of the resulting transition matrix. A choice of 1 yields a uniform distribution. Values greater than 1 produce a dense matrix, in which the transition probabilities between pairs of states are likely to be nearly equal. Values less than 1 result in a sparse matrix in which, for each given source state, only a small number of destination states have non-negligible transition probabilities. It is also possible to use a two-level prior Dirichlet distribution, in which one Dirichlet distribution (the upper distribution) governs the parameters of another Dirichlet distribution (the lower distribution), which in turn governs the transition probabilities. The upper distribution governs the overall distribution of states, determining how likely each state is to occur; its concentration parameter determines the density or sparseness of states. Such a two-level prior distribution, where both concentration parameters are set to produce sparse distributions, might be useful for example in unsupervised part-of-speech tagging, where some parts of speech occur much more commonly than others; learning algorithms that assume a uniform prior distribution generally perform poorly on this task. The parameters of models of this sort, with non-uniform prior distributions, can be learned using Gibbs sampling or extended versions of the expectation-maximization algorithm.

An extension of the previously described hidden Markov models with Dirichlet priors uses a Dirichlet process in place of a Dirichlet distribution. This type of model allows for an unknown and potentially infinite number of states. It is common to use a two-level Dirichlet process, similar to the previously described model with two levels of Dirichlet distributions. Such a model is called a *hierarchical Dirichlet process hidden Markov model*, or *HDP-HMM* for short. It was originally described under the name "Infinite Hidden Markov Model" and was further formalized in.

A different type of extension uses a discriminative model in place of the generative model of standard HMMs. This type of model directly models the conditional distribution of the hidden states given the observations, rather than modeling the joint distribution. An example of this model is the so-called *maximum entropy Markov model* (MEMM), which models the conditional distribution of the states using logistic regression (also known as a "maximum entropy model"). The advantage of this type of model is that arbitrary features (i.e. functions) of the observations can be modeled, allowing domain-specific knowledge of the problem at hand to be injected into the model. Models of this sort are not limited to modeling direct dependencies between a hidden state and its associated observation; rather, features of nearby observations, of combinations of the associated observation and nearby observations, or in fact of arbitrary observations at any distance from a given hidden state can be included in the process used to determine the value of a hidden state. Furthermore, there is no need for these features to be statistically independent of each other, as would be the case if such features were used in a generative model. Finally, arbitrary features over pairs of adjacent hidden states can be used rather than simple transition probabilities. The disadvantages of such models are: (1) The types of prior distributions that can be placed on hidden states are severely limited; (2) It is not possible to predict the probability of seeing an arbitrary observation. This second limitation is often not an issue in practice, since many common usages of HMM's do not require such predictive probabilities.

A variant of the previously described discriminative model is the linear-chain conditional random field. This uses an undirected graphical model (aka Markov random field) rather than the directed graphical models of MEMM's and similar models. The advantage of this type of model is that it does not suffer from the so-called *label bias* problem of MEMM's, and thus may make more accurate predictions. The disadvantage is that training can be slower than for MEMM's.

Yet another variant is the *factorial hidden Markov model*, which allows for a single observation to be conditioned on the corresponding hidden variables of a set of K independent Markov chains, rather than a single Markov chain. It is equivalent to a single HMM, with N^K states (assuming there are N states for each chain), and therefore, learning in such a model is difficult: for a sequence of length T, a straightforward Viterbi algorithm has complexity $O(N^{2K}T)$. To find an exact solution, a junction tree algorithm could be used, but it results in an $O(N^{K+1}KT)$ complexity. In practice, approximate techniques, such as variational approaches, could be used.

All of the above models can be extended to allow for more distant dependencies among hidden states, e.g. allowing for a given state to be dependent on the previous two or three states rather than a single previous state; i.e. the transition probabilities are extended to encompass sets of three or four adjacent states (or in general K adjacent states). The disadvantage of such models is that dynamic-programming algorithms for training them have an $O(N^K T)$ running time, for K adjacent states and T total observations (i.e. a length-T Markov chain).

Another recent extension is the *triplet Markov model*, in which an auxiliary underlying process is added to model some data specificities. Many variants of this model have been proposed. One should also mention the interesting link that has been established between the *theory of evidence* and the *triplet Markov models* and which allows to fuse data in Markovian context and to model nonstationary data.

Metabolic Control Analysis

Metabolic control analysis (MCA) is a mathematical framework for describing metabolic, signaling, and genetic pathways. MCA quantifies how variables, such as fluxes and species concentrations, depend on network parameters. In particular it is able to describe how network dependent properties, called control coefficients, depend on local properties called elasticities.

MCA was originally developed to describe the control in metabolic pathways but was subsequently extended to describe signaling and genetic networks. MCA has sometimes also been referred to as *Metabolic Control Theory* but this terminology was rather strongly opposed by Henrik Kacser, one of the founders.

More recent work has shown that MCA can be mapped directly on to classical control theory and are as such equivalent.

Biochemical systems theory is a similar formalism, though with a rather different objectives. Both are evolutions of an earlier theoretical analysis by Joseph Higgins.

Control Coefficients

A control coefficient measures the relative steady state change in a system variable, e.g. pathway flux (J) or metabolite concentration (S), in response to a relative change in a parameter, e.g. enzyme activity or the steady-state rate (v_i) of step i. The two main control coefficients are the flux and concentration control coefficients. Flux control coefficients are defined by:

$$C_{v_i}^J = \left(\frac{dJ}{dp} \frac{p}{J} \right) / \left(\frac{\partial v_i}{\partial p} \frac{p}{v_i} \right) = \frac{d \ln J}{d \ln v_i}$$

and concentration control coefficients by:

$$C_{v_i}^S = \left(\frac{dS}{dp} \frac{p}{S} \right) / \left(\frac{\partial v_i}{\partial p} \frac{p}{v_i} \right) = \frac{d \ln S}{d \ln v_i}$$

Summation Theorems

The flux control summation theorem was discovered independently by the Kacser/ Burns group and the Heinrich/Rapoport group in the early 1970s and late 1960s. The flux control summation theorem implies that metabolic fluxes are systemic properties and that their control is shared by all reactions in the system. When a single reaction changes its control of the flux this is compensated by changes in the control of the same flux by all other reactions.

$$\sum_i C_{v_i}^J = 1$$

$$\sum_i C_{v_i}^S = 0$$

Elasticity Coefficients

The elasticity coefficient measures the local response of an enzyme or other chemical reaction to changes in its environment. Such changes include factors such as substrates, products or effector concentrations.

Connectivity Theorems

The connectivity theorems are specific relationships between elasticities and control coefficients. They are useful because they highlight the close relationship between the kinetic properties of individual reactions and the system properties of a pathway. Two basic sets of theorems exists, one for flux and another for concentrations. The concentration connectivity theorems are divided again depending on whether the system species S_n is different from the local species S_m.

$$\sum_i C_i^J \varepsilon_S^i = 0$$

$$\sum_i C_i^{S_n} \varepsilon_{S_m}^i = 0 \quad n \neq m$$

$$\sum_i C_i^{S_n} \varepsilon_{S_m}^i = -1 \quad n = m$$

Control Equations

It is possible to combine the summation with the connectivity theorems to obtain closed expressions that relate the control coefficients to the elasticity coefficients. For example, consider the simplest non-trivial pathway:

$$X_o \to S \to X_1$$

We assume that X_o and X_1 are fixed boundary species so that the pathway can reach a steady state. Let the first step have a rate v_1 and the second step v_2. Focusing on the flux control coefficients, we can write one summation and one connectivity theorem for this simple pathway:

$$C_{v_1}^J + C_{v_2}^J = 1$$

$$C_{v_1}^J \varepsilon_S^{v_1} + C_{v_2}^J \varepsilon_S^{v_2} = 0$$

Using these two equations we can solve for the flux control coefficients to yield:

$$C_{v_1}^J = \frac{\varepsilon_S^2}{\varepsilon_S^2 - \varepsilon_S^1}$$

$$C_{v_2}^J = \frac{-\varepsilon_S^1}{\varepsilon_S^2 - \varepsilon_S^1}$$

Using these equations we can look at some simple extreme behaviors. For example, let us assume that the first step is completely insensitive to its product (i.e. not reacting with it), S, then $\varepsilon_S^{v_1} = 0$.. In this case, the control coefficients reduce to:

$$C_{v_1}^J = 1$$

$$C_{v_2}^J = 0$$

That is all the control (or sensitivity) is on the first step. This situation represents the classic rate-limiting step that is frequently mentioned in text books. The flux through the pathway is completely dependent on the first step. Under these conditions, no other step in the pathway can affect the flux. The effect is however dependent on the complete insensitivity of the first step to its product. Such a situation is likely to be rare in real pathways. In fact the classic rate limiting step has almost never been observed experimentally. Instead, a range of limitingness is observed, with some steps having more limitingness (control) than others.

We can also derive the concentration control coefficients for the simple two step pathway:

$$C_{v_1}^S = \frac{1}{\varepsilon_S^2 - \varepsilon_S^1}$$

$$C_{v_2}^{S} = \frac{-1}{\varepsilon_S^2 - \varepsilon_S^1}$$

An alternative approach to deriving the control equations is to consider the perturbations explicitly. Consider making a perturbation to E_1 which changes the local rate v_1. The effect on the steady-state to a small change in E_1 is to increase the flux and concentration of S. We can express these changes locally by describing the change in v_1 and v_2 using the expressions:

$$\frac{\delta v_1}{v_1} = \varepsilon_{E_1}^1 \frac{\delta E_1}{E_1} + \varepsilon_S^1 \frac{\delta S}{S}$$

$$\frac{\delta v_2}{v_2} = \varepsilon_S^2 \frac{\delta S}{S}$$

The local changes in rates are equal to the global changes in flux, J. In addition if we assume that the enzyme elasticity of v_1 with respect to E_1 is unity, then

$$\frac{\delta J}{J} = \frac{\delta E_1}{E_1} + \varepsilon_S^1 \frac{\delta S}{S}$$

$$\frac{\delta J}{J} = \varepsilon_S^2 \frac{\delta S}{S}$$

Dividing both sides by the fractional change in E_1 and taking the limit $\delta E_1 \to 0$ yields:

$$C_{E_1}^{J} = 1 + \varepsilon_S^1 C_{E_1}^{S}$$

$$C_{E_1}^{J} = \varepsilon_S^2 C_{E_1}^{S}$$

From these equations we can choose either to eliminate $C_{E_1}^{J}$ or $C_{E_1}^{S}$ to yield the control equations given earlier. We can do the same kind of analysis for the second step to obtain the flux control coefficient for E_2. Note that we have expressed the control coefficients relative to   and E_2 but if we assume that $\delta v_i / v_i = \delta E_i / E_i$ then the control coefficients can be written with respect to v_i as before.

Three Step Pathway

Consider the simple three step pathway:

$$X_o \to S_1 \to S_2 \to X_1$$

where X_o and X_1 are fixed boundary species, the control equations for this pathway can be derived in a similar manner to the simple two step pathway although it is somewhat more tedious.

$$C_{E_1}^J = \varepsilon_1^2 \varepsilon_2^3 / D$$

$$C_{E_2}^J = -\varepsilon_1^1 \varepsilon_2^3 / D$$

$$C_{E_3}^J = \varepsilon_1^1 \varepsilon_2^2 / D$$

where D the denominator is given by:

$$D = \varepsilon_1^2 \varepsilon_2^3 - \varepsilon_1^1 \varepsilon_2^3 + \varepsilon_1^1 \varepsilon_2^2$$

Note that every term in the numerator appears in the denominator, this ensures that the flux control coefficient summation theorem is satisfied.

Likewise the concentration control coefficients can also be derived, for S_1

$$C_{E_1}^{S_1} = (\varepsilon_2^3 - \varepsilon_2^2) / D$$

$$C_{E_2}^{S_1} = -\varepsilon_2^3 / D$$

$$C_{E_3}^{S_1} = \varepsilon_2^2 / D$$

And for S_2

$$C_{E_1}^{S_2} = \varepsilon_1^2 / D$$

$$C_{E_2}^{S_2} = -\varepsilon_1^1 / D$$

$$C_{E_3}^{S_2} = (\varepsilon_1^1 - \varepsilon_1^2) / D$$

Note that the denominators remain the same as before and behave as a normalizing factor.

Derivation using Perturbations

Control equations can also be derived by considering the effect of perturbations on the system. Consider that reaction rates v_1 and v_2 are determined by two enzymes e_1 and e_2 respectively. Changing either enzyme will result in a change to the steady state level of x and the steady state reaction rates v. Consider a small change in e_1 of magnitude δe_1. This will have a number of effects, it will increase v_1 which in turn will increase x which in turn will increase v_2. Eventually the system will settle to a new steady state. We can describe these changes by focusing on the change in v_1 and v_2. The change in v_2, which we designate δv_2, came about as a result of the change δx. Because we are only considering small changes we can express the change δv_2 in terms of δx using the relation:

$$\delta v_2 = \frac{\partial v_2}{\partial x} \delta x$$

where the derivative $\partial v_2 / \partial x$ measures how responsive v_2 is to changes in x. The derivative can be computed if we know the rate law for v_2. For example, if we assume that the rate law is $v_2 = k_2 x$ then the derivative is k_2. We can also use a similar strategy to compute the change in v_1 as a result of the change δe_1. This time the change in v_1 is a result of two changes, the change in e_1 itself and the change in x. We can express these changes by summing the two individual contributions:

$$\delta v_1 = \frac{\partial v_1}{\partial e_1} \delta e_1 + \frac{\partial v_1}{\partial x} \delta x$$

We have two equations, one describing the change in v_1 and the other in v_2. Because we allowed the system to settle to a new steady state we can also state that the change in reaction rates must be the same (otherwise it wouldn't be at steady state). That is we can assert that $\delta v_1 = \delta v_2$. With this in mind we equate the two equations and write:

$$\frac{\partial v_2}{\partial x} \delta x = \frac{\partial v_1}{\partial e_1} \delta e_1 + \frac{\partial v_1}{\partial x} \delta x$$

Solving for the ratio $\delta x / \delta e_1$ we obtain:

$$\frac{\delta x}{\delta e_1} = \frac{-\dfrac{\partial v_1}{\partial e_1}}{\dfrac{\partial v_2}{\partial x} - \dfrac{\partial v_1}{\partial x}}$$

In the limit, as we make the change δe_1 smaller and smaller, the left-hand side converges to the derivative dx / de_1:

$$\lim_{\delta e_1 \to 0} \frac{\delta x}{\delta e_1} = \frac{dx}{de_1} = \frac{-\dfrac{\partial v_1}{\partial e_1}}{\dfrac{\partial v_2}{\partial x} - \dfrac{\partial v_1}{\partial x}}$$

We can go one step further and scale the derivatives to eliminate units. Multiplying both sides by e_1 and dividing both sides by x yields the scaled derivatives:

$$\frac{dx}{de_1}\frac{e_1}{x} = \frac{-\frac{\partial v_1}{\partial e_1}\frac{e_1}{v_1}}{\frac{\partial v_2}{\partial x}\frac{x}{v_2} - \frac{\partial v_1}{\partial x}\frac{x}{v_1}}$$

The scaled derivatives on the right-hand side are the elasticities, ε_x^v and the scaled left-hand term is the scaled sensitivity coefficient or concentration control coefficient, C_e^x

$$C_{e_1}^x = \frac{\varepsilon_{e_1}^1}{\varepsilon_x^2 - \varepsilon_x^1}$$

We can simplify this expression further. The reaction rate v_1 is usually a linear function of e_1. For example in the Briggs-Haldane equation, the reaction rate is given by $v = e_1 k_{cat} x / (K_m + x)$. Differentiating this rate law with respect to e_1 and scaling yields: $\varepsilon_{e_1}^{v_1} = 1$.

Using this result gives:

$$C_{e_1}^x = \frac{1}{\varepsilon_x^2 - \varepsilon_x^1}$$

A similar analysis can be done where e_2 is perturbed. In this case we obtain the sensitivity of x with respect to e_2 :

$$C_{e_2}^x = -\frac{1}{\varepsilon_x^2 - \varepsilon_x^1}$$

The above expressions measure how much enzymes e_1 and e_2 control the steady state concentration of intermediate x. We can also consider how the steady state reaction rates v_1 and v_2 are affected by perturbations in e_1 and e_2. This is often of importance to metabolic engineers who are interested in increasing rates of production. At steady state the reaction rates are often called the fluxes and abbreviated to J_1 and J_2. For a linear pathway such this example, both fluxes are equal at steady state so that the flux through the pathway is simply referred to as J. Expressing the change in flux as a result of a per-

turbations in e_1 and taking the limit as before we obtain: $C_{e_1}^J = \frac{\varepsilon_x^1}{\varepsilon_x^2 - \varepsilon_x^1}$, $C_{e_2}^J = \frac{-\varepsilon_x^1}{\varepsilon_x^2 - \varepsilon_x^1}$

The above expressions tell us how much enzymes e_1 and e_2 control the steady state flux. The key point here is that changes in enzyme concentration, or equivalently the enzyme activity, must be brought about by an external action.

Flux Balance Analysis

Flux balance analysis (FBA) is a mathematical method for simulating metabolism in genome-scale reconstructions of metabolic networks. In comparison to traditional methods of modeling, FBA is less intensive in terms of the input data required for constructing the model. Simulations performed using FBA are computationally inexpensive and can calculate steady-state metabolic fluxes for large models (over 2000 reactions) in a few seconds on modern personal computers.

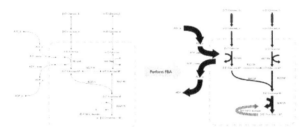

The results of FBA on a prepared metabolic network of the top six reactions of glycolysis. The predicted flux through each reaction is proportional to the width of the line. Objective function in red, constraints on alpha-D-glucose and beta-D-glucose import represented as red bars.

FBA finds applications in bioprocess engineering to systematically identify modifications to the metabolic networks of microbes used in fermentation processes that improve product yields of industrially important chemicals such as ethanol and succinic acid. It has also been used for the identification of putative drug targets in cancer and pathogens, rational design of culture media, and more recently host–pathogen interactions. The results of FBA can be visualized using flux maps similar to the image on the right, which illustrates the steady-state fluxes carried by reactions in glycolysis. The thickness of the arrows is proportional to the flux through the reaction.

FBA formalizes the system of equations describing the concentration changes in a metabolic network as the dot product of a matrix of the stoichiometric coefficients (the stoichiometric matrix S) and the vector v of the unsolved fluxes. The right-hand side of the dot product is a vector of zeros representing the system at steady state. Linear programming is then used to calculate a solution of fluxes corresponding to the steady state.

History

Some of the earliest work in FBA dates back to the early 1980s. Papoutsakis demonstrated that it was possible to construct flux balance equations using a metabolic map. It was Watson, however, who first introduced the idea of using linear programming and an objective function to solve for the fluxes in a pathway. The first significant study was subsequently published by Fell and Small, who used flux balance analysis together with more elaborate objective functions to study the constraints in fat synthesis.

Simulations

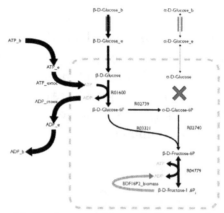

An example of a non lethal gene deletion in a sample metabolic network with fluxes shown by the weight of the reaction lines as calculated by FBA. Here the flux through the objective function is halved but is still present.

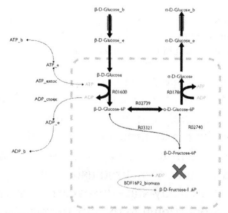

An example of a lethal gene deletion in a sample metabolic network with fluxes shown by the weight of the reaction lines as calculated by FBA. Here there is no flux through the objective function, simulating that the pathway is no longer functional.

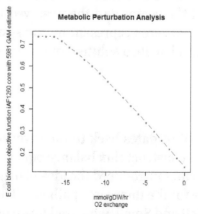

Reaction inhibition: Plot of FBA predicted growth rate (y-axis) to decreasing influx of Oxygen (x-axis) in an E.coli FBA model.

A 3-D Phenotypic Phase Plane showing the effect of varying glucose and glycerol input fluxes on the growth rate of Mycobacterium tuberculosis. The X axis represents glycerol influx and the Y axis represents glucose influx, the height of the surface (red) represents the value of the growth flux for each combination of the input fluxes.

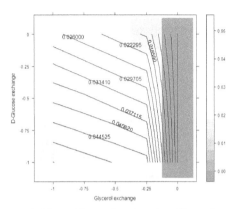

A levelplot version of the Phenotypic Phase Plane showing the effect of varying glucose and glycerol input fluxes on the growth rate of Mycobacterium tuberculosis. The X axis represents glycerol influx and the Y axis represents glucose influx, the color represents the value of the growth flux.

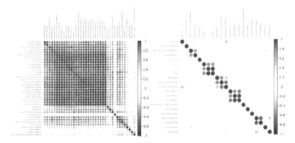

Comparison of correlation plots of lethal Pairwise reaction deletions across different subsystems for E.coli(left) and M.tuberculosis(right).

FBA is not computationally intensive, taking on the order of seconds to calculate optimal fluxes for biomass production for a typical network (around 2000 reactions). This means that the effect of deleting reactions from the network and/or changing flux constraints can be sensibly modelled on a single computer.

Gene/Reaction Deletion and Perturbation Studies

Single Reaction Deletion

A frequently used technique to search a metabolic network for reactions that are particularly critical to the production of biomass. By removing each reaction in a network in turn and measuring the predicted flux through the biomass function, each reaction can be classified as either essential (if the flux through the biomass function is substantially reduced) or non-essential (if the flux through the biomass function is unchanged or only slightly reduced).

Pairwise Reaction Deletion

Pairwise reaction deletion of all possible pairs of reactions is useful when looking for drug targets, as it allows the simulation of multi-target treatments, either by a single drug with multiple targets or by drug combinations. Double deletion studies can also quantify the synthetic lethal interactions between different pathways providing a measure of the contribution of the pathway to overall network robustness.

Single and Multiple Gene Deletions

Genes are connected to enzyme-catalyzed reactions by Boolean expressions known as Gene-Protein-Reaction expressions (GPR). Typically a GPR takes the form (Gene A AND Gene B) to indicate that the products of genes A and B are protein sub-units that assemble to form the complete protein and therefore the absence of either would result in deletion of the reaction. On the other hand, if the GPR is (Gene A OR Gene B) it implies that the products of genes A and B are isozymes.

Therefore, it is possible to evaluate the effect of single or multiple gene deletions by evaluation of the GPR as a Boolean expression. If the GPR evaluates to false, the reaction is constrained to zero in the model prior to performing FBA. Thus gene knockouts can be simulated using FBA.

Interpretation of Gene and Reaction Deletion Results

The utility of reaction inhibition and deletion analyses becomes most apparent if a gene-protein-reaction matrix has been assembled for the network being studied with FBA. The gene-protein-reaction matrix is a binary matrix connecting genes with the proteins made from them. Using this matrix, reaction essentiality can be converted into gene essentiality indicating the gene defects which may cause a certain disease phenotype or the proteins/enzymes which are essential (and thus what enzymes are the most promising drug targets in pathogens). However, the gene-protein-reaction matrix does not specify the Boolean relationship between genes with respect to the enzyme, instead it merely indicates an association between them. Therefore, it should be used only if the Boolean GPR expression is unavailable.

Reaction Inhibition

The effect of inhibiting a reaction, rather than removing it entirely, can be simulated in FBA by restricting the allowed flux through it. The effect of an inhibition can be classified as lethal or non-lethal by applying the same criteria as in the case of a deletion where a suitable threshold is used to distinguish "substantially reduced" from "slightly reduced". Generally the choice of threshold is arbitrary but a reasonable estimate can be obtained from growth experiments where the simulated inhibitions/deletions are actually performed and growth rate is measured.

Growth Media Optimization

To design optimal growth media with respect to enhanced growth rates or useful by-product secretion, it is possible to use a method known as Phenotypic Phase Plane analysis. PhPP involves applying FBA repeatedly on the model while co-varying the nutrient uptake constraints and observing the value of the objective function (or by-product fluxes). PhPP makes it possible to find the optimal combination of nutrients that favor a particular phenotype or a mode of metabolism resulting in higher growth rates or secretion of industrially useful by-products. The predicted growth rates of bacteria in varying media have been shown to correlate well with experimental results. as well as to define precise minimal media for the culture of *Salmonella typhimurium*.

Mathematical Description

In contrast to the traditionally followed approach of metabolic modeling using coupled ordinary differential equations, flux balance analysis requires very little information in terms of the enzyme kinetic parameters and concentration of metabolites in the system. It achieves this by making two assumptions, steady state and optimality. The first assumption is that the modeled system has entered a steady state, where the metabolite concentrations no longer change, i.e. in each metabolite node the producing and consuming fluxes cancel each other out. The second assumption is that the organism has been optimized through evolution for some biological goal, such as optimal growth or conservation of resources. The steady-state assumption reduces the system to a set of linear equations, which is then solved to find a flux distribution that satisfies the steady-state condition subject to the stoichiometry constraints while maximizing the value of a pseudo-reaction (the objective function) representing the conversion of biomass precursors into biomass.

The steady-state assumption dates to the ideas of material balance developed to model the growth of microbial cells in fermenters in bioprocess engineering. During microbial growth, a substrate consisting of a complex mixture of carbon, hydrogen, oxygen and nitrogen sources along with trace elements are consumed to generate biomass. The material balance model for this process becomes:

$$Input = Output + Accumulation$$

If we consider the system of microbial cells to be at steady state then we may set the accumulation term to zero and reduce the material balance equations to simple algebraic equations. In such a system, substrate becomes the input to the system which is consumed and biomass is produced becoming the output from the system. The material balance may then be represented as:

$$Input = Output$$

$$Input - Output = 0$$

Mathematically, the algebraic equations can be represented as a dot product of a matrix of coefficients and a vector of the unknowns. Since the steady-state assumption puts the accumulation term to zero. The system can be written as:

$$A \cdot \mathbf{x} = \mathbf{0}$$

Extending this idea to metabolic networks, it is possible to represent a metabolic network as a stoichiometry balanced set of equations. Moving to the matrix formalism, we can represent the equations as the dot product of a matrix of stoichiometry coefficients (stoichiometric matrix S) and the vector of fluxes $\mathbf{v}$ as the unknowns and set the right hand side to 0 implying the steady state.

$$S \cdot \mathbf{v} = \mathbf{0}$$

Metabolic networks typically have more reactions than metabolites and this gives an under-determined system of linear equations containing more variables than equations. The standard approach to solve such under-determined systems is to apply linear programming.

Linear programs are problems that can be expressed in canonical form:

$$\begin{aligned} \text{maximize} \quad & \mathbf{c}^{\mathsf{T}}\mathbf{x} \\ \text{subject to} \quad & A\mathbf{x} \leq \mathbf{b} \\ \text{and} \quad & \mathbf{x} \geq \mathbf{0} \end{aligned}$$

where x represents the vector of variables (to be determined), c and b are vectors of (known) coefficients, A is a (known) matrix of coefficients, and $(\cdot)^{\mathsf{T}}$ is the matrix transpose. The expression to be maximized or minimized is called the *objective function* ($\mathbf{c}^{\mathsf{T}}\mathbf{x}$ in this case). The inequalities $A\mathbf{x} \leq \mathbf{b}$ are the constraints which specify a convex polytope over which the objective function is to be optimized.

Linear Programming requires the definition of an objective function. The optimal solution to the LP problem is considered to be the solution which maximizes or minimizes the value of the objective function depending on the case in point. In the case of flux balance analysis, the objective function Z for the LP is often defined as biomass production. Biomass production is simulated by an equation representing a lumped reaction that converts various biomass precursors into one unit of biomass.

Therefore, the canonical form of a Flux Balance Analysis problem would be:

$$\begin{aligned} \text{maximize} \quad & \mathbf{c}^{\mathsf{T}}\mathbf{v} \\ \text{subject to} \quad & S\mathbf{v} = \mathbf{0} \\ \text{and} \quad & \mathbf{lowerbound} \leq \mathbf{v} \leq \mathbf{upperbound} \end{aligned}$$

where   represents the vector of fluxes (to be determined), S is a (known) matrix of coefficients. The expression to be maximized or minimized is called the *objective function* ($\mathbf{c}^T\mathbf{v}$ in this case). The inequalities **lowerbound** $\leq \mathbf{v}$ and $\mathbf{v} \leq$ **upperbound** define, respectively, the minimal and the maximal rates of flux for every reaction corresponding to the columns of the S matrix. These rates can be experimentally determined to constrain and improve the predictive accuracy of the model even further or they can be specified to an arbitrarily high value indicating no constraint on the flux through the reaction.

The main advantage of the flux balance approach is that it does not require any knowledge of the metabolite concentrations, or more importantly, the enzyme kinetics of the system; the homeostasis assumption precludes the need for knowledge of metabolite concentrations at any time as long as that quantity remains constant, and additionally it removes the need for specific rate laws since it assumes that at steady state, there is no change in the size of the metabolite pool in the system. The stoichiometric coefficients alone are sufficient for the mathematical maximization of a specific objective function.

The objective function is essentially a measure of how each component in the system contributes to the production of the desired product. The product itself depends on the purpose of the model, but one of the most common examples is the study of total biomass. A notable example of the success of FBA is the ability to accurately predict the growth rate of the prokaryote *E. coli* when cultured in different conditions. In this case, the metabolic system was optimized to maximize the biomass objective function. However this model can be used to optimize the production of any product, and is often used to determine the output level of some biotechnologically relevant product. The model itself can be experimentally verified by cultivating organisms using a chemostat or similar tools to ensure that nutrient concentrations are held constant. Measurements of the production of the desired objective can then be used to correct the model.

A good description of the basic concepts of FBA can be found in the freely available supplementary material to Edwards et al. 2001 which can be found at the Nature website. Further sources include the book "Systems Biology" by B. Palsson dedicated to the subject and a useful tutorial and paper by J. Orth. Many other sources of information on the technique exist in published scientific literature including Lee et al. 2006, Feist et al. 2008, and Lewis et al. 2012.

Model Preparation and Refinement

A comprehensive guide to creating, preparing and analysing a metabolic model using FBA, in addition to other techniques, was published by Thiele and Palsson in 2010. The key parts of model preparation are: creating a metabolic network without gaps, adding constraints to the model, and finally adding an objective function (often called the Biomass function), usually to simulate the growth of the organism being modelled.

Metabolic Network and Software Tools

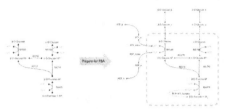

The first six reactions in Glycolysis prepared for FBA through the addition of an objective function (red) and the import and export of nutrients (ATP, ADP, BDG, ADG) across the system boundary (dashed green line).

Metabolic networks can vary in scope from those describing a single pathway, up to the cell, tissue or organism. The main requirement of a metabolic network that forms the basis of an FBA-ready network is that it contains no gaps. This typically means that extensive manual curation is required, making the preparation of a metabolic network for flux-balance analysis a process that can take months or years. However, recent advances such as so-called gap-filling methods can reduce the required time to weeks or months.

Software packages for creation of FBA models include Pathway Tools/MetaFlux, Simpheny, and MetNetMaker.

Generally models are created in BioPAX or SBML format so that further analysis or visualization can take place in other software although this is not a requirement.

Constraints

A key part of FBA is the ability to add constraints to the flux rates of reactions within networks, forcing them to stay within a range of selected values. This lets the model more accurately simulate real metabolism. The constraints belong to two subsets from a biological perspective; boundary constraints that limit nutrient uptake/excretion and internal constraints that limit the flux through reactions within the organism. In mathematical terms, the application of constraints can be considered to reduce the solution space of the FBA model. In addition to constraints applied at the edges of a metabolic network, constraints can be applied to reactions deep within the network. These constraints are usually simple; they may constrain the direction of a reaction due to energy considerations or constrain the maximum speed of a reaction due to the finite speed of all reactions in nature.

Growth Media Constraints

Organisms, and all other metabolic systems, require some input of nutrients. Typically the rate of uptake of nutrients is dictated by their availability (a nutrient that is not present cannot be absorbed), their concentration and diffusion constants (higher concentrations of quickly-diffusing metabolites are absorbed more quickly) and the method of absorption (such as active transport or facilitated diffusion versus simple diffusion).

If the rate of absorption (and/or excretion) of certain nutrients can be experimentally measured then this information can be added as a constraint on the flux rate at the edges of a metabolic model. This ensures that nutrients that are not present or not absorbed by the organism do not enter its metabolism (the flux rate is constrained to zero) and also means that known nutrient uptake rates are adhered to by the simulation. This provides a secondary method of making sure that the simulated metabolism has experimentally verified properties rather than just mathematically acceptable ones.

Thermodynamical Reaction Constraints

In principle, all reactions are reversible however in practice reactions often effectively occur in only one direction. This may be due to significantly higher concentration of reactants compared to the concentration of the products of the reaction. But more often it happens because the products of a reaction have a much lower free energy than the reactants and therefore the forward direction of a reaction is favored more.

For ideal reactions,

$$-\infty < v_i < \infty$$

For certain reactions a thermodynamic constraint can be applied implying direction (in this case forward)

$$0 < v_i < \infty$$

Realistically the flux through a reaction cannot be infinite (given that enzymes in the real system are finite) which implies that,

$$0 < v_i < v_{max}$$

Experimentally Measured Flux Constraints

Certain flux rates can be measured experimentally ($v_{i,m}$) and the fluxes within a metabolic model can be constrained, within some error (ε), to ensure these known flux rates are accurately reproduced in the simulation.

$$v_{i,m} - \varepsilon < v_i < v_{i,m} + \varepsilon$$

Flux rates are most easily measured for nutrient uptake at the edge of the network. Measurements of internal fluxes is possible using radioactively labelled or NMR visible metabolites.

Constrained FBA-ready metabolic models can be analyzed using software such as the COBRA toolbox(requires MATLAB), SurreyFBA, or the web-based FAME. Additional software packages have been listed elsewhere. A comprehensive review of all such software and their functionalities has been recently reviewed.

An open-source alternative is available in the R (programming language) as the packages abcdeFBA or sybil for performing FBA and other constraint based modeling techniques.

Objective Function

FBA can give a large number of mathematically acceptable solutions to the steady-state problem $(S\vec{v} = 0)$. However solutions of biological interest are the ones which produce the desired metabolites in the correct proportion. The objective function defines the proportion of these metabolites. For instance when modelling the growth of an organism the objective function is generally defined as biomass. Mathematically, it is a column in the stoichiometry matrix the entries of which place a "demand" or act as a "sink" for biosynthetic precursors such as fatty acids, amino acids and cell wall components which are present on the corresponding rows of the S matrix. These entries represent experimentally measured, dry weight proportions of cellular components. Therefore, this column becomes a lumped reaction that simulates growth and reproduction. Therefore, the accuracy of experimental measurements plays an essential role in the correct definition of the biomass function and makes the results of FBA biologically applicable by ensuring that the correct proportion of metabolites are produced by metabolism.

When modeling smaller networks the objective function can be changed accordingly. An example of this would be in the study of the carbohydrate metabolism pathways where the objective function would probably be defined as a certain proportion of ATP and NADH and thus simulate the production of high energy metabolites by this pathway.

Optimization of the Objective/Biomass Function

Linear programming can be used to find a single optimal solution. The most common biological optimization goal for a whole-organism metabolic network would be to choose the flux vector $\vec{v}$ that maximises the flux through a biomass function composed of the constituent metabolites of the organism placed into the stoichiometric matrix and denoted $v_{biomass}$ or simply v_b

$$\max_{\vec{v}} v_b \qquad \text{s.t.} \qquad S\vec{v} = 0$$

In the more general case any reaction can be defined and added to the biomass function with either the condition that it be maximised or minimised if a single "optimal" solution is desired. Alternatively, and in the most general case, a vector $\vec{c}$ can be introduced, which defines the weighted set of reactions that the linear programming model should aim to maximise or minimise,

$$\max{}_{\vec{v}} \; \vec{v} \cdot \vec{c} \quad \text{s.t.} \quad \mathbf{S}\vec{v} = 0.$$

In the case of there being only a single separate biomass function/reaction within the stoichiometric matrix $\vec{c}$ would simplify to all zeroes with a value of 1 (or any non-zero value) in the position corresponding to that biomass function. Where there were multiple separate objective functions $\vec{c}$ would simplify to all zeroes with weighted values in the positions corresponding to all objective functions.

Reducing the Solution Space – biological Considerations for the System

The analysis of the null space of matrices is implemented in software packages specialized for matrix operations such as Matlab and Octave. Determination of the null space of $\mathbf{S}$ tells us all the possible collections of flux vectors (or linear combinations thereof) that balance fluxes within the biological network. The advantage of this approach becomes evident in biological systems which are described by differential equation systems with many unknowns. The velocities in the differential equations above - v_1 and v_2 - are dependent on the reaction rates of the underlying equations. The velocities are generally taken from the Michaelis–Menten kinetic theory, which involves the kinetic parameters of the enzymes catalyzing the reactions and the concentration of the metabolites themselves. Isolating enzymes from living organisms and measuring their kinetic parameters is a difficult task, as is measuring the internal concentrations and diffusion constants of metabolites within an organism. Therefore, the differential equation approach to metabolic modeling is beyond the current scope of science for all but the most studied organisms. FBA avoids this impediment by applying the homeostatic assumption, which is a reasonably approximate description of biological systems.

Although FBA avoids that biological obstacle, the mathematical issue of a large solution space remains. FBA has a two-fold purpose. Accurately representing the biological limits of the system and returning the flux distribution closest to the natural fluxes within the target system/organism. Certain biological principles can help overcome the mathematical difficulties. While the stoichiometric matrix is almost always under-determined initially (meaning that the solution space to $\mathbf{S}\vec{v} = 0$ is very large), the size of the solution space can be reduced and be made more reflective of the biology of the problem through the application of certain constraints on the solutions.

Extensions

The success of FBA and the realization of its limitations has led to extensions that attempt to mediate the limitations of the technique.

Flux Variability Analysis

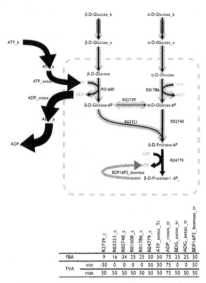

	R2739_c	R03321_c	R02740_c	R01600_c	R01786_c	R04779_c	ATP_extoc_Tr	ADP_ctoec_tr	BDG_extoc_tr	ADG_extoc_tr	BDF16P2_biomass_tr
FBA	9	16	34	25	25	50	50	75	25	25	50
FVA min	-50	0	0	0	0	50	50	75	0	0	50
FVA max	50	50	50	50	50	50	50	75	50	50	50

Visual and numerical representation of FVA on a complete network.

The optimal solution to the flux-balance problem is rarely unique with many possible, and equally optimal, solutions existing. Flux variability analysis (FVA), built into virtually all current analysis software, returns the boundaries for the fluxes through each reaction that can, paired with the right combination of other fluxes, produce the optimal solution.

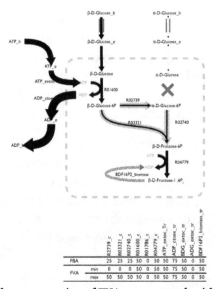

	R2739_c	R03321_c	R02740_c	R01600_c	R01786_c	R04779_c	ATP_extoc_Tr	ADP_ctoec_tr	BDG_extoc_tr	ADG_extoc_tr	BDF16P2_biomass_tr
FBA	25	25	25	50	0	50	50	75	50	0	50
FVA min	0	0	0	50	0	50	50	75	50	0	50
FVA max	50	50	50	50	0	50	50	75	50	0	50

Visual and numerical representation of FVA on a network with non-lethal deletion.

Reactions which can support a low variability of fluxes through them are likely to be of a higher importance to an organism and FVA is a promising technique for the identification of reactions that are highly important.

Minimization of Metabolic Adjustment (MOMA)

When simulating knockouts or growth on media, FBA gives the final steady-state flux distribution. This final steady state is reached in varying time-scales. For example, the predicted growth rate of *E. coli* on glycerol as the primary carbon source did not match the FBA predictions, however on sub-culturing for 40 days or 700 generations the growth rate adaptively evolved to match the FBA prediction.

Sometimes it is of interest to find out what is the immediate effect of a perturbation or knockout, since it takes time for regulatory changes to occur and for the organism to re-organize fluxes to optimally utilize a different carbon source or circumvent the effect of the knockout. MOMA predicts the immediate sub-optimal flux distribution following the perturbation by minimizing the distance (Euclidean) between the wild-type FBA flux distribution and the mutant flux distribution using quadratic programming. This yields an optimization problem of the form.

$$\min \| \mathbf{v_w} - \mathbf{v_d} \|^2 \qquad s.t. \quad \mathbf{S} \cdot \mathbf{v_d} = 0$$

where $\mathbf{v_w}$ represents the wild-type (or unperturbed state) flux distribution and $\mathbf{v_d}$ represents the flux distribution on gene deletion that is to be solved for. This simplifies to:

$$\min \frac{1}{2} \mathbf{v_d}^T \mathbf{I} \mathbf{v_d} + (-\mathbf{v_w}) \cdot \mathbf{v_d} \qquad s.t. \quad \mathbf{S} \cdot \mathbf{v_d} = 0$$

This is the MOMA solution which represents the flux distribution immediately post-perturbation.

Regulatory On-Off Minimization (ROOM)

ROOM attempts to improve the prediction of the metabolic state of an organism after a gene knockout. It follows the same premise as MOMA that an organism would try to restore a flux distribution as close as possible to the wild-type after a knockout. However it further hypothesizes that this steady state would be reached through a series of transient metabolic changes by the regulatory network and that the organism would try to minimize the number of regulatory changes required to reach the wild-type state. Instead of using a distance metric minimization however it uses a Mixed Integer Linear Programming method.

Dynamic FBA

Dynamic FBA attempts to add the ability for models to change over time, thus in some ways avoiding the strict steady state condition of pure FBA. Typically the technique involves running an FBA simulation, changing the model based on the outputs of that simulation, and rerunning the simulation. By repeating this process an element of feed-back is achieved over time.

Comparison with Other Techniques

FBA provides a less simplistic analysis than Choke Point Analysis while requiring far less information on reaction rates and a much less complete network reconstruction than a full dynamic simulation would require. In filling this niche, FBA has been shown to be a very useful technique for analysis of the metabolic capabilities of cellular systems.

Choke Point Analysis

Unlike choke point analysis which only considers points in the network where metabolites are produced but not consumed or vice versa, FBA is a true form of metabolic network modelling because it considers the metabolic network as a single complete entity (the stoichiometric matrix) at all stages of analysis. This means that network effects, such as chemical reactions in distant pathways affecting each other, can be reproduced in the model. The upside to the inability of choke point analysis to simulate network effects is that it considers each reaction within a network in isolation and thus can suggest important reactions in a network even if a network is highly fragmented and contains many gaps.

Dynamic Metabolic Simulation

Unlike dynamic metabolic simulation, FBA assumes that the internal concentration of metabolites within a system stays constant over time and thus is unable to provide anything other than steady-state solutions. It is unlikely that FBA could, for example, simulate the functioning of a nerve cell. Since the internal concentration of metabolites is not considered within a model, it is possible that an FBA solution could contain metabolites at a concentration too high to be biologically acceptable. This is a problem that dynamic metabolic simulations would probably avoid. One advantage of the simplicity of FBA over dynamic simulations is that they are far less computationally expensive, allowing the simulation of large numbers of perturbations to the network. A second advantage is that the reconstructed model can be substantially simpler by avoiding the need to consider enzyme rates and the effect of complex interactions on enzyme kinetics.

Weighted Correlation Network Analysis

Weighted correlation network analysis, also known as weighted gene co-expression network analysis (WGCNA), is a widely used data mining method especially for studying biological networks based on pairwise correlations between variables. While it can be applied to most high-dimensional data sets, it has been most widely used in genomic applications. It allows one to define modules (clusters), intramodular hubs, and network nodes with regard to module membership, to study the relationships between co-expression modules, and to compare the network topology of different networks (differential network analysis). WGCNA can be used as data reduction technique (related to oblique factor analysis), as clustering method (fuzzy clustering), as feature selection method (e.g. as gene screening method), as framework for integrating complementary (genomic) data (based on weighted correlations between quantitative variables), and as data exploratory technique. Although WGCNA incorporates traditional data exploratory techniques, its intuitive network language and analysis framework transcend any standard analysis technique. Since it uses network methodology and is well suited for integrating complementary genomic data sets, it can be interpreted as systems biologic or systems genetic data analysis method. By selecting intramodular hubs in consensus modules, WGCNA also gives rise to network based meta analysis techniques

History

The WGCNA method was developed by Steve Horvath, a professor of human genetics at the David Geffen School of Medicine at UCLA and of biostatistics at the UCLA Fielding School of Public Health and his colleagues at UCLA, and (former) lab members (in particular Peter Langfelder, Bin Zhang, Jun Dong). Much of the work arose from collaborations with applied researchers. In particular, weighted correlation networks were developed in joint discussions with cancer researchers Paul Mischel, Stanley F. Nelson, and neuroscientists Daniel H. Geschwind, Michael C. Oldham (according to the acknowledgement section in). There is a vast literature on dependency networks, scale free networks and coexpression networks.

Comparison between Weighted and Unweighted Correlation Networks

A weighted correlation network can be interpreted as special case of a weighted network, dependency network or correlation network. Weighted correlation network analysis can be attractive for the following reasons:

- The network construction (based on soft thresholding the correlation coefficient) preserves the continuous nature of the underlying correlation information. For example, weighted correlation networks that are constructed on the basis of correlations between numeric variables do not require the choice of a hard threshold. Dichotomizing information and (hard)-thresholding may lead to information loss.

- The network construction is highly robust results with respect to different choices of the soft threshold. In contrast, results based on unweighted networks, constructed by thresholding a pairwise association measure, often strongly depend on the threshold.

- Weighted correlation networks facilitate a geometric interpretation based on the angular interpretation of the correlation, chapter 6 in.

- Resulting network statistics can be used to enhance standard data-mining methods such as cluster analysis since (dis)-similarity measures can often be transformed into weighted networks., chapter 6 in

- WGCNA provides powerful module preservation statistics which can be used to quantify whether can be found in another condition. Also module preservation statistics allow one to study differences between the modular structure of networks.

- Weighted networks and correlation networks can often be approximated by "factorizable" networks. Such approximations are often difficult to achieve for sparse, unweighted networks. Therefore, weighted (correlation) networks allow for a parsimonious parametrization (in terms of modules and module membership) (chapters 2, 6 in) and

Method

First, one defines a gene co-expression similarity measure which is used to define the network. We denote the gene co-expression similarity measure of a pair of genes i and j by s_{ij}. Many co-expression studies use the absolute value of the correlation as an unsigned co-expression similarity measure,

$$s_{ij}^{unsigned} = |cor(x_i, x_j)|$$

where gene expression profiles x_i and x_j consist of the expression of genes i and j across multiple samples. However, using the absolute value of the correlation may obfuscate biologically relevant information, since no distinction is made between gene repression and activation. In contrast, in signed networks the similarity between genes reflects the sign of the correlation of their expression profiles. To define a signed co-expression measure between gene expression profiles x_i and x_j, one can use a simple transformation of the correlation:

$$s_{ij}^{signed} = 0.5 + 0.5cor(x_i, x_j)$$

As the unsigned measure $s_{ij}^{unsigned}$, the signed similarity s_{ij}^{signed} takes on a value between 0 and 1. Note that the unsigned similarity between two oppositely expressed genes ($cor(x_i, x_j) = -1$) equals 1 while it equals 0 for the signed similarity. Similarly, while the unsigned co-expression measure of two genes with zero correlation remains zero, the signed similarity equals 0.5.

Next, an adjacency matrix (network), $A = [a_{ij}]$, is used to quantify how strongly genes are connected to one another. A is defined by thresholding the co-expression similarity matrix $S = [s_{ij}]$. 'Hard' thresholding (dichotomizing) the similarity measure S results in an unweighted gene co-expression network. Specifically an unweighted network adjacency is defined to be 1 if $s_{ij} > \tau$ and 0 otherwise. Because hard thresholding encodes gene connections in a binary fashion, it can be sensitive to the choice of the threshold and result in the loss of co-expression information. The continuous nature of the co-expression information can be preserved by employing soft thresholding, which results in a weighted network. Specifically, WGCNA uses the following power function assess their connection strength:

$$a_{ij} = (s_{ij})^\beta,$$

where the power β is the soft thresholding parameter. The default values $\beta = 6$ and $\beta = 12$ are used for unsigned and signed networks, respectively. Alternatively, β can be chosen using the scale-free topology criterion which amounts to choosing the smallest value of β such that approximate scale free topology is reached.

Since $log(a_{ij}) = \beta log(s_{ij})$, the weighted network adjacency is linearly related to the co-expression similarity on a logarithmic scale. Note that a high power β transforms high similarities into high adjacencies, while pushing low similarities towards 0. Since this soft-thresholding procedure applied to a pairwise correlation matrix leads to weighted adjacency matrix, the ensuing analysis is referred to as weighted gene co-expression network analysis.

A major step in the module centric analysis is to cluster genes into network modules using a network proximity measure. Roughly speaking, a pair of genes has a high proximity if it is closely interconnected. By convention, the maximal proximity between two genes is 1 and the minimum proximity is 0. Typically, WGCNA uses the define the topological overlap measure (TOM) as proximity. which can also be defined for weighted networks. The TOM combines the adjacency of two genes and the connection strengths these two genes share with other "third party" genes. The TOM is a highly robust measure of network interconnectedness (proximity). This proximity is used as input of average linkage hierarchical clustering. Modules are defined as branches of the resulting cluster tree using the dynamic branch cutting approach Next the genes inside a given module are summarize with the module eigengene, which can be considered as the best summary of the standardized module expression data. The module eigengene of a given module is defined as the first principal component of the standardized expression profiles. To find modules that relate to a clinical trait of interest, module eigengenes are correlated with the clinical trait of interest, which gives rise to an eigengene significance measure. One can also construct co-expression networks between module eigengenes (eigengene networks), i.e. networks whose nodes are modules To identify intramodular hub genes inside a given module, one can use two types of connectivity measures. The first, referred to as $kME_i = cor(x_i, ME)$, , is defined based on correlating each gene with the respective module eigengene. The second, referred to as kIN, is defined as a sum of adjacencies with respect to the module genes. In practice, these two measures are equivalent. To test whether a module is preserved in another data set, one can use various network statistics, e.g. *Zsummary*.

Applications

WGCNA has been widely used for analyzing gene expression data (i.e. transcriptional data), e.g. to find intramodular hub genes.

It is often used as data reduction step in systems genetic applications where modules are represented by "module eigengenes" e.g. Module eigengenes can be used to correlate modules with clinical traits. Eigengene networks are coexpression networks between module eigengenes (i.e. networks whose nodes are modules) . WGCNA is widely used in neuroscientific applications, e.g. and for analyzing genomic data including microarray data (Kadarmideen et al. 2011), single cell RNA-Seq data (Kogelman et al. 2014) DNA methylation data, miRNA data, peptide counts and microbiota data (16S rRNA gene sequencing). Other applications include brain imaging data, e.g. functional MRI data

R Software Package

The WGCNA R software package provides functions for carrying out all aspects of weighted network analysis (module construction, hub gene selection, module preservation statistics, differential network analysis, network statistics). The WGCNA package is available from the Comprehensive R Archive Network (CRAN), the standard repository for R add-on packages.

Gene Prediction

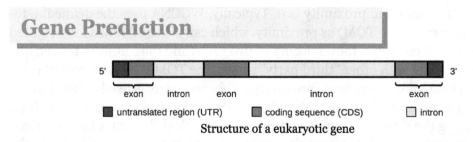

Structure of a eukaryotic gene

In computational biology gene prediction or gene finding refers to the process of identifying the regions of genomic DNA that encode genes. This includes protein-coding genes as well as RNA genes, but may also include prediction of other functional elements such as regulatory regions. Gene finding is one of the first and most important steps in understanding the genome of a species once it has been sequenced.

In its earliest days, "gene finding" was based on painstaking experimentation on living cells and organisms. Statistical analysis of the rates of homologous recombination of several different genes could determine their order on a certain chromosome, and information from many such experiments could be combined to create a genetic map specifying the rough location of known genes relative to each other. Today, with comprehensive genome sequence and powerful computational resources at the disposal of the research community, gene finding has been redefined as a largely computational problem.

Determining that a sequence is functional should be distinguished from determining the function of the gene or its product. Predicting the function of a gene and confirming that the gene prediction is accurate still demands *in vivo* experimentation through gene knockout and other assays, although frontiers of bioinformatics research are making it increasingly possible to predict the function of a gene based on its sequence alone.

Gene prediction is one of the key steps in genome annotation, following sequence assembly, the filtering of non-coding regions and repeat masking.

Gene prediction is closely related to the so-called 'target search problem' investigating how DNA-binding proteins (transcription factors) locate specific binding sites within the genome. Many aspects of structural gene prediction are based on current understanding of underlying biochemical processes in the cell such as gene transcription, translation, protein–protein interactions and regulation processes, which are subject of active research in the various omics fields such as transcriptomics, proteomics, metabolomics, and more generally structural and functional genomics.

Empirical Methods

In empirical (similarity, homology or evidence-based) gene finding systems, the target genome is searched for sequences that are similar to extrinsic evidence in the form of the known expressed sequence tags, messenger RNA (mRNA), protein products, and homologous or orthologous sequences. Given an mRNA sequence, it is trivial to derive a unique genomic DNA sequence from which it had to have been transcribed. Given a protein sequence, a family of possible coding DNA sequences can be derived by reverse translation of the genetic code. Once candidate DNA sequences have been determined, it is a relatively straightforward algorithmic problem to efficiently search a target genome for matches, complete or partial, and exact or inexact. Given a sequence, local alignment algorithms such as BLAST, FASTA and Smith-Waterman look for regions of similarity between the target sequence and possible candidate matches. Matches can be complete or partial, and exact or inexact. The success of this approach is limited by the contents and accuracy of the sequence database.

A high degree of similarity to a known messenger RNA or protein product is strong evidence that a region of a target genome is a protein-coding gene. However, to apply this approach systemically requires extensive sequencing of mRNA and protein products. Not only is this expensive, but in complex organisms, only a subset of all genes in the organism's genome are expressed at any given time, meaning that extrinsic evidence for many genes is not readily accessible in any single cell culture. Thus, to collect extrinsic evidence for most or all of the genes in a complex organism requires the study of many hundreds or thousands of cell types, which presents further difficulties. For example, some human genes may be expressed only during development as an embryo or fetus, which might be difficult to study for ethical reasons.

Despite these difficulties, extensive transcript and protein sequence databases have been generated for human as well as other important model organisms in biology, such as mice and yeast. For example, the RefSeq database contains transcript and protein sequence from many different species, and the Ensembl system comprehensively maps this evidence to human and several other genomes. It is, however, likely that these databases are both incomplete and contain small but significant amounts of erroneous data.

New high-throughput transcriptome sequencing technologies such as RNA-Seq and ChIP-sequencing open opportunities for incorporating additional extrinsic evidence into gene prediction and validation, and allow structurally rich and more accurate alternative to previous methods of measuring gene expression such as expressed sequence tag or DNA microarray.

Major challenges involved in gene prediction involve dealing with sequencing errors in raw DNA data, dependence on the quality of the sequence assembly, handling short reads, Frameshift mutations, overlapping genes and incomplete genes.

In prokaryotes it's essential to consider horizontal gene transfer when searching for gene sequence homology. An additional important factor underused in current gene detection tools is existence of gene clusters—operons in both prokaryotes and eukaryotes. Most popular gene detectors treat each gene in isolation, independent of others, which is not biologically accurate.

Ab Initio Methods

Ab Initio gene prediction is an intrinsic method based on gene content and signal detection. Because of the inherent expense and difficulty in obtaining extrinsic evidence for many genes, it is also necessary to resort to *ab initio* gene finding, in which the genomic DNA sequence alone is systematically searched for certain tell-tale signs of protein-coding genes. These signs can be broadly categorized as either *signals*, specific sequences that indicate the presence of a gene nearby, or *content*, statistical properties of the protein-coding sequence itself. *Ab initio* gene finding might be more accurately characterized as gene *prediction*, since extrinsic evidence is generally required to conclusively establish that a putative gene is functional.

In the genomes of prokaryotes, genes have specific and relatively well-understood pro- moter sequences (signals), such as the Pribnow box and transcription factor binding sites, which are easy to systematically identify. Also, the sequence coding for a protein occurs as one contiguous open reading frame (ORF), which is typically many hundred or thousands of base pairs long. The statistics of stop codons are such that even find- ing an open reading frame of this length is a fairly informative sign. (Since 3 of the 64 possible codons in the genetic code are stop codons, one would expect a stop codon ap- proximately every 20–25 codons, or 60–75 base pairs, in a random sequence.) Further- more, protein-coding DNA has certain periodicities and other statistical properties that are easy to detect in sequence of this length. These characteristics make prokaryotic gene finding relatively straightforward, and well-designed systems are able to achieve high levels of accuracy.

Ab initio gene finding in eukaryotes, especially complex organisms like humans, is con- siderably more challenging for several reasons. First, the promoter and other regulatory signals in these genomes are more complex and less well-understood than in prokaryotes, making them more difficult to reliably recognize. Two classic examples of signals identified by eukaryotic gene finders are CpG islands and binding sites for a poly(A) tail.

Second, splicing mechanisms employed by eukaryotic cells mean that a particular pro- tein-coding sequence in the genome is divided into several parts (exons), separated by non-coding sequences (introns). (Splice sites are themselves another signal that eu- karyotic gene finders are often designed to identify.) A typical protein-coding gene in hu- mans might be divided into a dozen exons, each less than two hundred base pairs in length, and some as short as twenty to thirty. It is therefore much more difficult to detect periodic- ities and other known content properties of protein-coding DNA in eukaryotes.

Advanced gene finders for both prokaryotic and eukaryotic genomes typically use com- plex probabilistic models, such as hidden Markov models (HMMs) to combine infor- mation from a variety of different signal and content measurements. The GLIMMER system is a widely used and highly accurate gene finder for prokaryotes. GeneMark is another popular approach. Eukaryotic *ab initio* gene finders, by comparison, have achieved only limited success; notable examples are the GENSCAN and geneid pro- grams. The SNAP gene finder is HMM-based like Genscan, and attempts to be more adaptable to different organisms, addressing problems related to using a gene finder on a genome sequence that it was not trained against. A few recent approaches like mSplicer, CONTRAST, or mGene also use machine learning techniques like support vector machines for successful gene prediction. They build a discriminative model us- ing hidden Markov support vector machines or conditional random fields to learn an accurate gene prediction scoring function.

Ab Initio methods have been benchmarked, with some approaching 100% sensitivity, however as the sensitivity increases, accuracy suffers as a result of increased false pos- itives.

Other Signals

Among the derived signals used for prediction are statistics resulting from the sub-sequence statistics like k-mer statistics, Isochore (genetics) or Compositional domain GC composition/uniformity/entropy, sequence and frame length, Intron/Exon/Donor/Acceptor/Promoter and Ribosomal binding site vocabulary, Fractal dimension, Fourier transform of a pseudo-number-coded DNA, Z-curve parameters and certain run features.

It has been suggested that signals other than those directly detectable in sequences may improve gene prediction. For example, the role of secondary structure in the identification of regulatory motifs has been reported. In addition, it has been suggested that RNA secondary structure prediction helps splice site prediction.

Neural Networks

Neural networks are computational models that excel at machine learning and pattern recognition. Neural networks must be trained with example data before being able to generalise for experimental data, and tested against benchmark data. Neural networks are able to come up with approximate solutions to problems that are hard to solve algorithmically, provided there is sufficient training data. When applied to gene prediction, neural networks can be used alongside other *ab initio* methods to predict or identify biological features such as splice sites. One approach involves using a sliding window, which traverses the sequence data in an overlapping manner. The output at each position is a score based on whether the network thinks the window contains a donor splice site or an acceptor splice site. Larger windows offer more accuracy but also require more computational power. A neural network is an example of a signal sensor as its goal is to identify a functional site in the genome.

Combined Approaches

Programs such as Maker combine extrinsic and *ab initio* approaches by mapping protein and EST data to the genome to validate *ab initio* predictions. Augustus, which may be used as part of the Maker pipeline, can also incorporate hints in the form of EST alignments or protein profiles to increase the accuracy of the gene prediction.

Comparative Genomics Approaches

As the entire genomes of many different species are sequenced, a promising direction in current research on gene finding is a comparative genomics approach.

This is based on the principle that the forces of natural selection cause genes and other functional elements to undergo mutation at a slower rate than the rest of the genome, since mutations in functional elements are more likely to negatively impact the organism than mutations elsewhere. Genes can thus be detected by comparing the genomes of related species to detect this evolutionary pressure for conservation. This approach was first applied to the mouse and human genomes, using programs such as SLAM, SGP and TWINSCAN/N-SCAN and CONTRAST.

Multiple Informants

TWINSCAN examined only human-mouse synteny to look for orthologous genes. Programs such as N-SCAN and CONTRAST allowed the incorporation of alignments from multiple organisms, or in the case of N-SCAN, a single alternate organism from the target. The use of multiple informants can lead to significant improvements in accuracy.

CONTRAST is composed of two elements. The first is a smaller classifier, identifying donor splice sites and acceptor splice sites as well as start and stop codons. The second element involves constructing a full model using machine learning. Breaking the problem into two means that smaller targeted data sets can be used to train the classifiers, and that classifier can operate independently and be trained with smaller windows. The full model can use the independent classifier, and not have to waste computational time or model complexity re-classifying intron-exon boundaries. The paper in which CONTRAST is introduced proposes that their method (and those of TWINSCAN, etc.) be classified as *de novo* gene assembly, using alternate genomes, and identifying it as distinct from *ab initio*, which uses a target 'informant' genomes.

Comparative gene finding can also be used to project high quality annotations from one genome to another. Notable examples include Projector, GeneWise and GeneMapper. Such techniques now play a central role in the annotation of all genomes.

Pseudogene Prediction

Pseudogenes are close relatives of genes, sharing very high sequence homology, but being unable to code for the same protein product. Whilst once relegated as byproducts of gene sequencing, increasingly, as regulatory roles are being uncovered, they are becoming predictive targets in their own right. Pseudogene prediction utilises existing sequence similarity and ab initio methods, whilst adding additional filtering and methods of identifying pseudogene characteristics.

Sequence similarity methods can be customised for pseudogene prediction using additional filtering to find candidate pseudogenes. This could use disablement detection, which looks for nonsense or frameshift mutations that would truncate or collapse an otherwise functional coding sequence. Additionally, translating DNA into proteins sequences can be more effective than just straight DNA homology.

Content sensors can be filtered according to the differences in statistical properties between pseudogenes and genes, such as a reduced count of CpG islands in pseudogenes, or the differences in G-C content between pseudogenes and their neighbours. Signal sensors also can be honed to pseudogenes, looking for the absence of introns or polyadenine tails.

Metagenomic Gene Prediction

Metagenomics is the study of genetic material recovered from the environment, resulting in sequence information from a pool of organisms. Predicting genes is useful for comparative metagenomics.

Metagenomics tools also fall into the basic categories of using either sequence similarity approaches (MEGAN4) and ab initio techniques (GLIMMER-MG).

Glimmer-MG is an extension to GLIMMER that relies mostly on an ab initio approach for gene finding and by using training sets from related organisms. The prediction strategy is augmented by classification and clustering gene data sets prior to applying ab initio gene prediction methods. The data is clustered by species. This classification method leverages techniques from metagenomic phylogenetic classification. An example of software for this purpose is, Phymm, which uses interpolated markov models—and PhymmBL, which integrates BLAST into the classification routines.

MEGAN4 uses a sequence similarity approach, using local alignment against databases of known sequences, but also attempts to classify using additional information on functional roles, biological pathways and enzymes. As in single organism gene prediction, sequence similarity approaches are limited by the size of the database.

FragGeneScan and MetaGeneAnnotator are popular gene prediction programs based on Hidden Markov model. These predictors account for sequencing errors, partial genes and work for short reads.

References

- Afrajmovich, V. S.; Arnold, V. I.; et al. (1994). Bifurcation Theory and Catastrophe Theory. ISBN 3-540-65379-1.

- Wiggins, Stephen (1988). Global bifurcations and Chaos: Analytical Methods. New York: Springer. ISBN 0-387-96775-3.

- Xuedong Huang; M. Jack; Y. Ariki (1990). Hidden Markov Models for Speech Recognition. Edinburgh University Press. ISBN 0-7486-0162-7.

- Richard Durbin; Sean R. Eddy; Anders Krogh; Graeme Mitchison (1999). Biological Sequence Analysis: Probabilistic Models of Proteins and Nucleic Acids. Cambridge University Press. ISBN 0-521-62971-3.

- Horvath S (2011). Weighted Network Analysis: Applications in Genomics and Systems Biology. Springer Book. 1st Edition., 2011, XXII, 414 p Hardcover ISBN 978-1-4419-8818-8 website

- Baum, L. E.; Sell, G. R. (1968). "Growth transformations for functions on manifolds". Pacific Journal of Mathematics. 27 (2): 211–227. doi:10.2140/pjm.1968.27.211. Retrieved 28 November 2011.

- Baum, L. E.; Petrie, T. (1966). "Statistical Inference for Probabilistic Functions of Finite State Markov Chains". The Annals of Mathematical Statistics. 37 (6): 1554–1563. doi:10.1214/aoms/1177699147. Retrieved 28 November 2011.

3

Modelling Biological Systems: An Overview

Modelling biological system is an important part of computational biology. It helps in the development of algorithms and data structures. Some of the aspects of modelling biological systems explained are protein structure prediction, simulated growth of plants and epidemic model. This text is an overview of the subject matter incorporating all the major aspects of modelling biological systems.

Modelling Biological Systems

Modelling biological systems is a significant task of systems biology and mathematical biology. Computational systems biology aims to develop and use efficient algorithms, data structures, visualization and communication tools with the goal of computer modelling of biological systems. It involves the use of computer simulations of biological systems, including cellular subsystems (such as the networks of metabolites and enzymes which comprise metabolism, signal transduction pathways and gene regulatory networks), to both analyze and visualize the complex connections of these cellular processes.

Artificial life or virtual evolution attempts to understand evolutionary processes via the computer simulation of simple (artificial) life forms.

Overview

It is understood that an unexpected emergent property of a complex system is a result of the interplay of the cause-and-effect among simpler, integrated parts. Biological systems manifest many important examples of emergent properties in the complex interplay of components. Traditional study of biological systems requires reductive methods in which quantities of data are gathered by category, such as concentration over time in response to a certain stimulus. Computers are critical to analysis and modelling of these data. The goal is to create accurate real-time models of a system's response to environmental and internal stimuli, such as a model of a cancer cell in order to find weaknesses in its signalling pathways, or modelling of ion channel mutations to see effects on cardiomyocytes and in turn, the function of a beating heart.

Standards

By far the most widely accepted standard format for storing and exchanging models in the field is the Systems Biology Markup Language (SBML) The SBML.org website includes a guide to many important software packages used in computational systems biology. Other markup languages with different emphases include BioPAX and CellML.

Particular Tasks

Cellular Model

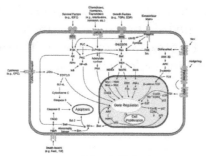

Part of the Cell Cycle

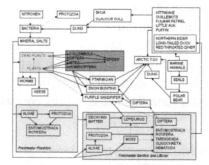

Summerhayes and Elton's 1923 food web of Bear Island (*Arrows represent an organism being consumed by another organism*).

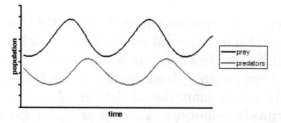

A sample time-series of the Lotka–Volterra model. Note that the two populations exhibit cyclic behaviour.

Creating a cellular model has been a particularly challenging task of systems biology and mathematical biology. It involves the use of computer simulations of the many cellular subsystems such as the networks of metabolites and enzymes which comprise metabolism, signal transduction pathways and gene regulatory networks to both ana-lyze and visualize the complex connections of these cellular processes.

The complex network of biochemical reaction/transport processes and their spatial organization make the development of a predictive model of a living cell a grand challenge for the 21st century, listed as such by the National Science Foundation (NSF) in 2006.

A whole cell computational model for the bacterium *Mycoplasma genitalium*, includ-ing all its 525 genes, gene products, and their interactions, was built by scientists from Stanford University and the J. Craig Venter Institute and published on 20 July 2012 in Cell.

A dynamic computer model of intracellular signaling was the basis for Merrimack Pharmaceuticals to discover the target for their cancer medicine MM-111.

Membrane computing is the task of modelling specifically a cell membrane.

Multi-cellular Organism Simulation

An open source simulation of C. elegans at the cellular level is being pursued by the OpenWorm community. So far the physics engine Gepetto has been built and mod-els of the neural connectome and a muscle cell have been created in the NeuroML format.

Protein Folding

Protein structure prediction is the prediction of the three-dimensional structure of a protein from its amino acid sequence—that is, the prediction of a protein's tertiary structure from its primary structure. It is one of the most important goals pursued by bioinformatics and theoretical chemistry. Protein structure prediction is of high im-portance in medicine (for example, in drug design) and biotechnology (for example, in the design of novel enzymes). Every two years, the performance of current methods is assessed in the CASP experiment.

Human Biological Systems

Brain Model

The Blue Brain Project is an attempt to create a synthetic brain by reverse-engineering the mammalian brain down to the molecular level. The aim of the project, founded in May 2005 by the Brain and Mind Institute of the *École Polytechnique* in Lausanne, Switzerland, is to study the brain's architectural and functional principles. The project is headed by the Institute's director, Henry Markram. Using a Blue Gene supercomput-er running Michael Hines's NEURON software, the simulation does not consist simply of an artificial neural network, but involves a partially biologically realistic model of neurons. It is hoped by its proponents that it will eventually shed light on the nature of consciousness. There are a number of sub-projects, including the Cajal Blue Brain, coordinated by the Supercomputing and Visualization Center of Madrid (CeSViMa), and others run by universities and independent laboratories in the UK, U.S., and Israel. The Human Brain Project builds on the work of the Blue Brain Project. It is one of six pilot projects in the Future Emerging Technologies Research Program of the European Commission, competing for a billion euro funding.

Model of the Immune System

The last decade has seen the emergence of a growing number of simulations of the immune system.

Virtual Liver

The Virtual Liver project is a 43 million euro research program funded by the German Government, made up of seventy research group distributed across Germany. The goal is to produce a virtual liver, a dynamic mathematical model that represents human liver physiology, morphology and function.

Tree Model

Electronic trees (e-trees) usually use L-systems to simulate growth. L-systems are very important in the field of complexity science and A-life. A universally accepted system for describing changes in plant morphology at the cellular or modular level has yet to be devised. The most widely implemented tree generating algorithms are described in the papers "Creation and Rendering of Realistic Trees", and Real-Time Tree Rendering

Ecological Models

Ecosystem models are mathematical representations of ecosystems. Typically they simplify complex foodwebs down to their major components or trophic levels, and quantify these as either numbers of organisms, biomass or the inventory/concentration of some pertinent chemical element (for instance, carbon or a nutrient species such as nitrogen or phosphorus).

Models in Ecotoxicology

The purpose of models in ecotoxicology is the understanding, simulation and prediction of effects caused by toxicants in the environment. Most current models describe effects on one of many different levels of biological organization (e.g. organisms or populations). A challenge is the development of models that predict effects across biological scales. Ecotoxicology and models discusses some types of ecotoxicological models and provides links to many others.

Modelling of Infectious Disease

It is possible to model the progress of most infectious diseases mathematically to discover the likely outcome of an epidemic or to help manage them by vaccination. This field tries to find parameters for various infectious diseases and to use those parameters to make useful calculations about the effects of a mass vaccination programme.

Cellular Model

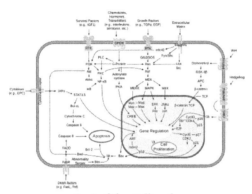

Part of the Cell cycle

Creating a cellular model has been a particularly challenging task of systems biology and mathematical biology. It involves developing efficient algorithms, data structures, visualization and communication tools to orchestrate the integration of large quantities of biological data with the goal of computer modeling.

It is also directly associated with bioinformatics, computational biology and Artificial life.

It involves the use of computer simulations of the many cellular subsystems such as the networks of metabolites and enzymes which comprise metabolism, signal transduction pathways and gene regulatory networks to both analyze and visualize the complex connections of these cellular processes.

The complex network of biochemical reaction/transport processes and their spatial organization make the development of a predictive model of a living cell a grand challenge for the 21st century.

Overview

The eukaryotic cell cycle is very complex and is one of the most studied topics, since its misregulation leads to cancers. It is possibly a good example of a mathematical model as it deals with simple calculus but gives valid results. Two research groups have produced several models of the cell cycle simulating several organisms. They have recently produced a generic eukaryotic cell cycle model which can represent a particular eukaryote depending on the values of the parameters, demonstrating that the idiosyncrasies of the individual cell cycles are due to different protein concentrations and affinities, while the underlying mechanisms are conserved (Csikasz-Nagy et al., 2006). By means of a system of ordinary differential equations these models show the change in time (dynamical system) of the protein inside a single typical cell; this type of model is called a deterministic process (whereas a model describing a statistical distribution of protein concentrations in a population of cells is called a stochastic process). To obtain these equations an iterative series of steps must be done: first the several models and observations are combined to form a consensus diagram and the appropriate kinetic laws are chosen to write the differential equations, such as rate kinetics for stoichiometric reactions, Michaelis-Menten kinetics for enzyme substrate reactions and Goldbeter–Koshland kinetics for ultrasensitive transcription factors, afterwards the parameters of the equations (rate constants, enzyme efficiency coefficients and Michaelis constants) must be fitted to match observations; when they cannot be fitted the kinetic equation is revised and when that is not possible the wiring diagram is modified. The parameters are fitted and validated using observations of both wild type and mutants, such as protein half-life and cell size.In order to fit the parameters the differential equations need to be studied. This can be done either by simulation or by analysis.In a simulation, given a starting vector (list of the values of the variables), the progression of the system is calculated by solving the equations at each time-frame in small increments. In analysis, the properties of the equations are used to investigate the behavior of the system depending of the values of the parameters and variables. A system of differential equations can be represented as a vector field, where each vector described the change (in concentration of two or more protein) determining where and how fast the trajectory (simulation) is heading. Vector fields can have several special points: a stable point, called a sink, that attracts in all directions (forcing the concentrations to be at a certain value), an unstable point, either a source or a saddle point which repels (forcing the concentrations to change away from a certain value), and a limit cycle, a closed trajectory towards which several trajectories spiral towards (making the concentrations oscillate). A better representation which can handle the large number of variables and parameters is called a bifurcation diagram (bifurcation theory): the presence of these special steady-state points at certain values of a parameter (e.g. mass) is represented by a point and once the parameter passes a certain value, a qualitative change occurs, called a bifurcation, in which the nature of the space changes, with profound consequences for the protein concentrations: the cell cycle has phases (partially corresponding to G1 and G2) in which mass, via a stable point, controls cyclin levels, and phases (S and M phases) in which the concentrations change independently, but once the phase has changed at a bifurcation event (cell cycle checkpoint), the system cannot go back to the previous levels since at the current mass the vector field is profoundly different and the mass cannot be reversed back through the bifurcation event, making a checkpoint irreversible. In particular the S and M checkpoints are regulated by means of special bifurcations called a Hopf bifurcation and an infinite period bifurcation.

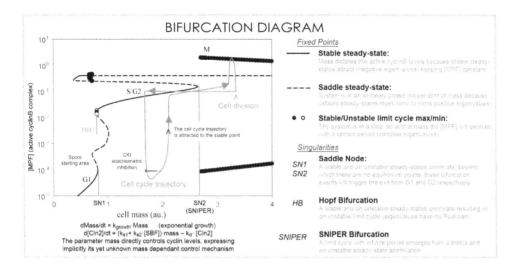

Molecular Level Simulations

Cell Collective is a modeling software that enables one to house dynamical biological data, build computational models, stimulate, break and recreate models. The development is led by Tomas Helikar, PhD Bioformatics, a researcher within the field of computational biology. It is designed for biologists, students learning about computational biology, teachers focused on teaching life sciences, and researchers within the field of life science. The complexities of math and computer science are built into the backend and one can learn about the methods used for modeling biological species, but complex math equations, algorithms, programming are not required and hence won't impede model building.

The mathematical framework behind Cell Collective is based on a common qualitative (discrete) modeling technique where the regulatory mechanism of each node is described with a logical function.

Model validation The model was constructed using local (e.g., protein–protein interaction) information from the primary literature. In other words, during the construction phase of the model, there was no attempt to determine the local interactions based on any other larger phenotypes or phenomena. However, after the model was completed, verification of the accuracy of the model involved testing it for the ability to reproduce complex input–output phenomena that have been observed in the laboratory. To do this, the T-cell model was simulated under a multitude of cellular conditions and analyzed in terms of input–output dose–response curves to determine whether the model behaves as expected, including various downstream effects as a result of activation of the TCR, G-protein-coupled receptor, cytokine, and integrin pathways.

E-Cell Project aims "to make precise whole cell simulation at the molecular level possible".

CytoSolve - developed by V. A. Shiva Ayyadurai and C. Forbes Dewey, Jr. of Department of Biological Engineering at the Massachusetts Institute of Technology - provided a method to model the whole cell by dynamically integrating multiple molecular pathway models. .''

In the July 2012 issue of *Cell*, a team led by Markus Covert at Stanford published the most complete computational model of a cell to date. The model of the roughly 500-gene *Mycoplasma genitalium* contains 28 algorithmically-independent components incorporating work from over 900 sources. It accounts for interactions of the complete genome, transcriptome, proteome, and metabolome of the organism, marking a significant advancement for the field.

Most attempts at modeling cell cycle processes have focused on the broad, complicated molecular interactions of many different chemicals, including several cyclin and cyclin-dependent kinase molecules as they correspond to the S, M, G1 and G2 phases of the cell cycle. In a 2014 published article in PLOS computational biology, collaborators at University of Oxford, Virginia Tech and Institut de Génétique et Développement de Rennes produced a simplified model of the cell cycle using only one cyclin/CDK interaction. This model showed the ability to control totally functional cell division through regulation and manipulation only the one interaction, and even allowed researchers to skip phases through varying the concentration of CDK. This model could help understand how the relatively simple interactions of one chemical translate to a cellular level model of cell division.

Projects

Multiple projects are in progress.

- CytoSolve
- Synthecell
- Karyote - Indiana University
- E-Cell Project
- Virtual Cell - University of Connecticut Health Center
- Silicon Cell
- WholeCell - Stanford University

Protein Structure Prediction

Protein structure prediction is the inference of the three-dimensional structure of a protein from its amino acid sequence — that is, the prediction of its folding and its secondary and tertiary structure from its primary structure. Structure prediction is fundamentally different from the inverse problem of protein design. Protein structure prediction is one of the most important goals pursued by bioinformatics and theoretical chemistry; it is highly important in medicine (for example, in drug design) and biotechnology (for example, in the design of novel enzymes). Every two years, the performance of current methods is assessed in the CASP experiment (Critical Assessment of Techniques for Protein Structure Prediction). A continuous evaluation of protein structure prediction web servers is performed by the community project CAMEO3D.

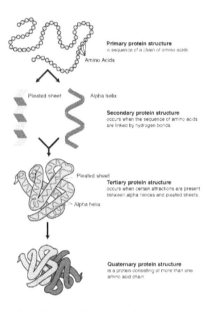

Constituent amino-acids can be analyzed to predict secondary, tertiary and quaternary protein structure.

Protein Structure and Terminology

Proteins are chains of amino acids joined together by peptide bonds. Many conformations of this chain are possible due to the rotation of the chain about each Cα atom. It is these conformational changes that are responsible for differences in the three dimensional structure of proteins. Each amino acid in the chain is polar, i.e. it has separated positive and negative charged regions with a free C=O group, which can act as hydrogen bond acceptor and an NH group, which can act as hydrogen bond donor. These groups can therefore interact in the protein structure. The 20 amino acids can be classified according to the chemistry of the side chain which also plays an important structural role. Glycine takes on a special position, as it has the smallest side chain, only one Hydrogen atom, and therefore can increase the local flexibility in the protein structure. Cysteine on the other hand can react with another cysteine residue and thereby form a cross link stabilizing the whole structure.

The protein structure can be considered as a sequence of secondary structure elements, such as α helices and β sheets, which together constitute the overall three-dimensional configuration of the protein chain. In these secondary structures regular patterns of H bonds are formed between neighboring amino acids, and the amino acids have similar Φ and Ψ angles.

Bond angles for ψ and ω

The formation of these structures neutralizes the polar groups on each amino acid. The secondary structures are tightly packed in the protein core in a hydrophobic environment. Each amino acid side group has a limited volume to occupy and a limited number of possible interactions with other nearby side chains, a situation that must be taken into account in molecular modeling and alignments.

α Helix

The α helix is the most abundant type of secondary structure in proteins. The α helix has 3.6 amino acids per turn with an H bond formed between every fourth residue; the average length is 10 amino acids (3 turns) or 10 Å but varies from 5 to 40 (1.5 to 11 turns). The alignment of the H bonds creates a dipole moment for the helix with a resulting partial positive charge at the amino end of the helix. Because this region has free NH2 groups, it will interact with negatively charged groups such as phosphates. The most common location of α helices is at the surface of protein cores, where they provide an interface with the aqueous environment. The inner-facing side of the helix tends to have hydrophobic amino acids and the outer-facing side hydrophilic amino acids. Thus, every third of four amino acids along the chain will tend to be hydrophobic, a pattern that can be quite readily detected. In the leucine zipper motif, a repeating pattern of leucines on the facing sides of two adjacent helices is highly predictive of the motif. A helical-wheel plot can be used to show this repeated pattern. Other α helices buried in the protein core or in cellular membranes have a higher and more regular distribution of hydrophobic amino acids, and are highly predictive of such structures. Helices exposed on the surface have a lower proportion of hydrophobic amino acids. Amino acid content can be predictive of an α -helical region. Regions richer in alanine (A), glutamic acid (E), leucine (L), and methionine (M) and poorer in proline (P), glycine (G), tyrosine (Y), and serine (S) tend to form an α helix. Proline destabilizes or breaks an α helix but can be present in longer helices, forming a bend.

An alpha-helix with hydrogen bonds (yellow dots)

B Sheet

β sheets are formed by H bonds between an average of 5–10 consecutive amino acids in one portion of the chain with another 5–10 farther down the chain. The interacting regions may be adjacent, with a short loop in between, or far apart, with other structures in between. Every chain may run in the same direction to form a parallel sheet, every other chain may run in the reverse chemical direction to form an anti parallel sheet, or the chains may be parallel and anti parallel to form a mixed sheet.The pattern of H bonding is different in the parallel and anti parallel configurations. Each amino acid in the interior strands of the sheet forms two H bonds with neighboring amino acids, whereas each amino acid on the outside strands forms only one bond with an interior strand. Looking across the sheet at right angles to the strands, more distant strands are rotated slightly counterclockwise to form a left-handed twist. The Cα atoms alternate above and below the sheet in a pleated structure, and the R side groups of the amino acids alternate above and below the pleats. The Φ and Ψ angles of the amino acids in sheets vary considerably in one region of the Ramachandran plot. It is more difficult to predict the location of β sheets than of α helices. The situation improves somewhat when the amino acid variation in multiple sequence alignments is taken into account.

Loop

Loops are regions of a protein chain that are (1) between α helices and β sheets, (2) of various lengths and three-dimensional configurations, and (3) on the surface of the structure. Hairpin loops that represent a complete turn in the polypeptide chain joining two antiparallel β strands may be as short as two amino acids in length. Loops interact with the surrounding aqueous environment and other proteins. Because amino acids in loops are not constrained by space and environment as are amino acids in the core region, and do not have an effect on the arrangement of secondary structures in the core, more substitutions, insertions, and deletions may occur. Thus, in a sequence alignment, the presence of these features may be an indication of a loop. The positions of introns in genomic DNA sometimes correspond to the locations of loops in the encoded protein. Loops also tend to have charged and polar amino acids and are frequently a component of active sites. A detailed examination of loop structures has shown that they fall into distinct families.

Coils

A region of secondary structure that is not a α helix, a β sheet, or a recognizable turn is commonly referred to as a coil.

Protein Classification

Proteins may be classified according to both structural and sequence similarity. For structural classification, the sizes and spatial arrangements of secondary structures described in the above paragraph are compared in known three-dimensional structures. Classification based on sequence similarity was historically the first to be used. Initially, similarity based on alignments of whole sequences was performed. Later, proteins were classified on the basis of the occurrence of conserved amino acid patterns. Databases that classify proteins by one or more of these schemes are available. In considering protein classification schemes, it is important to keep several observations in mind. First, two entirely different protein sequences from different evolutionary origins may fold into a similar structure. Conversely, the sequence of an ancient gene for a given structure may have diverged considerably in different species while at the same time maintaining the same basic structural features. Recognizing any remaining sequence similarity in such cases may be a very difficult task. Second, two proteins that share a significant degree of sequence similarity either with each other or with a third sequence also share an evolutionary origin and should share some structural features also. However, gene duplication and genetic rearrangements during evolution may give rise to new gene copies, which can then evolve into proteins with new function and structure.

Terms Used for Classifying Protein Structures and Sequences

The more commonly used terms for evolutionary and structural relationships among proteins are listed below. Many additional terms are used for various kinds of structural features found in proteins. Descriptions of such terms may be found at the CATH Web site the Structural Classification of Proteins (SCOP) Web site and a Glaxo-Wellcome tutorial on the Swiss bioinformatics Expasy Web site.

active site

> a localized combination of amino acid side groups within the tertiary (three-dimensional) or quaternary (protein subunit) structure that can interact with a chemically specific substrate and that provides the protein with biological ac-

tivity. Proteins of very different amino acid sequences may fold into a structure that produces the same active site.

architecture

> the relative orientations of secondary structures in a three-dimensional structure without regard to whether or not they share a similar loop structure.

fold

> a type of architecture that also has a conserved loop structure.

blocks

> a conserved amino acid sequence pattern in a family of proteins. The pattern includes a series of possible matches at each position in the represented sequences, but there are not any inserted or deleted positions in the pattern or in the sequences. By way of contrast, sequence profiles are a type of scoring matrix that represents a similar set of patterns that includes insertions and deletions.

class

> a term used to classify protein domains according to their secondary structural content and organization. Four classes were originally recognized by Levitt and Chothia (1976), and several others have been added in the SCOP database. Three classes are given in the CATH database: mainly-α, mainly-β, and α–β, with the α–β class including both alternating α/β and $\alpha+\beta$ structures.

core

> the portion of a folded protein molecule that comprises the hydrophobic interior of α-helices and β-sheets. The compact structure brings together side groups of amino acids into close enough proximity so that they can interact. When comparing protein structures, as in the SCOP database, core is the region common to most of the structures that share a common fold or that are in the same superfamily. In structure prediction, core is sometimes defined as the arrangement of secondary structures that is likely to be conserved during evolutionary change.

domain (sequence context)

> a segment of a polypeptide chain that can fold into a three-dimensional structure irrespective of the presence of other segments of the chain. The separate domains of a given protein may interact extensively or may be joined only by a length of polypeptide chain. A protein with several domains may use these domains for functional interactions with different molecules.

family (sequence context)

> a group of proteins of similar biochemical function that are more than 50% identical when aligned. This same cutoff is still used by the Protein Information Resource (PIR). A protein family comprises proteins with the same function in different organisms (orthologous sequences) but may also include proteins in the same organism (paralogous sequences) derived from gene duplication and rearrangements. If a multiple sequence alignment of a protein family reveals a common level of similarity throughout the lengths of the proteins, PIR refers to the family as a homeomorphic family. The aligned region is referred to as a homeomorphic domain, and this region may comprise several smaller homology domains that are shared with other families. Families may be further subdivided into subfamilies or grouped into superfamilies based on respective higher or lower levels of sequence similarity. The SCOP database reports 1296 families and the CATH database (version 1.7 beta), reports 1846 families.

> When the sequences of proteins with the same function are examined in greater detail, some are found to share high sequence similarity. They are obviously members of the same family by the above criteria. However, others are found that have very little, or even insignificant, sequence similarity with other family members. In such cases, the family relationship between two distant family members A and C can often be demonstrated by finding an additional family member B that shares significant similarity with both A and C. Thus, B provides a connecting link between A and C. Another approach is to examine distant alignments for highly conserved matches.

> At a level of identity of 50%, proteins are likely to have the same three-dimensional structure, and the identical atoms in the sequence alignment will also superimpose within approximately 1 Å in the structural model. Thus, if the structure of one member of a family is known, a reliable prediction may be made for a second member of the family, and the higher the identity level, the more reliable the prediction. Protein structural modeling can be performed by examining how well the amino acid substitutions fit into the core of the three-dimensional structure.

family (structural context)

> as used in the FSSP database (Families of structurally similar proteins) and the DALI/FSSP Web site, two structures that have a significant level of structural similarity but not necessarily significant sequence similarity.

fold

> similar to structural motif, includes a larger combination of secondary structural units in the same configuration. Thus, proteins sharing the same fold have the same combination of secondary structures that are connected by similar loops.

An example is the Rossman fold comprising several alternating α helices and parallel β strands. In the SCOP, CATH, and FSSP databases, the known protein structures have been classified into hierarchical levels of structural complexity with the fold as a basic level of classification.

homologous domain (sequence context)

an extended sequence pattern, generally found by sequence alignment methods, that indicates a common evolutionary origin among the aligned sequences. A homology domain is generally longer than motifs. The domain may include all of a given protein sequence or only a portion of the sequence. Some domains are complex and made up of several smaller homology domains that became joined to form a larger one during evolution. A domain that covers an entire sequence is called the homeomorphic domain by PIR (Protein Information Resource).

module

a region of conserved amino acid patterns comprising one or more motifs and considered to be a fundamental unit of structure or function. The presence of a module has also been used to classify proteins into families.

motif (sequence context)

a conserved pattern of amino acids that is found in two or more proteins. In the Prosite catalog, a motif is an amino acid pattern that is found in a group of proteins that have a similar biochemical activity, and that often is near the active site of the protein. Examples of sequence motif databases are the Prosite catalog and the Stanford Motifs Database.

motif (structural context)

a combination of several secondary structural elements produced by the folding of adjacent sections of the polypeptide chain into a specific three-dimensional configuration. An example is the helix-loop-helix motif. Structural motifs are also referred to as supersecondary structures and folds.

position-specific scoring matrix (sequence context, also known as weight or scoring matrix)

represents a conserved region in a multiple sequence alignment with no gaps. Each matrix column represents the variation found in one column of the multiple sequence alignment.

Position-specific scoring matrix—3D (structural context) represents the amino acid variation found in an alignment of proteins that fall into the same structural class. Matrix columns represent the amino acid variation found at one amino acid position in the aligned structures.

primary structure

> the linear amino acid sequence of a protein, which chemically is a polypeptide chain composed of amino acids joined by peptide bonds.

profile (sequence context)

> a scoring matrix that represents a multiple sequence alignment of a protein family. The profile is usually obtained from a well-conserved region in a multiple sequence alignment. The profile is in the form of a matrix with each column representing a position in the alignment and each row one of the amino acids. Matrix values give the likelihood of each amino acid at the corresponding position in the alignment. The profile is moved along the target sequence to locate the best scoring regions by a dynamic programming algorithm. Gaps are allowed during matching and a gap penalty is included in this case as a negative score when no amino acid is matched. A sequence profile may also be represented by a hidden Markov model, referred to as a profile HMM (hidden markov model).

profile (structural context)

> a scoring matrix that represents which amino acids should fit well and which should fit poorly at sequential positions in a known protein structure. Profile columns represent sequential positions in the structure, and profile rows represent the 20 amino acids. As with a sequence profile, the structural profile is moved along a target sequence to find the highest possible alignment score by a dynamic programming algorithm. Gaps may be included and receive a penalty. The resulting score provides an indication as to whether or not the target protein might adopt such a structure.

quaternary structure

> the three-dimensional configuration of a protein molecule comprising several independent polypeptide chains.

secondary structure

> the interactions that occur between the C, O, and NH groups on amino acids in a polypeptide chain to form α-helices, β-sheets, turns, loops, and other forms, and that facilitate the folding into a three-dimensional structure.

superfamily

> a group of protein families of the same or different lengths that are related by distant yet detectable sequence similarity. Members of a given superfamily thus have a common evolutionary origin. Originally, Dayhoff defined the cutoff for superfamily status as being the chance that the sequences are not related of 10 6, on the basis of an alignment score (Dayhoff et al. 1978). Proteins with few identities in an

alignment of the sequences but with a convincingly common number of structural and functional features are placed in the same superfamily. At the level of three-dimensional structure, superfamily proteins will share common structural features such as a common fold, but there may also be differences in the number and arrangement of secondary structures. The PIR resource uses the term *homeomorphic superfamilies* to refer to superfamilies that are composed of sequences that can be aligned from end to end, representing a sharing of single sequence homology domain, a region of similarity that extends throughout the alignment. This domain may also comprise smaller homology domains that are shared with other protein families and superfamilies. Although a given protein sequence may contain domains found in several superfamilies, thus indicating a complex evolutionary history, sequences will be assigned to only one homeomorphic superfamily based on the presence of similarity throughout a multiple sequence alignment. The superfamily alignment may also include regions that do not align either within or at the ends of the alignment. In contrast, sequences in the same family align well throughout the alignment.

supersecondary structure

a term with similar meaning to a structural motif. Tertiary structure is the three-dimensional or globular structure formed by the packing together or folding of secondary structures of a polypeptide chain.

Secondary Structure

Secondary structure prediction is a set of techniques in bioinformatics that aim to predict the local secondary structures of proteins based only on knowledge of their amino acid sequence. For proteins, a prediction consists of assigning regions of the amino acid sequence as likely alpha helices, beta strands (often noted as "extended" conformations), or turns. The success of a prediction is determined by comparing it to the results of the DSSP algorithm (or similar e.g. STRIDE) applied to the crystal structure of the protein. Specialized algorithms have been developed for the detection of specific well-defined patterns such as transmembrane helices and coiled coils in proteins.

The best modern methods of secondary structure prediction in proteins reach about 80% accuracy; this high accuracy allows the use of the predictions as feature improving fold recognition and ab initio protein structure prediction, classification of structural motifs, and refinement of sequence alignments. The accuracy of current protein secondary structure prediction methods is assessed in weekly benchmarks such as LiveBench and EVA.

Background

Early methods of secondary structure prediction, introduced in the 1960s and early 1970s, focused on identifying likely alpha helices and were based mainly on helix-coil transition models. Significantly more accurate predictions that included beta sheets were introduced in the 1970s and relied on statistical assessments based on proba- bility parameters derived from known solved structures. These methods, applied to a single sequence, are typically at most about 60-65% accurate, and often underpredict beta sheets. The evolutionary conservation of secondary structures can be exploited by simultaneously assessing many homologous sequences in a multiple sequence align- ment, by calculating the net secondary structure propensity of an aligned column of amino acids. In concert with larger databases of known protein structures and mod- ern machine learning methods such as neural nets and support vector machines, these methods can achieve up 80% overall accuracy in globular proteins. The theoretical up- per limit of accuracy is around 90%, partly due to idiosyncrasies in DSSP assignment near the ends of secondary structures, where local conformations vary under native conditions but may be forced to assume a single conformation in crystals due to packing constraints. Limitations are also imposed by secondary structure prediction's inability to account for tertiary structure; for example, a sequence predicted as a likely helix may still be able to adopt a beta-strand conformation if it is located within a beta-sheet region of the protein and its side chains pack well with their neighbors. Dramatic conformational chang- es related to the protein's function or environment can also alter local secondary structure.

Historical Perspective

To date, over 20 different secondary structure prediction methods have been developed. One of the first algorithms was Chou-Fasman method, which relies predominantly on probability parameters determined from relative frequencies of each amino acid's ap- pearance in each type of secondary structure. The original Chou-Fasman parameters, determined from the small sample of structures solved in the mid-1970s, produce poor results compared to modern methods, though the parameterization has been updated since it was first published. The Chou-Fasman method is roughly 50-60% accurate in predicting secondary structures.

The next notable program was the GOR method, named for the three scientists who de- veloped it — *G*arnier, *O*sguthorpe, and *R*obson, is an information theory-based meth- od. It uses the more powerful probabilistic technique of Bayesian inference. The GOR method takes into account not only the probability of each amino acid having a partic- ular secondary structure, but also the conditional probability of the amino acid assum- ing each structure given the contributions of its neighbors (it does not assume that the neighbors have that same structure). The approach is both more sensitive and more accurate than that of Chou and Fasman because amino acid structural propensities are only strong for a small number of amino acids such as proline and glycine. Weak contributions from each of many neighbors can add up to strong effects overall. The original GOR method was roughly 65% accurate and is dramatically more successful in predicting alpha helices than beta sheets, which it frequently mispredicted as loops or disorganized regions.

Another big step forward, was using machine learning methods. First artificial neural networks methods were used. As a training sets they use solved structures to identify common sequence motifs associated with particular arrangements of secondary structures. These methods are over 70% accurate in their predictions, although beta strands are still often underpredicted due to the lack of three-dimensional structural information that would allow assessment of hydrogen bonding patterns that can promote formation of the extended conformation required for the presence of a complete beta sheet. PSIPRED and JPRED are some of the most known programs based on neural networks for protein secondary structure prediction. Next, support vector machines have proven particularly useful for predicting the locations of turns, which are difficult to identify with statistical methods.

Extensions of machine learning techniques attempt to predict more fine-grained local properties of proteins, such as backbone dihedral angles in unassigned regions. Both SVMs and neural networks have been applied to this problem. More recently, real-value torsion angles can be accurately predicted by SPINE-X and successfully employed for ab initio structure prediction.

Other Improvements

It is reported that in addition to the protein sequence, secondary structure formation depends on other factors. For example, it is reported that secondary structure tendencies depend also on local environment, solvent accessibility of residues, protein structural class, and even the organism from which the proteins are obtained. Based on such observations, some studies have shown that secondary structure prediction can be improved by addition of information about protein structural class, residue accessible surface area and also contact number information.

Tertiary Structure

The practical role of protein structure prediction is now more important than ever. Massive amounts of protein sequence data are produced by modern large-scale DNA sequencing efforts such as the Human Genome Project. Despite community-wide efforts in structural genomics, the output of experimentally determined protein structures—typically by time-consuming and relatively expensive X-ray crystallography or NMR spectroscopy—is lagging far behind the output of protein sequences.

The protein structure prediction remains an extremely difficult and unresolved undertaking. The two main problems are calculation of protein free energy and finding the global minimum of this energy. A protein structure prediction method must explore the space of possible protein structures which is astronomically large. These problems can be partially bypassed in "comparative" or homology modeling and fold recognition methods, in which the search space is pruned by the assumption that the protein in question adopts a structure that is close to the experimentally determined structure of another homologous protein. On the other hand, the *de novo* or ab initio protein structure prediction methods must explicitly resolve these problems. The progress and challenges in protein structure prediction has been reviewed in Zhang 2008.

Ab Initio Protein Modelling

Energy- and Fragment-based Methods

Ab initio- or *de novo-* protein modelling methods seek to build three-dimensional protein models "from scratch", i.e., based on physical principles rather than (directly) on previously solved structures. There are many possible procedures that either attempt to mimic protein folding or apply some stochastic method to search possible solutions (i.e., global optimization of a suitable energy function). These procedures tend to require vast computational resources, and have thus only been carried out for tiny proteins. To predict protein structure *de novo* for larger proteins will require better algorithms and larger computational resources like those afforded by either powerful supercomputers (such as Blue Gene or MDGRAPE-3) or distributed computing (such as Folding@home, the Human Proteome Folding Project and Rosetta@Home). Although these computational barriers are vast, the potential benefits of structural genomics (by predicted or experimental methods) make *ab initio* structure prediction an active research field.

As of 2009, a 50-residue protein could be simulated atom-by-atom on a supercomputer for 1 millisecond. As of 2012, comparable stable-state sampling could be done on a standard desktop with a new graphics card and more sophisticated algorithms. A much larger simulation timescales can be achieved using coarse-grained modeling.

Evolutionary Covariation to Predict 3D Contacts

As sequencing became more commonplace in the 1990s several groups used protein sequence alignments to predict correlated mutations and it was hoped that these coevolved residues could be used to predict tertiary structure (using the analogy to distance constraints from experimental procedures such as NMR). The assumption is when single residue mutations are slightly deleterious, compensatory mutations may occur to restabilize residue-residue interactions. This early work used what are known as *local* methods to calculate correlated mutations from protein sequences, but suffered from indirect false correlations which result from treating each pair of residues as independent of all other pairs.

In 2011, a different, and this time *global* statistical approach, demonstrated that predicted coevolved residues were sufficient to predict the 3D fold of a protein, providing there are enough sequences available (>1,000 homologous sequences are needed). The method, EVfold, uses no homology modeling, threading or 3D structure fragments and can be run on a standard personal computer even for proteins with hundreds of residues. The accuracy of the contacts predicted using this and related approaches has now been demonstrated on many known structures and contact maps, including the prediction of experimentally unsolved transmembrane proteins.

Comparative Protein Modeling

Comparative protein modelling uses previously solved structures as starting points, or templates. This is effective because it appears that although the number of actual proteins is vast, there is a limited set of tertiary structural motifs to which most proteins belong. It has been suggested that there are only around 2,000 distinct protein folds in nature, though there are many millions of different proteins.

These methods may also be split into two groups:

Homology modeling

> is based on the reasonable assumption that two homologous proteins will share very similar structures. Because a protein's fold is more evolutionarily conserved than its amino acid sequence, a target sequence can be modeled with reasonable accuracy on a very distantly related template, provided that the relationship between target and template can be discerned through sequence alignment. It has been suggested that the primary bottleneck in comparative modelling arises from difficulties in alignment rather than from errors in structure prediction given a known-good alignment. Unsurprisingly, homology modelling is most accurate when the target and template have similar sequences.

Protein threading

> scans the amino acid sequence of an unknown structure against a database of solved structures. In each case, a scoring function is used to assess the compatibility of the sequence to the structure, thus yielding possible three-dimensional models. This type of method is also known as 3D-1D fold recognition due to its compatibility analysis between three-dimensional structures and linear protein sequences. This method has also given rise to methods performing an inverse folding search by evaluating the compatibility of a given structure with a large database of sequences, thus predicting which sequences have the potential to produce a given fold.

Side-chain Geometry Prediction

Accurate packing of the amino acid side chains represents a separate problem in protein structure prediction. Methods that specifically address the problem of predicting side-chain geometry include dead-end elimination and the self-consistent mean field methods. The side chain conformations with low energy are usually determined on the rigid polypeptide backbone and using a set of discrete side chain conformations known as "rotamers." The methods attempt to identify the set of rotamers that minimize the model's overall energy.

These methods use rotamer libraries, which are collections of favorable conformations for each residue type in proteins. Rotamer libraries may contain information about the conformation, its frequency, and the standard deviations about mean dihedral angles, which can be used in sampling. Rotamer libraries are derived from structural bioinformatics or other statistical analysis of side-chain conformations in known experimental structures of proteins, such as by clustering the observed conformations for tetrahedral carbons near the staggered (60°, 180°, -60°) values.

Rotamer libraries can be backbone-independent, secondary-structure-dependent, or backbone-dependent. Backbone-independent rotamer libraries make no reference to backbone conformation, and are calculated from all available side chains of a certain type (for instance, the first example of a rotamer library, done by Ponder and Richards at Yale in 1987). Secondary-structure-dependent libraries present different dihedral angles and/or rotamer frequencies for α-helix, β-sheet, or coil secondary structures. Backbone-dependent rotamer libraries present conformations and/or frequencies dependent on the local backbone conformation as defined by the backbone dihedral angles ϕ and ψ, regardless of secondary structure.

The modern versions of these libraries as used in most software are presented as multidimensional distributions of probability or frequency, where the peaks correspond to the dihedral-angle conformations considered as individual rotamers in the lists. Some versions are based on very carefully curated data and are used primarily for structure validation, while others emphasize relative frequencies in much larger data sets and are the form used primarily for structure prediction, such as the Dunbrack rotamer libraries.

Side-chain packing methods are most useful for analyzing the protein's hydrophobic core, where side chains are more closely packed; they have more difficulty addressing the looser constraints and higher flexibility of surface residues, which often occupy multiple rotamer conformations rather than just one.

Prediction of Structural Classes

Statistical methods have been developed for predicting structural classes of proteins based on their amino acid composition, pseudo amino acid composition and functional domain composition.

Quaternary Structure

In the case of complexes of two or more proteins, where the structures of the proteins are known or can be predicted with high accuracy, protein–protein docking methods can be used to predict the structure of the complex. Information of the effect of mutations at specific sites on the affinity of the complex helps to understand the complex structure and to guide docking methods.

Software

A great number of software tools for protein structure prediction exist. Approaches include homology modeling, protein threading, *ab initio* methods, secondary structure prediction, and transmembrane helix and signal peptide prediction. Two most successful methods based on CASP experiment are I-TASSER and HHpred.

Evaluation of Automatic Structure Prediction Servers

CASP, which stands for Critical Assessment of Techniques for Protein Structure Prediction, is a community-wide experiment for protein structure prediction taking place every two years since 1994. CASP provides with an opportunity to assess the quality of available human, non-automated methodology (human category) and automatic servers for protein structure prediction (server category, introduced in the CASP7). The official results of automated assessment in 2012 CASP10 are available at for automated servers and for human and server predictors. In December 2014 next CASP11 assessment will be publicly available.

The CAMEO3D Continuous Automated Model EvaluatiOn Server evaluates automated protein structure prediction servers on a weekly basis using blind predictions for newly release protein structures. CAMEO publishes the results on its website ().

Protein–protein Interaction Prediction

Protein–protein interaction prediction is a field combining bioinformatics and structural biology in an attempt to identify and catalog physical interactions between pairs or groups of proteins. Understanding protein–protein interactions is important for the investigation of intracellular signaling pathways, modelling of protein complex structures and for gaining insights into various biochemical processes. Experimentally, physical interactions between pairs of proteins can be inferred from a variety of experimental techniques, including yeast two-hybrid systems, protein-fragment complementation assays (PCA), affinity purification/mass spectrometry, protein microarrays, fluorescence resonance energy transfer (FRET), and Microscale Thermophoresis (MST). Efforts to experimentally determine the interactome of numerous species are ongoing, and a number of computational methods for interaction prediction have been developed in recent years.

Methods

Proteins that interact are more likely to co-evolve, therefore, it is possible to make inferences about interactions between pairs of proteins based on their phylogenetic distances. It has also been observed in some cases that pairs of interacting proteins have fused orthologues in other organisms. In addition, a number of bound protein complexes have been structurally solved and can be used to identify the residues that mediate the interaction so that similar motifs can be located in other organisms.

Phylogenetic Profiling

Phylogenetic profiling finds pairs of protein families with similar patterns of presence or absence across large numbers of species. This method is based on the hypothesis that potentially interacting proteins should co-evolve and should have orthologs in closely related species. That is, proteins that form complexes or are part of a pathway should be present simultaneously in order for them to function. A phylogenetic profile is constructed for each protein under investigation. The profile is basically a record of whether the protein is present in certain genomes. If two proteins are found to be present and absent in the same genomes, those proteins are deemed likely to be functionally related. A similar method can be applied to protein domains, where profiles are constructed for domains to determine if there are domain interactions. Some drawbacks with the phylogenetic profile methods are that they are computationally expensive to perform, they rely on homology detection between distant organisms, and they only identify if the proteins being investigated are functionally related (part of complex or in same pathway) and not if they have direct interactions.

Prediction of Co-evolved Protein Pairs Based on Similar Phylogenetic Trees

It was observed that the phylogenetic trees of ligands and receptors were often more similar than due to random chance. This is likely because they faced similar selection pressures and co-evolved. This method uses the phylogenetic trees of protein pairs to determine if interactions exist. To do this, homologs of the proteins of interest are found (using a sequence search tool such as BLAST) and multiple-sequence alignments are done (with alignment tools such as Clustal) to build distance matrices for each of the proteins of interest. The distance matrices should then be used to build phylogenetic trees. However, comparisons between phylogenetic trees are difficult, and current methods circumvent this by simply comparing distance matrices. The distance matrices of the proteins are used to calculate a correlation coefficient, in which a larger value corresponds to co-evolution. The benefit of comparing distance matrices instead of phylogenetic trees is that the results do not depend on the method of tree building that was used. The downside is that difference matrices are not perfect representations of phylogenetic trees, and inaccuracies may result from using such a shortcut. Another factor worthy of note is that there are background similarities between the phylogenetic trees of any protein, even ones that do not interact. If left unaccounted for, this could lead to a high false-positive rate. For this reason, certain methods construct a background tree using 16S rRNA sequences which they use as the canonical tree of life. The distance matrix constructed from this tree of life is then subtracted from the distance matrices of the proteins of interest. However, because RNA distance matrices and DNA distance matrices have different scale, presumably because RNA and DNA have different mutation rates, the RNA matrix needs to be rescaled before it can be subtracted from the DNA matrices. By using molecular clock proteins, the scaling coefficient for protein distance/RNA distance can be calculated. This coefficient is used to rescale the RNA matrix.

Rosetta Stone (Gene Fusion) Method

A Rosetta stone protein is a protein chain composed of two fused proteins. It is observed that proteins or domains that interact with one another tend to have homologs in other genomes that are fused into a Rosetta stone protein , such as might arise by gene fusion when two previously separate genes form a new composite one. This evolutionary mechanism can be used to predict protein interactions. If two proteins are separate in one organism but fused in the other, then it is very likely that they will interact in the case where they are expressed as two separate products. The STRING database makes use of this to predict protein-protein interactions. Gene fusion has been extensively studied and large amounts of data are available. Nonetheless, like phylogenetic profile methods, the Rosetta stone method does not necessarily find interacting proteins, as there can be other reasons for the fusion of two proteins, such as optimizing co-expression of the proteins. The most obvious drawback of this method is that there are many protein interactions that cannot be discovered this way; it relies on the presence of Rosetta stone proteins.

Classification Methods

Classification methods use data to train a program (classifier) to distinguish positive examples of interacting protein/domain pairs with negative examples of non-interacting pairs. Popular classifiers used are Random Forest Decision (RFD) and Support Vector Machines. RFD produces results based on the domain composition of interacting and non-interacting protein pairs. When given a protein pair to classify, RFD first creates a representation of the protein pair in a vector. The vector contains all the domain types used to train RFD, and for each domain type the vector also contains a value of 0, 1, or 2. If the protein pair does not contain a certain domain, then the value for that domain is 0. If one of the proteins of the pair contains the domain, then the value is 1. If both proteins contain the domain, then the value is 2. Using training data, RFD constructs a decision forest, consisting of many decision trees. Each decision tree evaluates several domains, and based on the presence or absence of interactions in these domains, makes a decision as to if the protein pair interacts. The vector representation of the protein pair is evaluated by each tree to determine if they are an interacting pair or a non-interacting pair. The forest tallies up all the input from the trees to come up with a final decision. The strength of this method is that it does not assume that domains interact independent of each other. This makes it so that multiple domains in proteins can be used in the prediction. This is a big step up from previous methods which could only predict based on a single domain pair. The limitation of this method is that it relies on the training dataset to produce results. Thus, usage of different training datasets could influence the results.

Inference of Interactions from Homologous Structures

This group of methods makes use of known protein complex structures to predict and structurally model interactions between query protein sequences. The prediction process generally starts by employing a sequence based method (e.g. Interolog) to search for protein complex structures that are homologous to the query sequences. These known complex structures are then used as templates to structurally model the interaction between query sequences. This method has the advantage of not only inferring protein interactions but also suggests models of how proteins interact structurally, which can provide some insights into the atomic level mechanism of that interaction. On the other hand, the ability for these methods to make a prediction is constrained by a limited number of known protein complex structures.

Association Methods

Association methods look for characteristic sequences or motifs that can help distinguish between interacting and non-interacting pairs. A classifier is trained by looking for sequence-signature pairs where one protein contains one sequence-signature, and its interacting partner contains another sequence-signature. They look specifically for sequence-signatures that are found together more often than by chance. This uses a log-odds score which is computed as $\log_2(Pij/PiPj)$, where Pij is the observed frequency of domains i and j occurring in one protein pair; Pi and Pj are the background frequencies of domains i and j in the data. Predicted domain interactions are those with positive log-odds scores and also having several occurrences within the database. The downside with this method is that it looks at each pair of interacting domains separately, and it assumes that they interact independently of each other.

Identification of Structural Patterns

This method builds a library of known protein–protein interfaces from the PDB, where the interfaces are defined as pairs of polypeptide fragments that are below a threshold slightly larger than the Van der Waals radius of the atoms involved. The sequences in the library are then clustered based on structural alignment and redundant sequences are eliminated. The residues that have a high (generally >50%) level of frequency for a given position are considered hotspots. This library is then used to identify potential interactions between pairs of targets, providing that they have a known structure (i.e. present in the PDB).

Bayesian Network Modelling

Bayesian methods integrate data from a wide variety of sources, including both experimental results and prior computational predictions, and use these features to assess the likelihood that a particular potential protein interaction is a true positive result. These methods are useful because experimental procedures, particularly the yeast two-hybrid experiments, are extremely noisy and produce many false positives, while the previously mentioned computational methods can only provide circumstantial evidence that a particular pair of proteins might interact.

Domain-pair Exclusion Analysis

The domain-pair exclusion analysis detects specific domain interactions that are hard to detect using Bayesian methods. Bayesian methods are good at detecting nonspecific promiscuous interactions and not very good at detecting rare specific interactions. The domain-pair exclusion analysis method calculates an E-score which measures if two domains interact. It is calculated as log(probability that the two proteins interact given that the domains interact/probability that the two proteins interact given that the domains don't interact). The probabilities required in the formula are calculated using an Expectation Maximization procedure, which is a method for estimating parameters in statistical models. High E-scores indicate that the two domains are likely to interact, while low scores indicate that other domains form the protein pair are more likely to be responsible for the interaction. The drawback with this method is that it does not take into account false positives and false negatives in the experimental data.

Supervised Learning Problem

The problem of PPI prediction can be framed as a supervised learning problem. In this paradigm the known protein interactions supervise the estimation of a function that can predict whether an interaction exists or not between two proteins given data about the proteins (e.g., expression levels of each gene in different experimental conditions, location information, phylogenetic profile, etc.).

Relationship to Docking Methods

The field of protein–protein interaction prediction is closely related to the field of protein–protein docking, which attempts to use geometric and steric considerations to fit two proteins of known structure into a bound complex. This is a useful mode of inquiry in cases where both proteins in the pair have known structures and are known (or at least strongly suspected) to interact, but since so many proteins do not have experimentally determined structures, sequence-based interaction prediction methods are especially useful in conjunction with experimental studies of an organism's interactome.

Simulated Growth of Plants

The simulated growth of plants is a significant task in of systems biology and mathematical biology, which seeks to reproduce plant morphology with computer software. Electronic trees (e-trees) usually use L-systems to simulate growth. L-systems are very important in the field of complexity science and A-life. A universally accepted system for describing changes in plant morphology at the cellular or modular level has yet to be devised. The most widely implemented tree-generating algorithms are described in the papers "Creation and Rendering of Realistic Trees", and Real-Time Tree Rendering

'Weeds', generated using an L-system in 3D.

The realistic modeling of plant growth is of high value to biology, but also for computer games.

Theory + Algorithms

A biologist, Aristid Lindenmayer (1925–1989) worked with yeast and filamentous fungi and studied the growth patterns of various types of algae, such as the blue/green bacteria *Anabaena catenula*. Originally the L-systems were devised to provide a formal description of the development of such simple multicellular organisms, and to illustrate the neighbourhood relationships between plant cells. Later on, this system was extended to describe higher plants and complex branching structures. Central to L-systems, is the notion of rewriting, where the basic idea is to define complex objects by successively replacing parts of a simple object using a set of rewriting rules or productions. The rewriting can be carried out recursively. L-Systems are also closely related to Koch curves.

Environmental Interaction

A challenge for plant simulations is to consistently integrate environmental factors, such as surrounding plants, obstructions, water and mineral availability, and lighting conditions. is to build virtual/environments with as many parameters as computationally feasible, thereby, not only simulating the growth of the plant, but also the environment it is growing within, and, in fact, whole ecosystems. Changes in resource availability influence plant growth, which in turn results in a change of resource availability. Powerful models and powerful hardware will be necessary to effectively simulate these recursive interactions of recursive structures.

Software

- Branching: L-system Tree   A Java applet and its source code (open source) of the botanical tree growth simulation using the L-system.

- Arbaro- opensource

- Treal- opensource

- L-arbor

- Genesis 3.0

- AmapSim - from Cirad

- GreenLab

- ONETREE -Accompanying the CDROM is a CO_2 meter that plugs into your local serial port. It is this that controls the growth rate of the trees. It is the actual carbon dioxide level right at your computer that controls the growth rate of these virtual trees.

- Powerplant

Ecosystem Model

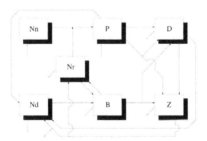

A structural diagram of the open ocean plankton ecosystem model of Fasham, Ducklow & McKelvie (1990).

An ecosystem model is an abstract, usually mathematical, representation of an ecological system (ranging in scale from an individual population, to an ecological community, or even an entire biome), which is studied to gain understanding of the real system.

Using data gathered from the field, ecological relationships — such as the relation of sunlight and water availability to photosynthetic rate, or that between predator and prey populations — are derived, and these are combined to form ecosystem models. These model systems are then studied in order to make predictions about the dynamics of the real system. Often, the study of inaccuracies in the model (when compared to empirical observations) will lead to the generation of hypotheses about possible ecological relations that are not yet known or well understood. Models enable researchers to simulate large-scale experiments that would be too costly or unethical to perform on a real ecosystem. They also enable the simulation of ecological processes over very long periods of time (i.e. simulating a process that takes centuries in reality, can be done in a matter of minutes in a computer model).

Ecosystem models have applications in a wide variety of disciplines, such as natural resource management, ecotoxicology and environmental health, agriculture, and wildlife conservation. It has also been applied to archaeology with varying degrees of success, through attempts to combine ecological models and archaeological models to explain mobility, diversity, etc. of stone tools

Types of Models

There are two major types of ecological models, which are generally applied to different types of problems: (1) *analytic* models and (2) *simulation/computational* models. Analytic models are often more complex mathematically, and work best when dealing with relatively simple (often linear) systems, specifically those that can be accurately described by a set of mathematical equations whose behavior is well known. Simulation models on the other hand, use numerical techniques to solve problems for which analytic solutions are impractical or impossible. Simulation models tend to be more widely used, and are generally considered more ecologically realistic, while analytic models are valued for their mathematical elegance and explanatory power. Ecopath is a powerful software system which uses simulation and computational methods to model marine ecosystems. It is widely used by marine and fisheries scientists as a tool for modelling and visualising the complex relationships that exist in real world marine ecosystems.

Model Design

The process of model design begins with a specification of the problem to be solved, and the objectives for the model.

Ecological systems are composed of an enormous number of biotic and abiotic factors that interact with each other in ways that are often unpredictable, or so complex as to be impossible to incorporate into a computable model. Because of this complexity, ecosystem models typically simplify the systems they are studying to a limited number of components that are well understood, and deemed relevant to the problem that the model is intended to solve.

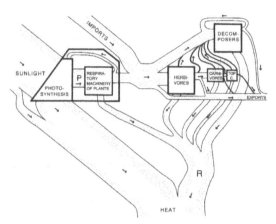

Diagram of the Silver Springs model (Odum, 1971). Note the aggregation into functional groups such as "herbivores" or "decomposers".

The process of simplification typically reduces an ecosystem to a small number of state variables and mathematical functions that describe the nature of the relationships between them. The number of ecosystem components that are incorporated into the model is limited by aggregating similar processes and entities into functional groups that are treated as a unit.

After establishing the components to be modeled and the relationships between them, another important factor in ecosystem model structure is the representation of space used. Historically, models have often ignored the confounding issue of space. However, for many ecological problems spatial dynamics are an important part of the problem, with different spatial environments leading to very different outcomes. *Spatially explicit models* (also called "spatially distributed" or "landscape" models) attempt to incorporate a heterogeneous spatial environment into the model. A spatial model is one that has one or more state variables that are a function of space, or can be related to other spatial variables.

Validation

After construction, models are *validated* to ensure that the results are acceptably accurate or realistic. One method is to test the model with multiple sets of data that are independent of the actual system being studied. This is important since certain inputs can cause a faulty model to output correct results. Another method of validation is to compare the model's output with data collected from field observations. Researchers frequently specify beforehand how much of a disparity they are willing to accept between parameters output by a model and those computed from field data.

Example: The Lotka–Volterra Equations

A sample time-series of the Lotka-Volterra model. Note that the two populations exhibit cyclic behaviour, and that the predator cycle lags behind that of the prey.

One of the earliest, and most well-known, ecological models is the predator-prey model of Alfred J. Lotka (1925) and Vito Volterra (1926). This model takes the form of a pair of ordinary differential equations, one representing a prey species, the other its predator.

$$\frac{dX}{dt} = \alpha.X - \beta.X.Y$$

$$\frac{dY}{dt} = \gamma.\beta.X.Y - \delta.Y$$

where,

• X is the number/concentration of the prey species;	• β is the predation rate of Y upon X ;
• Y is the number/concentration of the predator species;	• γ is the assimilation efficiency of Y ;
• α is the prey species' growth rate;	• δ is the mortality rate of the predator species

Volterra originally devised the model to explain fluctuations in fish and shark populations observed in the Adriatic Sea after the First World War (when fishing was curtailed). However, the equations have subsequently been applied more generally. Although simple, they illustrate some of the salient features of ecological models: modelled biological populations experience growth, interact with other populations (as either predators, prey or competitors) and suffer mortality.

A credible, simple alternative to the Lotka-Volterra predator-prey model and its common prey dependent generalizations is the ratio dependent or Arditi-Ginzburg model. The two are the extremes of the spectrum of predator interference models. According to the authors of the alternative view, the data show that true interactions in nature are so far from the Lotka-Volterra extreme on the interference spectrum that the model can simply be discounted as wrong. They are much closer to the ratio dependent extreme, so if a simple model is needed one can use the Arditi-Ginzburg model as the first approximation.

Mathematical Modelling of Infectious Disease

Mathematical models can project how infectious diseases progress to show the likely outcome of an epidemic and help inform public health interventions. Models use some basic assumptions and mathematics to find parameters for various infectious diseases and use those parameters to calculate the effects of possible interventions, like mass vaccination programmes.

History

Early pioneers in infectious disease modelling were William Hamer and Ronald Ross, who in the early twentieth century applied the law of mass action to explain epidemic behaviour. Lowell Reed and Wade Hampton Frost developed the Reed–Frost epidemic model to describe the relationship between susceptible, infected and immune individuals in a population.

Concepts

R_o, the basic reproduction number

The average number of other individuals each infected individual will infect in a population that has no immunity to the disease.

S

> The proportion of the population who are susceptible to the disease (neither immune nor infected).

A

> The average age at which the disease is contracted in a given population.

L

> The average life expectancy in a given population.

Assumptions

Models are only as good as the assumptions on which they are based. If a model makes predictions which are out of line with observed results and the mathematics is correct, the initial assumptions must change to make the model useful.

- Rectangular and stationary age distribution, i.e., everybody in the population lives to age L and then dies, and for each age (up to L) there is the same number of people in the population. This is often well-justified for developed countries where there is a low infant mortality and much of the population lives to the life expectancy.

- Homogeneous mixing of the population, i.e., individuals of the population under scrutiny assort and make contact at random and do not mix mostly in a smaller subgroup. This assumption is rarely justified because social structure is widespread, for example, most people in London, only make contact with other Londoners, and within London then there will be smaller subgroups such as the Turkish community or teenagers (just to give two examples) who will mix with each other more than people outside their group. However, homogeneous mixing is a standard assumption to make the mathematics tractable.

Endemic Steady State

An infectious disease is said to be endemic when it can be sustained in a population without the need for external inputs. This means that, on average, each infected person is infecting *exactly* one other person (any more and the number of people infected will grow exponentially and there will be an epidemic, any less and the disease will die out). In mathematical terms, that is:

$$R_0 = 1.$$

The basic reproduction number (R_0) of the disease, assuming everyone is susceptible, multiplied by the proportion of the population that is actually susceptible (S) must be one (since those who are not susceptible do not feature in our calculations as they cannot contract the disease). Notice that this relation means that for a disease to be in the endemic steady state, the higher the basic reproduction number, the lower the proportion of the population susceptible must be, and vice versa.

Assume the rectangular stationary age distribution and let also the ages of infection have the same distribution for each birth year. Let the average age of infection be A, for instance when individuals younger than A are susceptible and those older than A are immune (or infectious). Then it can be shown by an easy argument that the proportion of the population that is susceptible is given by:

$$S = \frac{A}{L}.$$

But the mathematical definition of the endemic steady state can be rearranged to give:

$$S = \frac{1}{R_0}.$$

Therefore, due to the transitive property:

$$\frac{1}{R_0} = \frac{A}{L} \Rightarrow R_0 = \frac{L}{A}.$$

This provides a simple way to estimate the parameter R_0 using easily available data.

For a population with an exponential age distribution,

$$R_0 = 1 + \frac{L}{A}.$$

This allows for the basic reproduction number of a disease given A and L in either type of population distribution.

Infectious Disease Dynamics

Mathematical models need to integrate the increasing volume of data being generated on host-pathogen interactions. Many theoretical studies of the population dynamics, structure and evolution of infectious diseases of plants and animals, including humans, are concerned with this problem.

Research topics include:

- transmission, spread and control of infection
- epidemiological networks
- spatial epidemiology
- persistence of pathogens within hosts
- intra-host dynamics
- immuno-epidemiology
- virulence
- Strain (biology) structure and interactions
- antigenic shift
- phylodynamics
- pathogen population genetics
- evolution and spread of resistance

- role of host genetic factors
- statistical and mathematical tools and innovations
- role and identification of infection reservoirs

Mathematics of Mass Vaccination

If the proportion of the population that is immune exceeds the herd immunity level for the disease, then the disease can no longer persist in the population. Thus, if this level can be exceeded by vaccination, the disease can be eliminated. An example of this being successfully achieved worldwide is the global smallpox eradication, with the last wild case in 1977. The WHO is carrying out a similar vaccination campaign to eradicate polio.

The herd immunity level will be denoted q. Recall that, for a stable state:

$$R_0 \cdot S = 1.$$

S will be $(1 - q)$, since q is the proportion of the population that is immune and $q + S$ must equal one (since in this simplified model, everyone is either susceptible or immune). Then:

$$R_0 \cdot (1 - q) = 1,$$

$$1 - q = \frac{1}{R_0},$$

$$q = 1 - \frac{1}{R_0}.$$

Remember that this is the threshold level. If the proportion of immune individuals *exceeds* this level due to a mass vaccination programme, the disease will die out.

We have just calculated the critical immunisation threshold (denoted q_c). It is the minimum proportion of the population that must be immunised at birth (or close to birth) in order for the infection to die out in the population.

$$q_c = 1 - \frac{1}{R_0}$$

When Mass Vaccination cannot Exceed the Herd Immunity

If the vaccine used is insufficiently effective or the required coverage cannot be reached (for example due to popular resistance), the programme may fail to exceed q_c. Such a programme can, however, disturb the balance of the infection without eliminating it, often causing unforeseen problems.

Suppose that a proportion of the population q (where $q < q_c$) is immunised at birth against an infection with $R_0 > 1$. The vaccination programme changes R_0 to R_q where

$$R_q = R_0(1-q)$$

This change occurs simply because there are now fewer susceptibles in the population who can be infected. R_q is simply R_0 minus those that would normally be infected but that cannot be now since they are immune.

As a consequence of this lower basic reproduction number, the average age of infection A will also change to some new value A_q in those who have been left unvaccinated.

Recall the relation that linked R_0, A and L. Assuming that life expectancy has not changed, now:

$$R_q = \frac{L}{A_q},$$

$$A_q = \frac{L}{R_q} = \frac{L}{R_0(1-q)}.$$

But $R_0 = L/A$ so:

$$A_q = \frac{L}{(L/A)(1-q)} = \frac{AL}{L(1-q)} = \frac{A}{1-q}.$$

Thus the vaccination programme will raise the average age of infection, another mathematical justification for a result that might have been intuitively obvious. Unvaccinated individuals now experience a reduced force of infection due to the presence of the vaccinated group.

However, it is important to consider this effect when vaccinating against diseases that are more severe in older people. A vaccination programme against such a disease that does not exceed q_c may cause more deaths and complications than there were before the programme was brought into force as individuals will be catching the disease later in life. These unforeseen outcomes of a vaccination programme are called perverse effects.

When Mass Vaccination Exceeds the Herd Immunity

If a vaccination programme causes the proportion of immune individuals in a population to exceed the critical threshold for a significant length of time, transmission of the infectious disease in that population will stop. This is known as elimination of the infection and is different from eradication.

Elimination

> Interruption of endemic transmission of an infectious disease, which occurs if each infected individual infects less than one other, is achieved by maintaining vaccination coverage to keep the proportion of immune individuals above the critical immunisation threshold.

Eradication

> Reduction of infective organisms in the wild worldwide to zero. So far, this has only been achieved for smallpox and rinderpest. To get to eradication, elimination in all world regions must be achieved.

Epidemic Model

An epidemic model is a simplified means of describing the transmission of communicable disease through individuals.

Introduction

The modeling of infectious diseases is a tool which has been used to study the mechanisms by which diseases spread, to predict the future course of an outbreak and to evaluate strategies to control an epidemic (Daley & Gani, 2005).

The first scientist who systematically tried to quantify causes of death was John Graunt in his book *Natural and Political Observations made upon the Bills of Mortality*, in 1662. The bills he studied were listings of numbers and causes of deaths published weekly. Graunt's analysis of causes of death is considered the beginning of the "theory of competing risks" which according to Daley and Gani (Daley & Gani, 2005, p. 2) is "a theory that is now well established among modern epidemiologists".

The earliest account of mathematical modeling of spread of disease was carried out in 1766 by Daniel Bernoulli. Trained as a physician, Bernoulli created a mathematical model to defend the practice of inoculating against smallpox (Hethcote, 2000). The calculations from this model showed that universal inoculation against smallpox would increase the life expectancy from 26 years 7 months to 29 years 9 months (Bernoulli & Blower, 2004).

Daniel Bernoulli's work preceded our modern understanding of germ theory, and it was not until the research of Ronald Ross into the spread of malaria, that modern theoretical epidemiology began. This was soon followed by the work of A. G. McKendrick and

W. O. Kermack, whose paper *A Contribution to the Mathematical Theory of Epidemics* was published in 1927. A simple deterministic (compartmental) model was formulated in this paper. The model was successful in predicting the behavior of outbreaks very similar to that observed in many recorded epidemics (Brauer & Castillo-Chavez, 2001).

Types of Epidemic Models

Stochastic

"Stochastic" means being or having a random variable. A stochastic model is a tool for estimating probability distributions of potential outcomes by allowing for random variation in one or more inputs over time. Stochastic models depend on the chance variations in risk of exposure, disease and other illness dynamics. They are used when these fluctuations are important, as in small populations (Trottier & Philippe, 2001).

Deterministic

When dealing with large populations, as in the case of tuberculosis, deterministic or compartmental mathematical models are used. In the deterministic model, individuals in the population are assigned to different subgroups or compartments, each representing a specific stage of the epidemic. Letters such as M, S, E, I, and R are often used to represent different stages.

The transition rates from one class to another are mathematically expressed as derivatives, hence the model is formulated using differential equations. While building such models, it must be assumed that the population size in a compartment is differentiable with respect to time and that the epidemic process is deterministic. In other words, the changes in population of a compartment can be calculated using only the history used to develop the model (Brauer & Castillo-Chavez, 2001).

Another approach is through discrete analysis on a lattice (such as a two-dimensional square grid), where the updating is done through asynchronous single-site updates (Kinetic Monte Carlo) or synchronous updating (Cellular Automata). The lattice approach enables inhomogeneities and clustering to be taken into account. Lattice systems are usually studied through computer simulation.

Terminology

The following is a summary of the notation used in this and the next sections.

- M : Passively immune infants
- S : Susceptibles
- E : Exposed individuals in the latent period
- I : Infectives

- R : Recovered with immunity

- β : Contact rate

- μ : Average death rate

- B : Average birth rate

- $1/\varepsilon$: Average latent period

- $1/\gamma$: Average infectious period

- R_0 : Basic reproduction number

- N : Total population

- f : Average loss of immunity rate of recovered individuals

- δ : Average temporary immunity period

Deterministic Compartmental Models

The SIR Model

In 1927, W. O. Kermack and A. G. McKendrick created a model in which they considered a fixed population with only three compartments: susceptible, $S(t)$; infected, $I(t)$; and removed, $R(t)$. The compartments used for this model consist of three classes:

- $S(t)$ is used to represent the number of individuals not yet infected with the disease at time t, or those susceptible to the disease.

- $I(t)$ denotes the number of individuals who have been infected with the disease and are capable of spreading the disease to those in the susceptible category.

- $R(t)$ is the compartment used for those individuals who have been infected and then removed from the disease, either due to immunization or due to death. Those in this category are not able to be infected again or to transmit the infection to others.

The flow of this model may be considered as follows:

$$\mathcal{S} \to \mathcal{I} \to \mathcal{R}$$

Using a fixed population, $N = S(t) + I(t) + R(t)$, Kermack and McKendrick derived the following equations:

$$\frac{dS}{dt} = -\frac{\beta SI}{N}$$

$$\frac{dI}{dt} = \frac{\beta SI}{N} - \gamma I$$

$$\frac{dR}{dt} = \gamma I$$

Several assumptions were made in the formulation of these equations: First, an individual in the population must be considered as having an equal probability as every other individual of contracting the disease with a rate of β, which is considered the contact or infection rate of the disease. Therefore, an infected individual makes contact and is able to transmit the disease with βN others per unit time and the fraction of contacts by an infected with a susceptible is $S >$. The number of new infections in unit time per infective then is $\beta N(S / N)$, giving the rate of new infections (or those leaving the susceptible category) as $\beta N(S / N)I = \beta SI$ (Brauer & Castillo-Chavez, 2001). For the second and third equations, consider the population leaving the susceptible class as equal to the number entering the infected class. However, a number equal to the fraction (γ which represents the mean recovery/death rate, or $1/\gamma$ the mean infective period) of infectives are leaving this class per unit time to enter the removed class. These processes which occur simultaneously are referred to as the Law of Mass Action, a widely accepted idea that the rate of contact between two groups in a population is proportional to the size of each of the groups concerned (Daley & Gani, 2005). Finally, it is assumed that the rate of infection and recovery is much faster than the time scale of births and deaths and therefore, these factors are ignored in this model.

The SIR Model with Births and Deaths

Using the case of for example, there is an arrival of new susceptible individuals into the population. For this type of situation births and deaths must be included in the model. The following differential equations represent this model, assuming a death rate μ and birth rate equal to the death rate:

$$\frac{dS}{dt} = -\frac{\beta SI}{N} + \mu(N - S)$$

$$\frac{dI}{dt} = \frac{\beta SI}{N} - \gamma I - \mu I$$

$$\frac{dR}{dt} = \gamma I - \mu R$$

The SIS Model with Births and Deaths

The SIS model can be easily derived from the SIR model by simply considering that the individuals recover with no immunity to the disease, that is, individuals are immediately susceptible once they have recovered.

$$\mathcal{S} \to \mathcal{I} \to \mathcal{S}$$

Removing the equation representing the recovered population from the SIR model and adding those removed from the infected population into the susceptible population gives the following differential equations:

$$\frac{dS}{dt} = -\frac{\beta SI}{N} + \mu(N-S) + \gamma I$$

$$\frac{dI}{dt} = \frac{\beta SI}{N} - \gamma I - \mu I$$

The SIRS Model

This model is simply an extension of the SIR model as we will see from its construction.

$$\mathcal{S} \to \mathcal{I} \to \mathcal{R} \to \mathcal{S}$$

The only difference is that it allows members of the recovered class to be free of infection and rejoin the susceptible class.

$$\frac{dS}{dt} = -\frac{\beta SI}{N} + \mu(N-S) + fR$$

$$\frac{dI}{dt} = \frac{\beta SI}{N} - \gamma I - \mu I$$

$$\frac{dR}{dt} = \gamma I - \mu R - fR$$

Models with more compartments

The SEIS Model

The SEIS model takes into consideration the exposed or latent period of the disease, giving an additional compartment, E(t).

$$\mathcal{S} \to \mathcal{E} \to \mathcal{I} \to \mathcal{S}$$

In this model an infection does not leave any immunity thus individuals that have recovered return to being susceptible again, moving back into the $S(t)$ compartment. The following differential equations describe this model:

$$\frac{dS}{dT} = B - \beta SI - \mu S + \gamma I$$

$$\frac{dE}{dT} = \beta SI - (\epsilon + \mu)E$$

$$\frac{dI}{dT} = \varepsilon E - (\gamma + \mu)I$$

The SEIR Model

The SIR model discussed above takes into account only those diseases which cause an individual to be able to infect others immediately upon their infection. Many diseases have what is termed a latent or exposed phase, during which the individual is said to be infected but not infectious.

$$\mathcal{S} \to \mathcal{E} \to \mathcal{I} \to \mathcal{R}$$

In this model the host population (N) is broken into four compartments: susceptible, exposed, infectious, and recovered, with the numbers of individuals in a compartment, or their densities denoted respectively by $S(t)$, $E(t)$, $I(t)$, $R(t)$, that is $N = S(t) + E(t) + I(t) + R(t)$

$$\frac{dS}{dT} = B - \beta SI - \mu S$$

$$\frac{dE}{dT} = \beta SI - (\varepsilon + \mu)E$$

$$\frac{dI}{dT} = \varepsilon E - (\gamma + \mu)I$$

$$\frac{dR}{dT} = \gamma I - \mu R$$

The MSIR Model

There are several diseases where an individual is born with a passive immunity from its mother.

$$\mathcal{M} \to \mathcal{S} \to \mathcal{I} \to \mathcal{R}$$

To indicate this mathematically, an additional compartment is added, M(t), which results in the following differential equations:

$$\frac{dM}{dT} = B - \delta M - \mu M$$

$$\frac{dS}{dT} = \delta M - \beta SI - \mu S$$

$$\frac{dI}{dT} = \beta SI - \gamma I - \mu I$$

$$\frac{dR}{dT} = \gamma I - \mu R$$

The MSEIR Model

For the case of a disease, with the factors of passive immunity, and a latency period there is the MSEIR model.

$$\mathcal{M} \to \mathcal{S} \to \mathcal{E} \to \mathcal{I} \to \mathcal{R}$$

$$\frac{dM}{dT} = B - \delta M - \mu M$$

$$\frac{dS}{dT} = \delta M - \beta SI - \mu S$$

$$\frac{dE}{dT} = \beta SI - (\varepsilon + \mu)E$$

$$\frac{dI}{dT} = \varepsilon E - (\gamma + \mu)I$$

$$\frac{dR}{dT} = \gamma I - \mu R$$

The MSEIRS Model

An MSEIRS model is similar to the MSEIR, but the immunity in the R class would be temporary, so that individuals would regain their susceptibility when the temporary immunity ended.

$$\mathcal{M} \to \mathcal{S} \to \mathcal{E} \to \mathcal{I} \to \mathcal{R} \to \mathcal{S}$$

Reproduction Number

There is a threshold quantity which determines whether an epidemic occurs or the disease simply dies out. This quantity is called the basic reproduction number, denoted by R_0, which can be defined as the number of secondary infections caused by a single infective introduced into a population made up entirely of susceptible individuals (S(o) $\approx$ N) over the course of the infection of this single infective. This infective individual makes β contacts per unit time producing new infections with a mean infectious period of $1/\gamma$. Therefore, the basic reproduction number is

$$R_0 = \beta/\gamma$$

This value quantifies the transmission potential of a disease. If the basic reproduction number falls below one ($R_0 < 1$), i.e. the infective may not pass the infection on during the infectious period, the infection dies out. If $R_0 > 1$ there is an epidemic in the population. In cases where $R_0 = 1$, the disease becomes endemic, meaning the disease remains in the population at a consistent rate, as one infected individual transmits the disease to one susceptible (Trottier & Philippe, 2001).In cases of diseases with varying latent periods, the basic reproduction number can be calculated as the sum of the reproduction number for each transition time into the disease. An example of this is tuberculosis. Blower et al. (1995) calculated from a simple model of TB the following reproduction number:

$$R_0 = R_0^{FAST} + R_0^{SLOW}$$

In their model, it is assumed that the infected individuals can develop active TB by either direct progression (the disease develops immediately after infection) considered above as FAST tuberculosis or endogenous reactivation (the disease develops years after the infection) considered above as SLOW tuberculosis.

Other Considerations within Compartmental Epidemic Models

Vertical Transmission

In the case of some diseases such as AIDS and Hepatitis B, it is possible for the offspring of infected parents to be born infected. This transmission of the disease down from the mother is called Vertical Transmission. The influx of additional members into the infected category can be considered within the model by including a fraction of the newborn members in the infected compartment (Brauer & Castillo-Chavez, 2001).

Vector Transmission

Diseases transmitted from human to human indirectly, i.e. malaria spread by way of mosquitoes, are transmitted through a vector. In these cases, the infection transfers from human to insect and an epidemic model must include both species, generally requiring many more compartments than a model for direct transmission. For more information on this type of model see the reference *Population Dynamics of Infectious Diseases: Theory and Applications*, by R. M. Anderson (Brauer & Castillo-Chavez, 2001).

Others

Other occurrences (taken from *Mathematical Models in Population Biology and Epidemiology* by Fred Brauer and Carlos Castillo-Chávez) which may need to be considered when modeling an epidemic include things such as the following:

- Nonhomogeneous mixing
- Age-structured populations
- Variable infectivity
- Distributions that are spatially non-uniform
- Diseases caused by macroparasites
- Acquired immunity through vaccinations

References

- Mount DM (2004). Bioinformatics: Sequence and Genome Analysis. 2. Cold Spring Harbor Laboratory Press. ISBN 0-87969-712-1.

- Hall, Charles A.S. & Day, John W. (1990). Ecosytem Modeling in Theory and Practice: An Introduction with Case Histories. University Press of Colorado. pp. 7–8. ISBN 0-87081-216-5.

- Dale, Virginia (2003). "Opportunities for Using Ecological Models for Resource Management". Ecological modeling for resource management. Springer. p. 3. ISBN 978-0-387-95493-6.

- Pastorok, Robert A. (2002). "Introduction". Ecological modeling in risk assessment: chemical effects on populations, ecosystems, and landscapes. CRC Press. p. 7. ISBN 978-1-56670-574-5.

- Millspaugh, Joshua J. et al. (2008). "General Principles for Developing Landscape Models for Wildlife Conservation". Models for planning wildlife conservation in large landscapes. Academic Press. p. 1. ISBN 978-0-12-373631-4.

- Jørgensen, Sven Erik (1996). Handbook of environmental and ecological modeling. CRC Press. pp. 403–404. ISBN 978-1-56670-202-7.

- Grant, William Edward & Swannack, Todd M. (2008). Ecological modeling: a common-sense approach to theory and practice. John Wiley & Sons. p. 74. ISBN 978-1-4051-6168-8.

- Soetaert, Karline & Herman, Peter M.J. (2009). A practical guide to ecological modelling: using R as a simulation platform. Springer. p. 11. ISBN 978-1-4020-8623-6.

- Gillman, Michael & Hails, Rosemary (1997). An introduction to ecological modelling: putting practice into theory. Wiley-Blackwell. p. 4. ISBN 978-0-632-03634-9.

- Müller, Felix et al. (2011). "What are the General Conditions Under Which Ecological Models Can Be Applied". In Jopp, Fred et al. Modeling Complex Ecological Dynamics. Springer. pp. 13–14. ISBN 978-3-642-05028-2.

- McCallum, Hamish (2000). "Spatial Parameters". Population parameters: estimation for ecological models. Wiley-Blackwell. p. 184. ISBN 978-0-86542-740-2.

- Tenhunen, John D. et al, eds. (2001). Ecosystem approaches to landscape management in Central Europe. Springer. pp. 586–587. ISBN 978-3-540-67267-8.

- Jørgensen, Sven Erik & Bendoricchio, G. (2001). Fundamentals of ecological modelling. Gulf Professional Publishing. p. 79. ISBN 978-0-08-044028-6.

- Pastorok, Robert A. (2002). "Introduction". Ecological modeling in risk assessment: chemical effects on populations, ecosystems, and landscapes. CRC Press. p. 22. ISBN 978-1-56670-574-5.

- Voinov, Alexey (2008). Systems Science and Modeling for Ecological Economics. Academic Press. p. 131. ISBN 978-0-12-372583-7.

- Reuter, Hauke et al. (2011). "How Valid Are Model Results? Assumptions, Validity Range and Documentation". In Jopp, Fred et al. Modeling Complex Ecological Dynamics. Springer. p. 325. ISBN 978-3-642-05028-2.

- Arditi, R. and Ginzburg, L.R. (2012) How Species Interact: Altering the Standard View on Trophic Ecology Oxford University Press. ISBN 9780199913831.

Mathematical Modelling of Biological System

4

The topics that have been discussed in this chapter are metabolic network modelling, multi-compartment model, Wagner's gene network model and Morris-Lecar model. Metabolic network reconstruction and stimulation is used as an understanding of molecular mechanisms of any organism whereas multi-compartment model is used in explaining materials that are conveyed among the sections of a system. This section elucidates the crucial theories of mathematical modelling of biology system.

Metabolic Network Modelling

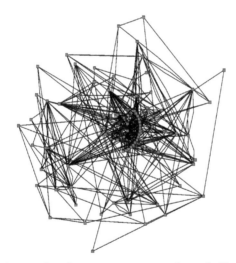

Metabolic network showing interactions between enzymes and metabolites in the *Arabidopsis thaliana* citric acid cycle. Enzymes and metabolites are the red dots and interactions between them are the lines.

Metabolic network reconstruction and simulation allows for an in-depth insight into the molecular mechanisms of a particular organism. In particular, these models correlate the genome with molecular physiology. A reconstruction breaks down metabolic pathways (such as glycolysis and the Citric acid cycle) into their respective reactions and enzymes, and analyzes them within the perspective of the entire network. In simplified terms, a reconstruction collects all of the relevant metabolic information of an organism and compiles it in a mathematical model. Validation and analysis of reconstructions can allow identification of key features of metabolism such as growth yield, resource distribution, network robustness, and gene essentiality. This knowledge can then be applied to create novel biotechnology.

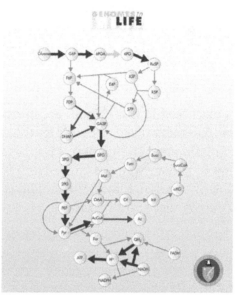

Metabolic Network Model for Escherichia coli.

In general, the process to build a reconstruction is as follows:

1. Draft a reconstruction

2. Refine the model

3. Convert model into a mathematical/computational representation

4. Evaluate and debug model through experimentation

Genome-Scale Metabolic Reconstruction

A metabolic reconstruction provides a highly mathematical, structured platform on which to understand the systems biology of metabolic pathways within an organism. The integration of biochemical metabolic pathways with rapidly available, unannotated genome sequences has developed what are called genome-scale metabolic models. Simply put, these models correspond metabolic genes with metabolic pathways. In general, the more information about physiology, biochemistry and genetics is available for the target organism, the better the predictive capacity of the reconstructed models. Mechanically speaking, the process of reconstructing prokaryotic and eukaryotic metabolic networks is essentially the same. Having said this, eukaryote reconstructions are typically more challenging because of the size of genomes, coverage of knowledge, and the multitude of cellular compartments. The first genome-scale metabolic model was generated in 1995 for *Haemophilus influenzae*. The first multicellular organism, *C. elegans*, was reconstructed in 1998. Since then, many reconstructions have been formed.

For a list of reconstructions that have been converted into a model and experimentally validated.

Organism	Genes in Genome	Genes in Model	Reactions	Metabolites	Date of reconstruction
Haemophilus influenzae	1,775	296	488	343	June 1999
Escherichia coli	4,405	660	627	438	May 2000
Saccharomyces cerevisiae	6,183	708	1,175	584	February 2003
Mus musculus	28,287	473	1220	872	January 2005
Homo sapiens	21,090	3,623	3,673	--	January 2007
Mycobacterium tuberculosis	4,402	661	939	828	June 2007
Bacillus subtilis	4,114	844	1,020	988	September 2007
Synechocystis sp. PCC6803	3,221	633	831	704	October 2008
Salmonella typhimurium	4,489	1,083	1,087	774	April 2009
Arabidopsis thaliana	27,379	1,419	1,567	1,748	February 2010

Drafting a Reconstruction

Resources

Because the timescale for the development of reconstructions is so recent, most reconstructions have been built manually. However, now, there are quite a few resources that allow for the semi-automatic assembly of these reconstructions that are utilized due to the time and effort necessary for a reconstruction. An initial fast reconstruction can be developed automatically using resources like PathoLogic or ERGO in combination with encyclopedias like MetaCyc, and then manually updated by using resources like PathwayTools. These semi-automatic methods allow for a fast draft to be created while allowing the fine tune adjustments required once new experimental data is found. It is only in this manner that the field of metabolic reconstructions will keep up with the ever-increasing numbers of annotated genomes.

Databases

- Kyoto Encyclopedia of Genes and Genomes (KEGG): a bioinformatics database containing information on genes, proteins, reactions, and pathways. The 'KEGG Organisms' section, which is divided into eukaryotes and prokaryotes, encompasses many organisms for which gene and DNA information can be searched by typing in the enzyme of choice.

- BioCyc, EcoCyc, and MetaCyc: BioCyc Is a collection of 3,000 pathway/genome databases (as of Oct 2013), with each database dedicated to one organism. For example, EcoCyc is a highly detailed bioinformatics database on the genome and metabolic reconstruction of *Escherichia coli*, including thorough descriptions of *E. coli* signaling pathways and regulatory network. The EcoCyc database can serve as a paradigm and model for any reconstruction. Additionally, MetaCyc, an encyclopedia of experimentally defined metabolic pathways and enzymes, contains 2,100 metabolic pathways and 11,400 metabolic reactions (Oct 2013).

- ENZYME: An enzyme nomenclature database (part of the ExPASy proteomics server of the Swiss Institute of Bioinformatics). After searching for a particular enzyme on the database, this resource gives you the reaction that is catalyzed. ENZYME has direct links to other gene/enzyme/literature databases such as KEGG, BRENDA, and PUBMED.

- BRENDA: A comprehensive enzyme database that allows for an enzyme to be searched by name, EC number, or organism.

- BiGG: A knowledge base of biochemically, genetically, and genomically structured genome-scale metabolic network reconstructions.

- metaTIGER: Is a collection of metabolic profiles and phylogenomic information on a taxonomically diverse range of eukaryotes which provides novel facilities for viewing and comparing the metabolic profiles between organisms.

Database	Scope				
	Enzymes	Genes	Reactions	Pathways	Metabolites
KEGG	X	X	X	X	X
BioCyc	X	X	X	X	X
MetaCyc	X		X	X	X
ENZYME	X		X		X
BRENDA	X		X		X
BiGG		X		X	X
This table quickly compares the scope of each database.					

Tools for Metabolic Modeling

- Pathway Tools: A bioinformatics software package that assists in the construction of pathway/genome databases such as EcoCyc. Developed by Peter Karp and associates at the SRI International Bioinformatics Research Group, Pathway Tools has several components. Its PathoLogic module takes an annotated genome for an organism and infers probable metabolic reactions and pathways to produce a new pathway/genome database. Its MetaFlux component can generate a quantitative metabolic model from that pathway/genome database using flux-balance analysis. Its Navigator component provides extensive query and visualization tools, such as visualization of metabolites, pathways, and the complete metabolic network.

- ERGO: A subscription-based service developed by Integrated Genomics. It integrates data from every level including genomic, biochemical data, literature, and high-throughput analysis into a comprehensive user friendly network of metabolic and nonmetabolic pathways.

- KEGGtranslator: an easy-to-use stand-alone application that can visualize and convert KEGG files (KGML formatted XML-files) into multiple output formats. Unlike other translators, KEGGtranslator supports a plethora of output formats, is able to augment the information in translated documents (e.g., MIRIAM annotations) beyond the scope of the KGML document, and amends missing components to fragmentary reactions within the pathway to allow simulations on those. KEGGtranslator converts these files to SBML, BioPAX, SIF, SBGN, SBML with qualitative modeling extension, GML, GraphML, JPG, GIF, LaTeX, etc.

KEGG pathways can directly be obtained from within the application.

- Model SEED: An online resource for the analysis, comparison, reconstruction, and curation of genome-scale metabolic models. Users can submit genome sequences to the RAST annotation system, and the resulting annotation can be automatically piped into the Model SEED to produce a draft metabolic model. The Model SEED automatically constructs a network of metabolic reactions, gene-protein-reaction associations for each reaction, and a biomass composition reaction for each genome to produce a model of microbial metabolism that can be simulated using Flux Balance Analysis.

- MetaMerge: algorithm for semi-automatically reconciling a pair of existing metabolic network reconstructions into a single metabolic network model.

Tools for Literature

- PUBMED: This is an online library developed by the National Center for Biotechnology Information, which contains a massive collection of medical journals. Using the link provided by ENZYME, the search can be directed towards the organism of interest, thus recovering literature on the enzyme and its use inside of the organism.

Methodology to Draft a Reconstruction

A reconstruction is built by compiling data from the resources above. Database tools such as KEGG and BioCyc can be used in conjunction with each other to find all the metabolic genes in the organism of interest. These genes will be compared to closely related organisms that have already developed reconstructions to find homologous genes and reactions. These homologous genes and reactions are carried over from the known reconstructions to form the draft reconstruction of the organism of interest. Tools such as ERGO, Pathway Tools and Model SEED can compile data into pathways to form a network of metabolic and non-metabolic pathways. These networks are then verified and refined before being made into a mathematical simulation.

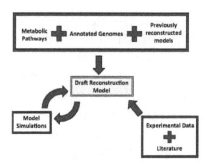

This is a visual representation of the metabolic network reconstruction process.

The predictive aspect of a metabolic reconstruction hinges on the ability to predict the biochemical reaction catalyzed by a protein using that protein's amino acid sequence as an input, and to infer the structure of a metabolic network based on the predicted set of reactions. A network of enzymes and metabolites is drafted to relate sequences and function. When an uncharacterized protein is found in the genome, its amino acid sequence is first compared to those of previously characterized proteins to search for homology. When a homologous protein is found, the proteins are considered to have a common ancestor and their functions are inferred as being similar. However, the quality of a reconstruction model is dependent on its ability to accurately infer phenotype directly from sequence, so this rough estimation of protein function will not be sufficient. A number of algorithms and bioinformatics resources have been developed for refinement of sequence homology-based assignments of protein functions:

InParanoid: Identifies eukaryotic orthologs by looking only at in-paralogs.

CDD: Resource for the annotation of functional units in proteins. Its collection of domain models utilizes 3D structure to provide insights into sequence/structure/function relationships.

InterPro: Provides functional analysis of proteins by classifying them into families and predicting domains and important sites.

STRING: Database of known and predicted protein interactions.

Once proteins have been established, more information about the enzyme structure, reactions catalyzed, substrates and products, mechanisms, and more can be acquired from databases such as KEGG, MetaCyc and NC-IUBMB. Accurate metabolic reconstructions require additional information about the reversibility and preferred physiological direction of an enzyme-catalyzed reaction which can come from databases such as BRENDA or MetaCyc database.

Model Refinement

An initial metabolic reconstruction of a genome is typically far from perfect due to the high variability and diversity of microorganisms. Often, metabolic pathway databases such as KEGG and MetaCyc will have "holes", meaning that there is a conversion from a substrate to a product (i.e., an enzymatic activity) for which there is no known protein in the genome that encodes the enzyme that facilitates the catalysis. What can also happen in semi-automatically drafted reconstructions is that some pathways are falsely predicted and don't actually occur in the predicted manner. Because of this, a systematic verification is made in order to make sure no inconsistencies are present and that all the entries listed are correct and accurate. Furthermore, previous literature can be researched in order to support any information obtained from one of the many metabolic reaction and genome databases. This provides an added level of assurance for the reconstruction that the enzyme and the reaction it catalyzes do actually occur in the organism.

Enzyme promiscuity and spontaneous chemical reactions can damage metabolites. This metabolite damage, and its repair or pre-emption, create energy costs that need to be incorporated into models. It is likely that many genes of unknown function encode proteins that repair or pre-empt metabolite damage, but most genome-scale metabolic reconstructions only include a fraction of all genes.

Any new reactions not present in the databases need to be added to the reconstruction. This is an iterative process that cycles between the experimental phase and the coding phase. As new information is found about the target organism, the model will be adjusted to predict the metabolic and phenotypical output of the cell. The presence or absence of certain reactions of the metabolism will affect the amount of reactants/products that are present for other reactions within the particular pathway. This is because products in one reaction go on to become the reactants for another reaction, i.e. products of one reaction can combine with other proteins or compounds to form new proteins/compounds in the presence of different enzymes or catalysts.

Francke *et al.* provide an excellent example as to why the verification step of the project needs to be performed in significant detail. During a metabolic network reconstruction of *Lactobacillus plantarum*, the model showed that succinyl-CoA was one of the reactants for a reaction that was a part of the biosynthesis of methionine. However, an understanding of the physiology of the organism would have revealed that due to an incomplete tricarboxylic acid pathway, *Lactobacillus plantarum* does not actually produce succinyl-CoA, and the correct reactant for that part of the reaction was acetyl-CoA.

Therefore, systematic verification of the initial reconstruction will bring to light several inconsistencies that can adversely affect the final interpretation of the reconstruction, which is to accurately comprehend the molecular mechanisms of the organism. Furthermore, the simulation step also ensures that all the reactions present in the reconstruction are properly balanced. To sum up, a reconstruction that is fully accurate can lead to greater insight about understanding the functioning of the organism of interest.

Metabolic Network Simulation

A metabolic network can be broken down into a stoichiometric matrix where the rows represent the compounds of the reactions, while the columns of the matrix correspond to the reactions themselves. Stoichiometry is a quantitative relationship between substrates of a chemical reaction. In order to deduce what the metabolic network suggests, recent research has centered on a few approaches, such as extreme pathways, elementary mode analysis, flux balance analysis, and a number of other constraint-based modeling methods.

Extreme Pathways

Price, Reed, and Papin, from the Palsson lab, use a method of singular value decomposition (SVD) of extreme pathways in order to understand regulation of a human red blood cell metabolism. Extreme pathways are convex basis vectors that consist of steady state functions of a metabolic network. For any particular metabolic network, there is always a unique set of extreme pathways available. Furthermore, Price, Reed, and Papin, define a constraint-based approach, where through the help of constraints like mass balance and maximum reaction rates, it is possible to develop a 'solution space' where all the feasible options fall within. Then, using a kinetic model approach, a single solution that falls within the extreme pathway solution space can be determined. Therefore, in their study, Price, Reed, and Papin, use both constraint and kinetic approaches to understand the human red blood cell metabolism. In conclusion, using extreme pathways, the regulatory mechanisms of a metabolic network can be studied in further detail.

Elementary Mode Analysis

Elementary mode analysis closely matches the approach used by extreme pathways. Similar to extreme pathways, there is always a unique set of elementary modes available for a particular metabolic network. These are the smallest sub-networks that allow a metabolic reconstruction network to function in steady state. According to Stelling (2002), elementary modes can be used to understand cellular objectives for the overall metabolic network. Furthermore, elementary mode analysis takes into account stoichiometrics and thermodynamics when evaluating whether a particular metabolic route or network is feasible and likely for a set of proteins/enzymes.

Minimal Metabolic Behaviors (MMBs)

In 2009, Larhlimi and Bockmayr presented a new approach called "minimal metabolic behaviors" for the analysis of metabolic networks. Like elementary modes or extreme pathways, these are uniquely determined by the network, and yield a complete description of the flux cone. However, the new description is much more compact. In contrast with elementary modes and extreme pathways, which use an inner description based on generating vectors of the flux cone, MMBs are using an outer description of the flux cone. This approach is based on sets of non-negativity constraints. These can be identified with irreversible reactions, and thus have a direct biochemical interpretation. One can characterize a metabolic network by MMBs and the reversible metabolic space.

Flux Balance Analysis

A different technique to simulate the metabolic network is to perform flux balance analysis. This method uses linear programming, but in contrast to elementary mode analysis and extreme pathways, only a single solution results in the end. Linear programming is usually used to obtain the maximum potential of the objective function that you are looking at, and therefore, when using flux balance analysis, a single solution is found to the optimization problem. In a flux balance analysis approach, exchange fluxes are assigned to those metabolites that enter or leave the particular network only. Those metabolites that are consumed within the network are not assigned any exchange flux value. Also, the exchange fluxes along with the enzymes can have constraints ranging from a negative to positive value (ex: -10 to 10).

Furthermore, this particular approach can accurately define if the reaction stoichiometry is in line with predictions by providing fluxes for the balanced reactions. Also, flux balance analysis can highlight the most effective and efficient pathway through the network in order to achieve a particular objective function. In addition, gene knockout studies can be performed using flux balance analysis. The enzyme that correlates to the gene that needs to be removed is given a constraint value of 0. Then, the reaction that the particular enzyme catalyzes is completely removed from the analysis.

Dynamic Simulation and Parameter Estimation

In order to perform a dynamic simulation with such a network it is necessary to construct an ordinary differential equation system that describes the rates of change in each metabolite's concentration or amount. To this end, a rate law, i.e., a kinetic equation that determines the rate of reaction based on the concentrations of all reactants is required for each reaction. Software packages that include numerical integrators, such as COPASI or SBMLsimulator, are then able to simulate the system dynamics given an initial condition. Often these rate laws contain kinetic parameters with uncertain values. In many cases it is desired to estimate these parameter values with respect to given time-series data of metabolite concentrations. The system is then supposed to reproduce the given data. For this purpose the distance between the given data set and the result of the simulation, i.e., the numerically or in few cases analytically obtained solution of the differential equation system is computed. The values of the parameters are then estimated to minimize this distance. One step further, it may be desired to estimate the mathematical structure of the differential equation system because the real rate laws are not known for the reactions within the system under study. To this end, the program SBMLsqueezer allows automatic creation of appropriate rate laws for all reactions with the network.

Synthetic Accessibility

Synthetic accessibility is a simple approach to network simulation whose goal is to predict which metabolic gene knockouts are lethal. The synthetic accessibility approach uses the topology of the metabolic network to calculate the sum of the minimum number of steps needed to traverse the metabolic network graph from the inputs, those metabolites available to the organism from the environment, to the outputs, metabolites needed by the organism to survive. To simulate a gene knockout, the reactions enabled by the gene are removed from the network and the synthetic accessibility metric is recalculated. An increase in the total number of steps is predicted to cause lethality. Wunderlich and Mirny showed this simple, parameter-free approach predicted knockout lethality in *E. coli* and *S. cerevisiae* as well as elementary mode analysis and flux balance analysis in a variety of media.

Applications of a Reconstruction

- Several inconsistencies exist between gene, enzyme, reaction databases, and published literature sources regarding the metabolic information of an organism. A reconstruction is a systematic verification and compilation of data from various sources that takes into account all of the discrepancies.

- The combination of relevant metabolic and genomic information of an organism.

- Metabolic comparisons can be performed between various organisms of the same species as well as between different organisms.

- Analysis of synthetic lethality

- Predict adaptive evolution outcomes

- Use in metabolic engineering for high value outputs

Reconstructions and their corresponding models allow the formulation of hypotheses about the presence of certain enzymatic activities and the production of metabolites that can be experimentally tested, complementing the primarily discovery-based approach of traditional microbial biochemistry with hypothesis-driven research. The results these experiments can uncover novel pathways and metabolic activities and decipher between discrepancies in previous experimental data. Information about the chemical reactions of metabolism and the genetic background of various metabolic properties (sequence to structure to function) can be utilized by genetic engineers to modify organisms to produce high value outputs whether those products be medically relevant like pharmaceuticals; high value chemical intermediates such as terpenoids and isoprenoids; or biotechnological outputs like biofuels.

Metabolic network reconstructions and models are used to understand how an organism or parasite functions inside of the host cell. For example, if the parasite serves to compromise the immune system by lysing macrophages, then the goal of metabolic reconstruction/simulation would be to determine the metabolites that are essential to the organism's proliferation inside of macrophages. If the proliferation cycle is inhibited, then the parasite would not continue to evade the host's immune system. A reconstruction model serves as a first step to deciphering the complicated mechanisms surrounding disease. These models can also look at the minimal genes necessary for a cell to maintain virulence. The next step would be to use the predictions and postulates generated from a reconstruction model and apply it to discover novel biological functions such as drug-engineering and drug delivery techniques.

Multi-compartment Model

A multi-compartment model is a type of mathematical model used for describing the way materials or energies are transmitted among the *compartments* of a system. Each compartment is assumed to be a homogeneous entity within which the entities being modelled are equivalent. For instance, in a pharmacokinetic model, the compartments may represent different sections of a body within which the concentration of a drug is assumed to be uniformly equal.

Hence a multi-compartment model is a lumped parameters model.

Multi-compartment models are used in many fields including pharmacokinetics, epidemiology, biomedicine, systems theory, complexity theory, engineering, physics, information science and social science. The circuits systems can be viewed as a multi-compartment model as well.

In systems theory, it involves the description of a network whose components are compartments that represent a population of elements that are equivalent with respect to the manner in which they process input signals to the compartment.

- Instant homogeneous distribution of materials or energies within a "compartment."

- The exchange rate of materials or energies among the compartments is related to the densities of these compartments.

- Usually, it is desirable that the materials do not undergo chemical reactions while transmitting among the compartments.

- When concentration of the cell is of interest, typically the volume is assumed to be constant over time, though this may not be totally true in reality.

Most commonly, the mathematics of multi-compartment models is simplified to provide only a single parameter—such as concentration—within a compartment.

Single-compartment Model

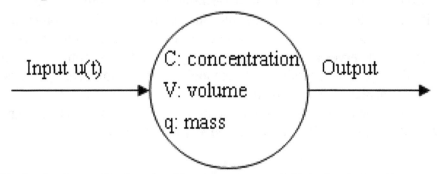

Possibly the simplest application of multi-compartment model is in the single-cell concentration monitoring (see the figure above). If the volume of a cell is V, the mass of solute is q, the input is $u(t)$ and the secretion of the solution is proportional to the density of it within the cell, then the concentration of the solution C within the cell over time is given by

$$\frac{dq}{dt} = u(t) - kq$$

$$C = \frac{q}{V}$$

where k is the proportionality.

As the number of compartments increases, the model can be very complex and the solutions usually beyond ordinary calculation. Below shows a three-cell model with interlinks among each other.

The formulae for n-cell multi-compartment models become:

$$\dot{q}_1 = q_1 k_{11} + q_2 k_{12} + \cdots + q_n k_{1n} + u_1(t)$$
$$\dot{q}_2 = q_1 k_{21} + q_2 k_{22} + \cdots + q_n k_{2n} + u_2(t)$$
$$\vdots$$
$$\dot{q}_n = q_1 k_{n1} + q_2 k_{n2} + \cdots + q_n k_{nn} + u_n(t)$$

Where

$$0 = \sum_{i=1}^{n} k_{ij} \text{ for } j = 1, 2, \ldots, n \text{ (as the total 'contents' of all compartments is constant in a}$$

closed system)

Or in matrix forms:

$$\dot{q} = Kq + u$$

Where

$$K = \begin{bmatrix} k_{11} & k_{12} & \cdots & k_{1n} \\ k_{21} & k_{22} & \cdots & k_{2n} \\ \vdots & \vdots & \ddots & \vdots \\ k_{n1} & k_{n2} & \cdots & k_{nn} \end{bmatrix} q = \begin{bmatrix} q_1 \\ q_2 \\ \vdots \\ q_n \end{bmatrix} u = \begin{bmatrix} u_1(t) \\ u_2(t) \\ \vdots \\ u_n(t) \end{bmatrix} \text{ and } \begin{bmatrix} 1 & 1 & \cdots & 1 \end{bmatrix} K = \begin{bmatrix} 0 & 0 & \cdots & 0 \end{bmatrix} \text{ (as}$$

the total 'contents' of all compartments is constant in a closed system)

In the special case of a closed system (see below) i.e. where $u = 0$ then there is a general solution.

$$q = c_1 e^{\lambda_1 t} v_1 + c_2 e^{\lambda_2 t} v_2 + \cdots + c_n e^{\lambda_n t} v_n$$

Where λ_1, λ_2, ... and λ_n are the eigenvalues of K; v_1, v_2, ... and v_n are the respective eigenvectors of K; and c_1, c_2, ... and c_n are constants.

However it can be shown that given the above requirement to ensure the 'contents' of a closed system are constant, then for every pair of eigenvalue and eigenvector then either $\lambda = 0$ or $\begin{bmatrix} 1 & 1 & \cdots & 1 \end{bmatrix} v = 0$ and also that one eigenvalue is 0, say λ_1

So

$$q = c_1 v_1 + c_2 e^{\lambda_2 t} v_2 + \cdots + c_n e^{\lambda_n t} v_n$$

Where

$$\begin{bmatrix} 1 & 1 & \cdots & 1 \end{bmatrix} v_i = 0 \text{ for } i = 2, 3, \ldots n$$

This solution can be rearranged:

$$q = \begin{bmatrix} v_1 \begin{bmatrix} c_1 & 0 & \cdots & 0 \end{bmatrix} + v_2 \begin{bmatrix} 0 & c_2 & \cdots & 0 \end{bmatrix} + \ldots + v_n \begin{bmatrix} 0 & 0 & \cdots & c_n \end{bmatrix} \end{bmatrix} \begin{bmatrix} 1 \\ e^{\lambda_2 t} \\ \vdots \\ e^{\lambda_n t} \end{bmatrix}$$

This somewhat inelegant equation demonstrates that all solutions of an *n-cell* multi-compartment model with constant or no inputs are of the form:

$$q = A \begin{bmatrix} 1 \\ e^{\lambda_2 t} \\ \vdots \\ e^{\lambda_n t} \end{bmatrix}$$

Where A is a *nxn* matrix and λ_2, λ_3, ... and λ_n are constants. Where $\begin{bmatrix} 1 & 1 & \cdots & 1 \end{bmatrix} A = \begin{bmatrix} a & 0 & \cdots & 0 \end{bmatrix}$

Model Topologies

Generally speaking, as the number of compartments increase, it is challenging both to find the algebraic and numerical solutions of the model. However, there are special cases of models, which rarely exist in nature, when the topologies exhibit certain regularities that the solutions become easier to find. The model can be classified according to the interconnection of cells and input/output characteristics:

1. Closed model: No sinks or source, lit. all $k_{oi} = 0$ and $u_i = 0$;

2. Open model: There are sinks or/and sources among cells.

3. Catenary model: All compartments are arranged in a chain, with each pool connecting only to its neighbors. This model has two or more cells.

4. Cyclic model: It's a special case of the catenary model, with three or more cells, in which the first and last cell are connected, i.e. $k_{1n} \neq 0$ or/and $k_{n1} \neq 0$.

5. Mammillary model: Consists of a central compartment with peripheral compartments connecting to it. There are no interconnections among other compartments.

6. Reducible model: It's a set of unconnected models. It bears great resemblance to the computer concept of forest as against trees.

Wagner's Gene Network Model

Wagner's gene network model is a computational model of artificial gene networks, which explicitly modeled the developmental and evolutionary process of genetic regulatory networks. A population with multiple organisms can be created and evolved from generation to generation. It was first developed by Andreas Wagner in 1996 and has been investigated by other groups to study the evolution of gene networks, gene expression, robustness, plasticity and epistasis.

Assumptions

The model and its variants have a number of simplifying assumptions. Three of them are listing below.

1. The organisms are modeled as gene regulatory networks. The models assume that gene expression is regulated exclusively at the transcriptional level;

2. The product of a gene can regulate the expression of (be a regulator of) that source gene or other genes. The models assume that a gene can only produce one active transcriptional regulator;

3. The effects of one regulator are independent of effects of other regulators on the same target gene.

Genotype

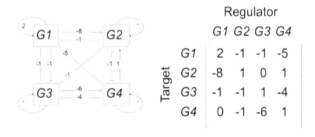

Gene network $\longrightarrow$ Regulatory matrix R

Network representation of the regulatory interactions between four genes (G1, G2, G3 and G4). Activations and repressions are denoted by arrows and bars, respectively. Numbers indicate the relative interaction strengths. Interaction matrix n on the right representing the network on the left.

The model represents individuals as networks of interacting transcriptional regulators. Each individual expresses n genes encoding transcription factors. The product of each gene can regulate the expression level of itself and/or the other genes through cis-regulatory elements. The interactions among genes constitute a gene network that is represented by a $N \times N$ regulatory matrix (R) in the model. The elements in matrix R represent the interaction strength. Positive values within the matrix represent the activation of the target gene, while negative ones represent repression. Matrix elements with value 0 indicate the absence of interactions between two genes.

Phenotype

An example of how the gene expression pattern modeled in Wagner model and its variants. G1, G2, G3 and G4 represent genes in the network. Filled box means the gene expression of that particular gene is on; open box means off. Gene expression patterns are represented by the state vector whose elements describe the expression states of gene .

$$S(t) \text{ Gene expression level}$$

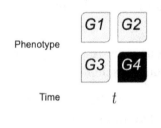

$$s_i(t) > 0 \ \text{ON (filled box)}$$

$$s_i(t) \leq 0 \ \text{OFF (open box)}$$

An example of how the gene expression pattern modeled in Wagner model and its variants. G1, G2, G3 and G4 represent genes in the network. Filled box means the gene expression of that particular gene is on; open box means off. Gene expression patterns are represented by the state vector S whose elements $s_i(t)$ describe the expression states of gene i .

The phenotype of each individual is modeled as the gene expression pattern at time t. It is represented by a state vector $S(t)$ in this model.

$$S(t) := (S_1(t), ..., S_N(t))$$

whose elements $s_i(t)$ denotes the expression states of gene i at time t. In the original Wagner model,

$$S(t) \in \{-1, 1\}$$

where 1 represents the gene is expressed while -1 implies the gene is not expressed. The expression pattern can only be ON or OFF. The continuous expression pattern between -1 (or 0) and 1 is also implemented in some other variants.

Development

The development process is modeled as the development of gene expression states.

The gene expression pattern $S(0)$ at time $t = 0$ is defined as the initial expression state. The interactions among genes change the expression states during the development process. This process is modeled by the following differential equations

$$S_i(t + \tau) = \sigma \left[\sum_{j=1}^{N} w_{ij} S_j(t)\right]$$

$$= \sigma [h_i](t)$$

where $S_i(t + \tau)$ represents the expression state of G_i at time t+τ. It is determined by a filter function $\sigma(x)$. $h_i(t)$ represents the weighted sum of regulatory effects (w_{ij}) of all genes on gene G_i at time t. In the original Wagner model, the filter function is a step function

$$\sigma(x) = -1 \text{ if } x < 0; 1 \text{ if } x > 0; 0 \text{ if } x = 0$$

In other variants, the filter function is implemented as a sigmoidal function

$$\sigma(x) = 2/(1 + e^{-ax}) - 1$$

In this way, the expression states will acquire a continuous distribution. The gene expression will reach the final state if it reaches a stable pattern.

Evolution

Evolutionary simulations are performed by reproduction-mutation-selection life cycle. Populations are fixed at size N and they will not go extinct. Non-overlapping generations are employed. In a typical evolutionary simulation, a single random viable individual that can produce a stable gene expression pattern is chosen as the founder. Cloned individuals are generated to create a population of N identical individuals. According to the asexual or sexual reproductive mode, offsprings are produced by randomly choosing (with replacement) parent individual(s) from current generation. Mutations can be acquired with probability μ and survive with probability equal to their fitness. This process is repeated until N individuals are produced that go on to found the following generation.

Fitness

Fitness in this model is the probability that an individual survives to reproduce. In the simplest implementation of the model, developmentally stable genotypes survive (i.e. their fitness is 1) and developmentally unstable ones do not (i.e. their fitness is 0).

Mutation

Mutations are modeled as the changes in gene regulation, i.e., the changes of the elements in the regulatory matrix .

Reproduction

Both sexual and asexual reproductions are implemented. Asexual reproduction is implemented as producing the offspring's genome (the gene network) by directly copying the parent's genome. Sexual reproduction is implemented as the recombination of the two parents' genomes.

Selection

An organism is considered viable if it reaches a stable gene expression pattern. An organism with oscillated expression pattern is discarded and cannot enter the next generation.

Biological Neuron Model

A biological neuron model, also known as a spiking neuron model, is a mathematical description of the properties of certain cells in the nervous system that generate sharp electrical potentials across their cell membrane, roughly one millisecond in duration, as shown in Fig. 1. Spiking neurons are known to be a major signaling unit of the nervous system, and for this reason characterizing their operation is of great importance. It is worth noting that not all the cells of the nervous system produce the type of spike that define the scope of the spiking neuron models. For example, cochlear hair cells, retinal receptor cells, and retinal bipolar cells do not spike. Furthermore, many cells in the nervous system are not classified as neurons but instead are classified as glia.

Ultimately, biological neuron models aim to explain the mechanisms underlying the operation of the nervous system for the purpose of restoring lost control capabilities such as perception (e.g. deafness or blindness), motor movement decision making, and continuous limb control. In that sense, biological neural models differ from artificial neuron models that do not presume to predict the outcomes of experiments involving the biological neural tissue (although artificial neuron models are also concerned with execution of perception and estimation tasks). Accordingly, an important aspect of biological neuron models is experimental validation, and the use of physical units to describe the experimental procedure associated with the model predictions.

Neuron models can be divided into two categories according to the physical units of the interface of the model. Each category could be further divided according to the abstraction/detail level:

Electrical input–output membrane voltage models – These models produce a prediction for membrane output voltage as function of electrical stimulation at the input stage (either voltage or current). The various models in this category differ in the exact functional relationship between the input current and the output voltage and in the level of details. Some models in this category are black box models and distinguish only between two measured voltage levels: the presence of a spike (also known as "action potential") or a quiescent state. Other models are more detailed and account for sub-cellular processes.

Natural or pharmacological input neuron models – These models were inspired from experiments involving either natural or pharmacological stimulation. The results of these experiment tend to vary from trial to trial, but the averaged response tends to converge to a clear pattern. Accordingly, the output of natural and pharmacological neuron models is the probability of a spike event as function of the input stimulus. Typically, the output probability is normalized (divided by) a time constant, and the resulting normalized probability is called the "firing rate" and has units of Hertz. The models in this category differ in the functional relationship connecting the input stimulus to the output probability. Models that are sub-categorized as Markov models are the simplest and yield the most tractable results.

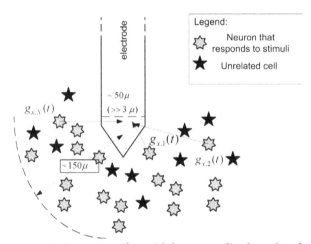

Extracellular measurement: Captures spikes with lower amplitudes, often from several spiking sources, depending on the size of the electrode and its proximity to the sources. Despite the decreased amplitude levels produced by this technique, it also has several advantages: 1) Is easier to obtain experimentally; 2) Is robust and lasts for a longer time; 3) Can reflect the dominant effect, especially when conducted in an anatomical region with many similar cells.

Although it is not unusual in science and engineering to have several descriptive models for different abstraction/detail levels, the number of different, sometimes contradicting, biological neuron models is exceptionally high. This situation is partly the result of the many different experimental settings, and the difficulty to separate the intrinsic properties of a single neuron from measurements effects and interactions of many cells (network effects). To accelerate the convergence to a unified theory, we list several models in each category, and where applicable, also references to supporting experiments.

Electrical Input–output Membrane Voltage Models

The models in this category describe the relationship between neuronal membrane currents at the input stage, and membrane voltage at the output stage. The most extensive experimental inquiry in this category of models was made by Hodgkin–Huxley in the early 1950s using an experimental setup that punctured the cell membrane and allowed to force a specific membrane voltage/current.

Most modern electrical neural interfaces apply extra-cellular electrical stimulation to avoid membrane puncturing which can lead to cell death and tissue damage. Hence, it is not clear to what extent the electrical neuron models hold for extra-cellular stimulation.

Integrate-and-fire

One of the earliest models of a neuron was first investigated in 1907 by Louis Lapicque. A neuron is represented in time by

$$I(t) = C_m \frac{dV_m(t)}{dt}$$

which is just the time derivative of the law of capacitance, $Q = CV$. When an input current is applied, the membrane voltage increases with time until it reaches a constant threshold V_{th}, at which point a delta function spike occurs and the voltage is reset to its resting potential, after which the model continues to run. The *firing frequency* of the model thus increases linearly without bound as input current increases.

The model can be made more accurate by introducing a refractory period t_{ref} that limits the firing frequency of a neuron by preventing it from firing during that period. Through some calculus involving a Fourier transform, the firing frequency as a function of a constant input current thus looks like

$$f(I) = \frac{I}{C_m V_{th} + t_{ref} I}.$$

A remaining shortcoming of this model is that it implements no time-dependent memory. If the model receives a below-threshold signal at some time, it will retain that voltage boost forever until it fires again. This characteristic is clearly not in line with observed neuronal behavior.

Hodgkin–Huxley Model

Experimental evidence supporting the model
Property of the H&H model
The shape of an individual spike
The identity of the ions involved
Spike speed across the axon

The Hodgkin–Huxley model (H&H model) is a model of the relationship between ion currents crossing the neuronal cell membrane and the membrane voltage. The model is based on experiments that allowed to force membrane voltage using an intra-cellular pipette. This model is based on the concept of membrane ion channels and relies on data from the squid giant axon. Hodgkin-Huxley was awarded the 1963 Nobel Prize in Physiology or Medicine for this model.

We note as before our voltage-current relationship, this time generalized to include multiple voltage-dependent currents:

$$C_m \frac{dV(t)}{dt} = -\sum_i I_i(t,V).$$

Each current is given by Ohm's Law as

$$I(t,V) = g(t,V) \cdot (V - V_{eq})$$

where $g(t,V)$ is the conductance, or inverse resistance, which can be expanded in terms of its constant average $\bar{g}$ and the activation and inactivation fractions m and h, respectively, that determine how many ions can flow through available membrane channels. This expansion is given by

$$g(t,V) = \bar{g} \cdot m(t,V)^p \cdot h(t,V)^q$$

and our fractions follow the first-order kinetics

$$\frac{dm(t,V)}{dt} = \frac{m_\infty(V) - m(t,V)}{\tau_m(V)} = \alpha_m(V) \cdot (1-m) - \beta_m(V) \cdot m$$

with similar dynamics for h, where we can use either τ and m_∞ or α and β to define our gate fractions.

With such a form, all that remains is to individually investigate each current one wants to include. Typically, these include inward Ca^{2+} and Na^+ input currents and several varieties of K^+ outward currents, including a "leak" current.

The end result can be at the small end 20 parameters which one must estimate or measure for an accurate model, and for complex systems of neurons not easily tractable by computer. Careful simplifications of the Hodgkin–Huxley model are therefore needed.

Leaky Integrate-and-fire

In the leaky integrate-and-fire model, the memory problem is solved by adding a "leak" term to the membrane potential, reflecting the diffusion of ions that occurs through the membrane when some equilibrium is not reached in the cell. The model looks like

$$I(t) - \frac{V_{\mathrm{m}}(t)}{R_{\mathrm{m}}} = C_{\mathrm{m}} \frac{dV_{\mathrm{m}}(t)}{dt}$$

where R_{m} is the membrane resistance, as we find it is not a perfect insulator as assumed previously. This forces the input current to exceed some threshold $I_{\mathrm{th}} = V_{\mathrm{th}} / R_{\mathrm{m}}$ in order to cause the cell to fire, else it will simply leak out any change in potential. The firing frequency thus looks like

$$f(I) = \begin{cases} 0, & I \leq I_{\mathrm{th}} \\ [t_{\mathrm{ref}} - R_{\mathrm{m}} C_{\mathrm{m}} \log(1 - \frac{V_{\mathrm{th}}}{IR_{\mathrm{m}}})]^{-1}, & I > I_{\mathrm{th}} \end{cases}$$

which converges for large input currents to the previous leak-free model with refractory period.

Galves-Löcherbach

The Galves-Löcherbach model is a specific development of the leaky integrate-and-fire model. It is inherently stochastic. It was developed by mathematicians Antonio Galves and Eva Löcherbach. Given the model specifications, the probability that a given neuron i spikes in a time period t may be described by

$$\mathrm{Prob}(X_t(i) = 1 \mid \mathcal{F}_{t-1}) = \phi_i\left(\sum_{j \in I} W_{j \to i} \sum_{s=L_t^i}^{t-1} g_j(t-s) X_s(j), t - L_t^i\right),$$

where $W_{j \to i}$ is a synaptic weight, describing the influence of neuron j on neuron i, g_j expresses the leak, and L_t^i provides the spiking history of neuron i before t, according to

$$L_t^i = \sup\{s < t : X_s(i) = 1\}.$$

Exponential Integrate-and-fire

In the Exponential Integrate-and-Fire, spike generation is exponential, following the equation:

$$\frac{dX}{dt} = \Delta_T \exp\left(\frac{X - X_T}{\Delta_T}\right).$$

where X is the membrane potential, X_T is the membrane potential threshold, and Δ_T is the sharpness of action potential initiation, usually around 1 mV for cortical pyramidal neurons. Once the membrane potential crosses X_T, it diverges to infinity in finite time.

FitzHugh–Nagumo

Sweeping simplifications to Hodgkin–Huxley were introduced by FitzHugh and Nagumo in 1961 and 1962. Seeking to describe "regenerative self-excitation" by a nonlinear positive-feedback membrane voltage and recovery by a linear negative-feedback gate voltage, they developed the model described by

$$\frac{dV}{dt} = V - V^3 - w + I_{ext}$$

$$\tau\frac{dw}{dt} = V - a - bw$$

where we again have a membrane-like voltage and input current with a slower general gate voltage w and experimentally-determined parameters $a = -0.7, b = 0.8, \tau = 1/0.08$. Although not clearly derivable from biology, the model allows for a simplified, immediately available dynamic, without being a trivial simplification.

Morris–Lecar

In 1981 Morris and Lecar combined Hodgkin–Huxley and FitzHugh–Nagumo into a voltage-gated calcium channel model with a delayed-rectifier potassium channel, represented by

$$C\frac{dV}{dt} = -I_{ion}(V,w) + I$$

$$\frac{dw}{dt} = \phi \cdot \frac{w_\infty - w}{\tau_w}$$

where $I_{ion}(V,w) = \overline{g}_{Ca}m_\infty \cdot (V - V_{Ca}) + \overline{g}_K w \cdot (V - V_K) + \overline{g}_L \cdot (V - V_L)$.

Hindmarsh–Rose

Building upon the FitzHugh–Nagumo model, Hindmarsh and Rose proposed in 1984 a model of neuronal activity described by three coupled first order differential equations:

$$\frac{dx}{dt} = y + 3x^2 - x^3 - z + I$$

$$\frac{dy}{dt} = 1 - 5x^2 - y$$

$$\frac{dz}{dt} = r \cdot (4(x + \tfrac{8}{5}) - z)$$

with $r^2 = x^2 + y^2 + z^2$, and $r \approx 10^{-2}$ so that the z variable only changes very slowly. This extra mathematical complexity allows a great variety of dynamic behaviors for the membrane potential, described by the x variable of the model, which include chaotic dynamics. This makes the Hindmarsh–Rose neuron model very useful, because being still simple, allows a good qualitative description of the many different patterns of the action potential observed in experiments.

Cable Theory

Cable theory describes the dendritic arbor as a cylindrical structure undergoing a regular pattern of bifurcation, like branches in a tree. For a single cylinder or an entire tree, the input conductance at the base (where the tree meets the cell body, or any such boundary) is defined as

$$G_{in} = \frac{G_\infty \tanh(L) + G_L}{1 + (G_L / G_\infty) \tanh(L)},$$

where L is the electrotonic length of the cylinder which depends on its length, diameter, and resistance. A simple recursive algorithm scales linearly with the number of branches and can be used to calculate the effective conductance of the tree. This is given by

$$G_D = G_m A_D \tanh(L_D)/L_D$$

where $A_D = \pi l d$ is the total surface area of the tree of total length l, and L_D is its total electrotonic length. For an entire neuron in which the cell body conductance is G_S and the membrane conductance per unit area is $G_{md} = G_m / A$, we find the total neuron conductance G_N for n dendrite trees by adding up all tree and soma conductances, given by

$$G_N = G_S + \sum_{j=1}^{n} A_{D_j} F_{dga_j},$$

where we can find the general correction factor F_{dga} experimentally by noting $G_D = G_{m-d} A_D F_{dga}$.

Compartmental Models

The cable model makes a number of simplifications to give closed analytic results, namely that the dendritic arbor must branch in diminishing pairs in a fixed pattern. A compartmental model allows for any desired tree topology with arbitrary branches and lengths, but makes simplifications in the interactions between branches to compensate. Thus, the two models give complementary results, neither of which is necessarily more accurate.

Each individual piece, or compartment, of a dendrite is modeled by a straight cylinder of arbitrary length l and diameter d which connects with fixed resistance to any number of branching cylinders. We define the conductance ratio of the ith cylinder as $B_i = G_i / G_\infty$, where $G_\infty = \frac{\pi d^{3/2}}{2\sqrt{R_i R_m}}$ and R_i is the resistance between the current compartment and the next. We obtain a series of equations for conductance ratios in and out of a compartment by making corrections to the normal dynamic $B_{out,i} = B_{in,i+1}$, as

- $$B_{out,i} = \frac{B_{in,i+1}(d_{i+1}/d_i)^{3/2}}{\sqrt{R_{m,i+1}/R_{m,i}}}$$

- $$B_{in,i} = \frac{B_{out,i} + \tanh X_i}{1 + B_{out,i}\tanh X_i}$$

- $$B_{out,par} = \frac{B_{in,dau1}(d_{dau1}/d_{par})^{3/2}}{\sqrt{R_{m,dau1}/R_{m,par}}} + \frac{B_{in,dau2}(d_{dau2}/d_{par})^{3/2}}{\sqrt{R_{m,dau2}/R_{m,par}}} + \dots$$

where the last equation deals with *parents* and *daughters* at branches, and $X_i = \frac{l_i\sqrt{4R_i}}{\sqrt{d_i R_m}}$.

We can iterate these equations through the tree until we get the point where the dendrites connect to the cell body (soma), where the conductance ratio is $B_{in,stem}$. Then our total neuron conductance is given by

$$G_N = \frac{A_{soma}}{R_{m,soma}} + \sum_j B_{in,stem,j} G_{\infty,j}.$$

An example of a compartmental model of a neuron, with an algorithm to reduce the number of compartments (increase the computational speed) and yet retain the salient electrical characteristics, can be found in.

Natural Input Stimulus Neuron Models

The models in this category were derived following experiments involving natural stimulation such as light, sound, touch, or odor. In these experiments, the spike pattern resulting from each stimulus presentation varies from trial to trial, but the averaged response from several trials often converges to a clear pattern. Consequently, the models in this category generate a probabilistic relationship between the input stimulus to spike occurrences.

The Non-homogeneous Poisson Process Model (Siebert)

Siebert modeled the neuron spike firing pattern using a non-homogeneous Poisson process model, following experiments involving the auditory system. According to Siebert, the probability of a spiking event at the time interval $[t, t + \Delta_t]$ is proportional to a non negative function $g[s(t)]$, where $s(t)$ is the raw stimulus.:

$$P_{spike}(t \in [t', t' + \Delta_t]) = \Delta_t \cdot g[s(t)]$$

Siebert considered several functions as $g[s(t)]$, including $g[s(t)] \propto s^2(t)$ for low stimulus intensities.

The main advantage of Siebert's model is its simplicity. The shortcomings of the model is its inability to reflect properly the following phenomena:

- The edge emphasizing property of the neuron in response to a stimulus pulse.

- The saturation of the firing rate.

- The values of inter-spike-interval-histogram at short intervals values (close to zero).

These shortcoming are addressed by the two state Markov Model.

The Two State Markov Model (Nossenson & Messer)

The spiking neuron model by Nossenson & Messer produces the probability of the neuron to fire a spike as a function of either an external or pharmacological stimulus. The model consists of a cascade of a receptor layer model and a spiking neuron model, as shown in Fig 4. The connection between the external stimulus to the spiking probability is made in two steps: First, a receptor cell model translates the raw external stimulus to neurotransmitter concentration, then, a spiking neuron model connects between neurotransmitter concentration to the firing rate (spiking probability). Thus, the spiking neuron model by itself depends on neurotransmitter concentration at the input stage.

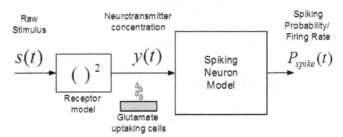

Fig 6: High level block diagram of the receptor layer and neuron model by Nossenson & Messer.

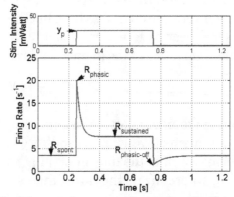

The prediction for the firing rate in response to a pulse stimulus as given by the model by Nossenson & Messer.

An important feature of this model is the prediction for neurons firing rate pattern which captures, using a low number of free parameters, the characteristic edge em-phasized response of neurons to a stimulus pulse, as shown in Fig. 5. The firing rate is identified both as a normalized probability for neural spike firing, and as a quantity proportional to the current of neurotransmitters released by the cell. The expression for the firing rate takes the following form:

$$R_{fire}(t) = \frac{P_{spike}(t;\Delta_t)}{\Delta_t} = [y(t) + R_0] \cdot P_0(t)$$

where,

P0 is the probability of the neuron to be "armed" and ready to fire. It is given by the following differential equation:

$$P_0 = -[y(t) + R_0 + R_1] \cdot P_0(t) + R_1$$

- P0 could be generally calculated recursively using Euler method, but in the case of a pulse of stimulus it yields a simple closed form expression.

- y(t) is the input of the model and is interpreted as the neurotransmitter con-centration on the cell surrounding (in most cases glutamate) . For an external stimulus it can be estimated through the receptor layer model:

$y(t) \simeq g_{gain} \cdot \langle s^2(t) \rangle$, with $\langle s^2(t) \rangle$ being short temporal average of stimulus power (given in Watt or other energy per time unit).

- R0 corresponds to the intrinsic spontaneous firing rate of the neuron.

- R1 is the recovery rate of the neuron from refractory state.

Other predictions by this model include:

1) The averaged Evoked Response Potential (ERP) due to population of many neurons in unfiltered measurements resembles the firing rate.

2) The voltage variance of activity due to multiple neuron activity resembles the firing rate (also known as Multi-Unit-Activity power or MUA).

3) The inter-spike-interval probability distribution takes the form a gamma-distribu-tion like function.

Experimental evidence supporting the model by Nossenson & Messer	
Property of the Model by Nossenson & Messer	Description of experimental evidence
The shape of the firing rate in response to an auditory stimulus pulse	The Firing Rate has the same shape of Fig 5.

The shape of the firing rate in response to a visual stimulus pulse	The Firing Rate has the same shape of Fig 5.
The shape of the firing rate in response to an olfactory stimulus pulse	The Firing Rate has the same shape of Fig 5.
The shape of the firing rate in response to a somato-sensory stimulus	The Firing Rate has the same shape of Fig 5.
The change in firing rate in response to neurotransmitter application (mostly glutamate)	Firing Rate change in response to neurotransmitter application (Glutamate)
Square dependence between an auditory stimulus pressure and the firing rate	Square Dependence between Auditory Stimulus pressure and the Firing Rate (- Linear dependence in pressure square (power)).
Square dependence between visual stimulus electric field (volts) and the firing rate	Square dependence between visual stimulus electric field (volts) - Linear Dependence between Visual Stimulus Power and the Firing Rate.
The shape of the Inter-Spike-Interval Statistics (ISI)	ISI shape resembles the gamma-function-like
The ERP resembles the firing rate in unfiltered measurements	The shape of the averaged evoked response potential in response to stimulus resembles the firing rate (Fig. 5).
MUA power resembles the firing rate	The shape of the empirical variance of extra-cellular measurements in response to stimulus pulse resembles the firing rate (Fig. 5).

Non-Markovian Models

The following is a list of published non-Markovian neuron models:

- Johnson, and Swami
- Berry and Meister
- Kass and Ventura

Pharmacological Input Stimulus Neuron Models

The models in this category produce predictions for experiments involving pharmacological stimulation.

Synaptic Transmission (Koch & Segev)

According to the model by Koch and Segev, the response of a neuron to individual neurotransmitters can be modeled as an extension of the classical Hodgkin–Huxley model with both standard and nonstandard kinetic currents. Four neurotransmitters primarily have influence in the CNS. AMPA/kainate receptors are fast excitatory mediators while NMDA receptors mediate considerably slower currents. Fast inhibitory currents go through GABA$_A$ receptors, while GABA$_B$ receptors mediate by secondary G-protein-activated potassium channels. This range of mediation produces the following current dynamics:

- $I_{AMPA}(t,V) = \bar{g}_{AMPA} \cdot [O] \cdot (V(t) - E_{AMPA})$

- $I_{NMDA}(t,V) = \bar{g}_{NMDA} \cdot B(V) \cdot [O] \cdot (V(t) - E_{NMDA})$

- $I_{GABA_A}(t,V) = \bar{g}_{GABA_A} \cdot ([O_1] + [O_2]) \cdot (V(t) - E_{Cl})$

- $I_{GABA_B}(t,V) = \bar{g}_{GABA_B} \cdot \dfrac{[G]^n}{[G]^n + K_d} \cdot (V(t) - E_K)$

where $\square$ is the maximal conductance (around 1S) and E is the equilibrium potential of the given ion or transmitter (AMDA, NMDA, Cl, or K), while $[O]$ describes the fraction of receptors that are open. For NMDA, there is a significant effect of *magnesium block* that depends sigmoidally on the concentration of intracellular magnesium by $B(V)$. For GABA$_B$, $[G]$ is the concentration of the G-protein, and K_d describes the dissociation of G in binding to the potassium gates.

The dynamics of this more complicated model have been well-studied experimentally and produce important results in terms of very quick synaptic potentiation and depression, that is, fast, short-term learning.

The Two State Markov Model (Nossenson & Messer)

The model by Nossenson and Messer translates neurotransmitter concentration at the input stage to the probability of releasing neurotransmitter at the output stage.

Applications

The question of neural modeling is at the heart of the following projects:

Conjectures Regarding the Role of the Neuron in the Wider Context of the Brain Principle of Operation

Conjecture 1: Relation between Artificial and Biological Neuron Models

The most basic model of a neuron consists of an input with some synaptic weight vector and an activation function or transfer function inside the neuron determining output.

This is the basic structure used in artificial neurons, which in a neural network often looks like

$$y_i = \phi\left(\sum_j w_{ij}x_j\right)$$

where y_i is the output of the i th neuron, x_j is the jth input neuron signal, w_{ij} is the synaptic weight (or strength of connection) between the neurons i and j, and φ is the activation function. While this model has seen success in machine-learning applications, it is a poor model for real (biological) neurons, because it lacks the time-dependence that real neurons exhibit. Some of the earliest biological models took this form until kinetic models such as the Hodgkin–Huxley model became dominant.

In the case of modelling a biological neuron, physical analogues are used in place of abstractions such as "weight" and "transfer function". A neuron is filled and surrounded with water containing ions, which carry electric charge. The neuron is bound by an insulating cell membrane and can maintain a concentration of charged ions on either side that determines a capacitance C_m. The firing of a neuron involves the movement of ions into the cell that occurs when neurotransmitters cause ion channels on the cell membrane to open. We describe this by a physical time-dependent current $I(t)$. With this comes a change in voltage, or the electrical potential energy difference between the cell and its surroundings, which is observed to sometimes result in a voltage spike called an action potential which travels the length of the cell and triggers the release of further neurotransmitters. The voltage, then, is the quantity of interest and is given by $V_m(t)$.

Conjecture 2: Loops of Spiking Neurons for Decision Making

Conjecture 3: The Neurotransmitter Based Energy Detection Scheme

The neurotransmitter based energy detection scheme suggests that the neural tissue chemically executes a Radar-like detection procedure. A list of experimental evidence supporting this conjecture is given in. This conjecture attributes active functional roles to non-spiking neurons and glia cells.

General Comments Regarding the Modern Perspective of Scientific and Engineering Models

- The models above are still idealizations. Corrections must be made for the increased membrane surface area given by numerous dendritic spines, temperatures significantly hotter than room-temperature experimental data, and nonuniformity in the cell's internal structure. Certain observed effects do not fit into some of these models. For instance, the temperature cycling (with minimal net temperature increase) of the cell membrane during action potential propagation not compatible with models which rely on modeling the membrane as a resistance which must dissipate energy when current flows through it. The transient thickening of the cell membrane during action potential propagation is also not predicted by these models, nor is the changing capacitance and voltage spike that results from this thickening incorporated into these models. The action of some anesthetics such as inert gases is problematic for these models as well. New models, such as the soliton model attempt to explain these phenomena, but are less developed than older models and have yet to be widely applied. Also improbable possibility of modelling of local chronobiology mechanisms.

- Modern views regarding of the role of the scientific model suggest that "All models are wrong but some are useful" (Box and Draper, 1987, Gribbin, 2009; Paninski et al., 2009).

Morris–Lecar Model

The Morris–Lecar model is a biological neuron model developed by Catherine Morris and Harold Lecar to reproduce the variety of oscillatory behavior in relation to Ca^{++} and K^+ conductance in the muscle fiber of the giant barnacle . Morris–Lecar neurons exhibit both class I and class II neuron excitability.

History

Catherine Morris (b. 24 December 1949) is a Canadian biologist. She won a Commonwealth scholarship to study at Cambridge University, where she earned her PhD in 1977. She became a professor at the University of Ottawa in the early 1980s. As of 2015, she is an emeritus professor at the University of Ottawa. Harold Lecar (18 Oct 1935-4 Feb 2014) was an American professor of biophysics and neurobiology at the University of California Berkeley. He graduated with his PhD in physics from Columbia University in 1963.

Experimental Method

The Morris–Lecar experiments relied on the current clamp method established by Keynes *et al.* (1973).

Large specimens of the barnacle *Balanus nubilus* (Pacific Bio-Marine Laboratories Inc., Venice, California) were used. The barnacle was sawed into lateral halves, and the depressor scutorum rostralis muscles were carefully exposed. Individual fibers were dissected, the incision starting from the tendon. The other end of the muscle was cut closc to its attachment on the shell and ligatured. Isolated fibers were either used immediately or kept for up to 30 min in standard artificial seawater before use. Experiments were carried out at room temperature of 22 C.

The Principal Assumptions Underlying the Morris–Lecar Model include

1. Equations apply to a spatially iso-potential patch of membrane. There are two persistent (non-inactivating) voltage-gated currents with oppositively biased reversal potentials. The depolarizing current is carried by Na+ or Ca2+ ions (or both), depending on the system to be modeled, and the hyperpolarizing current is carried by K+.

2. Activation gates follow changes in membrane potential sufficiently rapidly that the activating conductance can instantaneously relax to its steady-state value at any voltage.

3. The dynamics of the recovery variable can be approximated by a first-order linear differential equation for the probability of channel opening.

Physiological Description

The Morris–Lecar model is a two-dimensional system of nonlinear differential equations. It is considered a simplified model compared to the four-dimensional Hodgkin–Huxley model.

Qualitatively, this system of equations describes the complex relationship between membrane potential and the activation of ion channels within the membrane: the potential depends on the activity of the ion channels, and the activity of the ion channels depends on the voltage. As bifurcation parameters are altered, different classes of neuron behavior are exhibited. τ_N is associated with the relative time scales of the firing dynamics, which varies broadly from cell to cell and exhibits significant temperature dependency.

Quantitatively:

$$C\frac{dV}{dt}=I-g_{\mathrm{L}}(V-V_{\mathrm{L}})-g_{\mathrm{Ca}}M_{\mathrm{ss}}(V-V_{\mathrm{Ca}})-g_{\mathrm{K}}N(V-V_{\mathrm{K}})$$

$$\frac{dN}{dt}=\frac{N_{\mathrm{ss}}-N}{\tau_N}$$

where

$$M_{\mathrm{ss}}=\tfrac{1}{2}\cdot(1+\tanh[\tfrac{V-V_1}{V_2}])$$

$$N_{\mathrm{ss}}=\tfrac{1}{2}\cdot(1+\tanh[\tfrac{V-V_3}{V_4}])$$

$$\tau_N=1/(\phi\cosh[\tfrac{V-V_3}{2V_4}])$$

Note that the M_{ss} and N_{ss} equations may also be expressed as $M_{\mathrm{ss}} = (1 + \mathrm{Exp}[-2(V - V_1)/$

$V_2])^{-1}$ and $N_{ss} = (1 + \text{Exp}[-2(V - V_3) / V_4])^{-1}$, however most authors prefer the form using the hyperbolic functions.

Variables

- V : membrane potential
- N : recovery variable: the probability that the K+ channel is conducting

Parameters and Constants

- I : applied current
- C : membrane capacitance
- g_L, g_{Ca}, g_K : leak, Ca^{++}, and K$^+$ conductances through membranes channel
- V_L, V_{Ca}, V_K : equilibrium potential of relevant ion channels
- V_1, V_2, V_3, V_4: tuning parameters for steady state and time constant
- φ: reference frequency

Bifurcations

Bifurcation in the Morris–Lecar model have been analyzed with the applied current I, as the main bifurcation parameter and φ, g_{Ca}, V_3, V_4 as secondary parameters for phase plane analysis.

Possible Bifurcations

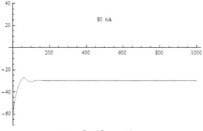

Hopf Bifurcation

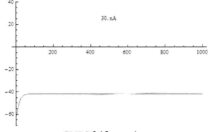

SNIC bifurcation

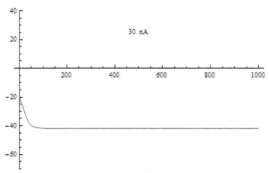

Homoclinic bifurcation

Current clamp simulations of the Morris–Lecar model. The injected current for the SNIC bifurcation and the homoclinic bifurcation is varied between 30 nA and 50 nA, while the current for the Hopf bifurcation is varied between 80nA and 100nA

Hindmarsh–Rose Model

The Hindmarsh–Rose model of neuronal activity is aimed to study the spiking-bursting behavior of the membrane potential observed in experiments made with a single neuron. The relevant variable is the membrane potential, $x(t)$, which is written in dimensionless units. There are two more variables, $y(t)$ and $z(t)$, which take into account the transport of ions across the membrane through the ion channels. The transport of sodium and potassium ions is made through fast ion channels and its rate is measured by $y(t)$, which is called the spiking variable. The transport of other ions is made through slow channels, and is taken into account through $z(t)$, which is called the bursting variable. Then, the Hindmarsh–Rose model has the mathematical form of a system of three nonlinear ordinary differential equations on the dimensionless dynamical variables $x(t)$, $y(t)$, and $z(t)$. They read:

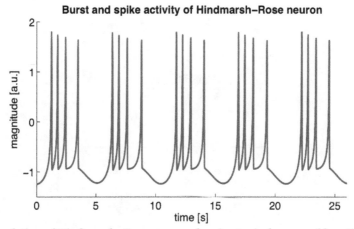

Simulation of Hindmarsh–Rose neuron showing typical neuronal bursting.

$$\frac{dx}{dt} = y + \phi(x) - z + I,$$

$$\frac{dy}{dt} = \psi(x) - y,$$

$$\frac{dz}{dt} = r[s(x - x_R) - z],$$

where

$$\phi(x) = -ax^3 + bx^2,$$

$$\psi(x) = c - dx^2.$$

The model has eight parameters: a, b, c, d, r, s, x_R and I. It is common to fix some of them and let the others be control parameters. Usually the parameter I, which means the current that enters the neuron, is taken as a control parameter. Other control parameters used often in the literature are a, b, c, d, or r, the first four modeling the working of the fast ion channels and the last one the slow ion channels, respectively. Frequently, the parameters held fixed are $s = 4$ and $x_R = -8/5$. When a, b, c, d are fixed the values given are $a = 1$, $b = 3$, $c = 1$, and $d = 5$. The parameter r is something of the order of 10^{-3}, and I ranges between -10 and 10.

The third state equation:

$$\frac{dz}{dt} = r[s(x - x_R) - z],$$

allows a great variety of dynamic behaviors of the membrane potential, described by variable x, including unpredictable behavior, which is referred to as chaotic dynamics. This makes the Hindmarsh–Rose model relatively simple and provides a good qualitative description of the many different patterns that are observed empirically.

References

- Ivanova, N.; A. Lykidis (2009). "Metabolic Reconstruction". Encyclopedia of Microbiology, 3rd Ed.: 607–621. doi:10.1016/B978-012373944-5.00010-9. ISBN 9780123739445.

- Anderson, D. H., Compartmental Modeling and Tracer Kinetics, Springer-Verlag Lecture Notes in Biomathematics #50, 1983 (ISBN 0-387-12303-2).

- Koch, Christof; Segev, Idan (1999). Methods in neuronal modeling : from ions to networks (2nd ed.). Cambridge, Massachusetts: MIT Press. p. 687. ISBN 0-262-11231-0.

- Ullah, E; Aeron S; Hassoun S (2015). "gEFM: An Algorithm for Computing Elementary Flux Modes Using Graph Traversal.". IEEE/ACM Transactions on Computational Biology and Bioinformatics: 1. doi:10.1109/TCBB.2015.2430344.

Computational Genomics: A Comprehensive Study

The computational analysis used to understand biology from the genome sequences is termed as computational genomics. Genome project and Mycoplasma laboratorium are one of the significant and important topics related to computational genomics. The following chapter unfolds its crucial aspects in a critical yet systematic manner.

Computational Genomics

Computational genomics (often referred to as Computational Genetics) refers to the use of computational and statistical analysis to decipher biology from genome sequences and related data, including both DNA and RNA sequence as well as other "post-genomic" data (i.e., experimental data obtained with technologies that require the genome sequence, such as genomic DNA microarrays). These, in combination with computational and statistical approaches to understanding the function of the genes and statistical association analysis, this field is also often referred to as Computational and Statistical Genetics/genomics. As such, computational genomics may be regarded as a subset of bioinformatics and computational biology, but with a focus on using whole genomes (rather than individual genes) to understand the principles of how the DNA of a species controls its biology at the molecular level and beyond. With the current abundance of massive biological datasets, computational studies have become one of the most important means to biological discovery.

History

The roots of computational genomics are shared with those of bioinformatics. During the 1960s, Margaret Dayhoff and others at the National Biomedical Research Foundation assembled databases of homologous protein sequences for evolutionary study. Their research developed a phylogenetic tree that determined the evolutionary changes that were required for a particular protein to change into another protein based on the underlying amino acid sequences. This led them to create a scoring matrix that assessed the likelihood of one protein being related to another.

Beginning in the 1980s, databases of genome sequences began to be recorded, but this presented new challenges in the form of searching and comparing the databases of gene information. Unlike text-searching algorithms that are used on websites such as Google or Wikipedia, searching for sections of genetic similarity requires one to find strings that are not simply identical, but similar. This led to the development of the Needleman-Wunsch algorithm, which is a dynamic programming algorithm for comparing sets of amino acid sequences with each other by using scoring matrices derived from the earlier research by Dayhoff. Later, the BLAST algorithm was developed for performing fast, optimized searches of gene sequence databases. BLAST and its derivatives are probably the most widely used algorithms for this purpose.

The emergence of the phrase "computational genomics" coincides with the availability of complete sequenced genomes in the mid-to-late 1990s. The first meeting of the Annual Conference on Computational Genomics was organized by scientists from The Institute for Genomic Research (TIGR) in 1998, providing a forum for this speciality and effectively distinguishing this area of science from the more general fields of Genomics or Computational Biology. The first use of this term in scientific literature, according to MEDLINE abstracts, was just one year earlier in Nucleic Acids Research. The final Computational Genomics conference was held in 2006, featuring a keynote talk by Nobel Laureate Barry Marshall, co-discoverer of the link between Helicobacter pylori and stomach ulcers. As of 2014, the leading conferences in the field include Intelligent Systems for Molecular Biology (ISMB) and RECOMB.

The development of computer-assisted mathematics (using products such as Mathematica or Matlab) has helped engineers, mathematicians and computer scientists to start operating in this domain, and a public collection of case studies and demonstrations is growing, ranging from whole genome comparisons to gene expression analysis. This has increased the introduction of different ideas, including concepts from systems and control, information theory, strings analysis and data mining. It is anticipated that computational approaches will become and remain a standard topic for research and teaching, while students fluent in both topics start being formed in the multiple courses created in the past few years.

Contributions of Computational Genomics Research to Biology

Contributions of computational genomics research to biology include:

- discovering subtle patterns in genomic sequences
- proposing cellular signalling networks
- proposing mechanisms of genome evolution
- predict precise locations of all human genes using comparative genomics techniques with several mammalian and vertebrate species
- predict conserved genomic regions that are related to early embryonic development

- discover potential links between repeated sequence motifs and tissue-specific gene expression

- measure regions of genomes that have undergone unusually rapid evolution

Latest Development (from 2012)

First Computer Model of an Organism

Researchers at Stanford University created the first software simulation of an entire organism. The smallest free-living organism, *Mycoplasma genitalium*, has 525 genes which are fully mapped. With data from more than 900 scientific papers reported on the bacterium, researchers developed the software model using the object-oriented programming approach. A series of modules mimic the various functions of the cell and then are integrated together into a whole simulated organism. The simulation runs on a single CPU, recreates the complete life span of the cell at the molecular level, reproducing the interactions of molecules in cell processes including metabolism and cell division.

The 'silicon cell' will act as computerized laboratories that could perform experiments which are difficult to do on an actual organism, or could carry out procedures much faster. The applications will include faster screening of new compounds, understanding of basic cellular principles and behavior.

Genome Project

When printed, the human genome sequence fills around 100 huge books of close print

Genome projects are scientific endeavours that ultimately aim to determine the complete genome sequence of an organism (be it an animal, a plant, a fungus, a bacterium, an archaean, a protist or a virus) and to annotate protein-coding genes and other important genome-encoded features. The genome sequence of an organism includes the collective DNA sequences of each chromosome in the organism. For a bacterium containing a single chromosome, a genome project will aim to map the sequence of that chromosome. For the human species, whose genome includes 22 pairs of autosomes and 2 sex chromosomes, a complete genome sequence will involve 46 separate chromosome sequences.

The Human Genome Project was a landmark genome project that is already having a major impact on research across the life sciences, with potential for spurring numerous medical and commercial developments.

Genome Assembly

Genome assembly refers to the process of taking a large number of short DNA sequences and putting them back together to create a representation of the original chromosomes from which the DNA originated. In a shotgun sequencing project, all the DNA from a source (usually a single organism, anything from a bacterium to a mammal) is first fractured into millions of small pieces. These pieces are then "read" by automated sequencing machines, which can read up to 1000 nucleotides or bases at a time. (The four bases are adenine, guanine, cytosine, and thymine, represented as AGCT.) A genome assembly algorithm works by taking all the pieces and aligning them to one another, and detecting all places where two of the short sequences, or *reads*, overlap. These overlapping reads can be merged, and the process continues.

Genome assembly is a very difficult computational problem, made more difficult because many genomes contain large numbers of identical sequences, known as repeats. These repeats can be thousands of nucleotides long, and some occur in thousands of different locations, especially in the large genomes of plants and animals.

The resulting (draft) genome sequence is produced by combining the information sequenced contigs and then employing linking information to create scaffolds. Scaffolds are positioned along the physical map of the chromosomes creating a "golden path".

Assembly Software

Originally, most large-scale DNA sequencing centers developed their own software for assembling the sequences that they produced. However, this has changed as the software has grown more complex and as the number of sequencing centers has increased. An example of such assembler *Short Oligonucleotide Analysis Package* developed by BGI for de novo assembly of human-sized genomes, alignment, SNP detection, resequencing, indel finding, and structural variation analysis.

Genome Annotation

Since the 1980s, molecular biology and bioinformatics have created the need for DNA annotation. DNA annotation or genome annotation is the process of identifying attaching biological information to sequences, and particularly in identifying the locations of genes and determining what those genes do. Kotgire Girish

When is a Genome Project Finished?

When sequencing a genome, there are usually regions that are difficult to sequence (often regions with highly repetitive DNA). Thus, 'completed' genome sequences are rarely ever complete, and terms such as 'working draft' or 'essentially complete' have been used to more accurately describe the status of such genome projects. Even when every base pair of a genome sequence has been determined, there are still likely to be errors present because DNA sequencing is not a completely accurate process. It could also be argued that a complete genome project should include the sequences of mitochondria and (for plants) chloroplasts as these organelles have their own genomes.

It is often reported that the goal of sequencing a genome is to obtain information about the complete set of genes in that particular genome sequence. The proportion of a genome that encodes for genes may be very small (particularly in eukaryotes such as humans, where coding DNA may only account for a few percent of the entire sequence). However, it is not always possible (or desirable) to only sequence the coding regions separately. Also, as scientists understand more about the role of this noncoding DNA (often referred to as junk DNA), it will become more important to have a complete genome sequence as a background to understanding the genetics and biology of any given organism.

In many ways genome projects do not confine themselves to only determining a DNA sequence of an organism. Such projects may also include gene prediction to find out where the genes are in a genome, and what those genes do. There may also be related projects to sequence ESTs or mRNAs to help find out where the genes actually are.

Historical and Technological Perspectives

Historically, when sequencing eukaryotic genomes (such as the worm *Caenorhabditis elegans*) it was common to first map the genome to provide a series of landmarks across the genome. Rather than sequence a chromosome in one go, it would be sequenced piece by piece (with the prior knowledge of approximately where that piece is located on the larger chromosome). Changes in technology and in particular improvements to the processing power of computers, means that genomes can now be 'shotgun sequenced' in one go (there are caveats to this approach though when compared to the traditional approach).

Improvements in DNA sequencing technology has meant that the cost of sequencing a new genome sequence has steadily fallen (in terms of cost per base pair) and newer technology has also meant that genomes can be sequenced far more quickly.

When research agencies decide what new genomes to sequence, the emphasis has been on species which are either high importance as model organism or have a relevance to human health (e.g. pathogenic bacteria or vectors of disease such as mosquitos) or species which have commercial importance (e.g. livestock and crop plants). Secondary emphasis is placed on species whose genomes will help answer important questions in molecular evolution (e.g. the common chimpanzee).

In the future, it is likely that it will become even cheaper and quicker to sequence a genome. This will allow for complete genome sequences to be determined from many different individuals of the same species. For humans, this will allow us to better understand aspects of human genetic diversity.

Example Genome Projects

L1 Dominette 01449, the Hereford who serves as the subject of the Bovine Genome Project

Many organisms have genome projects that have either been completed or will be completed shortly, including:

- Humans, Homo sapiens
- Humans, Homo sapiens
- Palaeo-Eskimo, an ancient-human
- Neanderthal, "*Homo neanderthalensis*" (partial)
- Common chimpanzee *Pan troglodytes*
- Domestic Cow
- Bovine Genome
- Honey Bee Genome Sequencing Consortium
- Horse genome
- Human microbiome project
- International Grape Genome Program
- International HapMap Project
- Tomato 150+ genome resequencing project

- 100K Genome Project

- Genomics England

Mycoplasma Laboratorium

Mycoplasma laboratorium is a designed, partially synthetic species of bacterium derived from the genome of *Mycoplasma genitalium*. This effort in synthetic biology is being undertaken at the J. Craig Venter Institute by a team of approximately 20 scientists headed by Nobel laureate Hamilton Smith, and including DNA researcher Craig Venter and microbiologist Clyde A. Hutchison III. *Mycoplasma genitalium* was chosen as it was the species with the smallest number of genes known at that time.

On May 21, 2010, *Science* reported that the Venter group had successfully synthesized the genome of the bacterium *Mycoplasma mycoides* from a computer record, and transplanted the synthesized genome into the existing cell of a *Mycoplasma capricolum* bacterium that had had its DNA removed. The "synthetic" bacterium was viable, i.e. capable of replicating billions of times. (The team had originally planned to use the *M. genitalium* bacterium they had previously been working with, but switched to *M. mycoides* because the latter bacterium grows much faster, which translated into quicker experiments.) Scientists who were not involved in the study caution that it is not a truly synthetic life form because its genome was put into an existing cell.

It is estimated that the synthetic genome cost US$40 million to make and took 20 people more than a decade of work. Despite the controversy, Venter has attracted over $110 million in investments so far for Synthetic Genomics, with a future deal with Exxon Mobil of $300 million in research to design algae for diesel fuel.

Mycoplasma

Mycoplasma genitalium was chosen as it was the species with the smallest number of genes known at that time.

Mycoplasma is a genus of bacteria of the class Mollicutes in the division Tenericutes, characterised by the lack of a cell wall (making it Gram negative) due to their parasitic or commensal lifestyle (extracellular and intracellular). In molecular biology, the genus has received much attention. Apart from being a notorious and hard to eradicate (immune to beta-lactam and other antibiotics) contaminant in mammalian cell cultures, it has also been used as a model organism: the second published complete bacterial genome sequence was that of *Mycoplasma genitalium*, which has one of the smallest genomes of free-living organisms. The *M. pneumoniae* genome sequence was published soon afterward and was the first genome sequence determined by primer walking of a cosmid library instead of the whole-genome shotgun method. Consequently, this species was chosen as a model for the minimal cell project, catalog the entire protein content of a cell.

Other Genera

Pelagibacter ubique (an α-proteobacterium of the order Rickettsiales) has the smallest known genome (1,308,759 base pairs) of any free living organism and is one of the smallest self-replicating cells known. It is possibly the most numerous bacterium in the world (perhaps 10^{28} individual cells) and, along with other members of the SAR11 clade, are estimated to make up between a quarter and a half of all bacterial or archaeal cells in the ocean. However, this species was identified only in 2002 by rRNA sequences and was fully sequenced in 2005, being an extremely hard to cultivate species which does not reach a high growth density, Additionally, several newly discovered species have fewer genes than *M. genitalium*, but many essential genes that are missing in *Hodgkinia cicadicola*, *Sulcia muelleri*, *Baumannia cicadellinicola* (symbionts of cicadas) and *Carsonella ruddi* (symbiote of hackberry petiole gall psyllid, *Pachypsylla venusta[*]*) may be encoded in the host nucleus as these endosymbionts are acquiring an organelle-like status in a similar way to mitochondria and chloroplasts.

species name	number of genes	size (Mbp)
Candidatus Hodgkinia cicadicola Dsem	169	0.14
Candidatus Carsonella ruddii PV	182	0.16
Candidatus Sulcia muelleri GWSS	227	0.25
Candidatus Sulcia muelleri SMDSEM	242	0.28
Buchnera aphidicola str. Cinara cedri	357	0.4261
Mycoplasma genitalium G37	475	0.58
Candidatus Phytoplasma Mali	479	0.6
Buchnera aphidicola str. Baizongia pistaciae	504	0.6224
Nanoarchaeum equitans Kin4-M	540	0.49

Minimal Genome Project

The team started with the bacterium *M. genitalium*, an obligate intracellular parasite whose genome consists of 482 genes comprising 582,970 base pairs, arranged on one circular chromosome (the smallest genome of any known natural organism that can be grown in free culture). They then systematically removed genes to find a minimal set of 382 genes that can sustain life. This effort was also known as the Minimal Genome Project.

The team intends to synthesize chromosome DNA sequences consisting of these 382 genes. Once a version of the minimal 382-gene chromosome has been synthesized, it is intended to be transplanted into a *M. genitalium* cell to create Mycoplasma laboratorium.

The resulting Mycoplasma laboratorium bacterium is expected to be able to replicate itself with its man-made DNA, making it the most synthetic organism to date, although the molecular machinery and chemical environment that would allow it to replicate would not be synthetic.

In December 2003, the team had reported a fast method of synthesizing a genome from scratch, producing the 5386-base genome of the bacteriophage Phi X 174 in about two weeks. However, the genome of Mycoplasma laboratorium is about 50 times larger. In January 2008, the team reported to have synthesized the complete 582,970 base pair chromosome of *M. genitalium*, with small modifications so that it won't be infectious and can be distinguished from the wild type. They named this genome *Mycoplasma genitalium JCVI-1.0*. The team had also demonstrated the process of transplanting a (non-synthetic) genome from one *Mycoplasma* species to another in June 2007. In May 2010 they showed that they were able to synthesize the 1,078,809 base pair genome of *Mycoplasma mycoides* from scratch and transplant it into a *Mycoplasma capricolum* cell; the new genome then took over the cell and the new organism multiplied. The new organism was nicknamed *Synthia*.

Venter hopes to eventually synthesize bacteria to manufacture hydrogen and biofuels, and also to absorb carbon dioxide and other greenhouse gases. George M. Church, another pioneer in synthetic biology, holds that *E. coli* is a more efficient organism than *M. genitalium* and that creating a fully synthetic genome is not necessary and too costly for such tasks; he points out that synthetic genes have already been incorporated into *E.coli* to perform some of the above tasks. On June 28, 2007, a team at the J. Craig Venter Institute published an article in *Science Express*, saying that they had successfully transplanted the natural DNA from a *Mycoplasma mycoides* bacterium into a *Mycoplasma capricolum* cell, creating a bacterium which behaved like a *M. mycoides*.

On Oct 6, 2007, Craig Venter announced in an interview with UK's *The Guardian* newspaper that the same team had synthesized a modified version of the single chromosome of *Mycoplasma genitalium* using chemicals. The chromosome was modified to eliminate all genes which tests in live bacteria had shown to be unnecessary. The next planned step in this *minimal genome project* is to transplant the synthesized minimal genome into a bacterial cell with its old DNA removed; the resulting bacterium will be called Mycoplasma laboratorium. The next day the Canadian bioethics group, ETC Group issued a statement through their representative, Pat Mooney, saying Venter's "creation" was "a chassis on which you could build almost anything". The synthesized genome had not yet been transplanted into a working cell.

On May 21, 2010, *Science* reported that the Venter group had successfully synthesized the genome of the bacterium *Mycoplasma mycoides* from a computer record, and transplanted the synthesized genome into the existing cell of a *Mycoplasma capricolum* bacterium that had had its DNA removed. The "synthetic" bacterium was viable, i.e. capable of replicating billions of times. The team had originally planned to use the

M. genitalium bacterium they had previously been working with, but switched to *M. mycoides* because the latter bacterium grows much faster, which translated into quicker experiments. They have also shown that the natural genome of *M. mycoides* can be transplanted but has yet to show that the same could be done for *M. genitalium*. Venter describes it as "the first species.... to have its parents be a computer". The transformed bacterium is dubbed "Synthia" by ETC. A Venter spokesperson has declined to confirm any breakthrough at the time of this writing, likely because similar genetic introduction techniques such as transfection, transformation, transduction and protofection have been a standard research practice for many years.

Now that the technique has been proven to work with the *M. mycoides* genome, the next project is presumably to go back to the minimized *M. genitalium* and transplant it into a cell to create the previously mentioned Mycoplasma laboratorium.

The creation of a new synthetic bacterium was announced in *Science* on March 25, 2016. It has only 473 genes, the fewest genes of any freely living organism. This fast growing new cell, called Syn 3.0, was created by transplanting the genome of Mycoplasma mycoides, with all the unessential DNA removed, into a Mycoplasma capricolum, which had been emptied of its own DNA.

M. genitalium was not used because it reproduces too slowly.

Bacterial Genome Transplantation

In order to propagate a synthetic genome, the technique to transplant an intact whole bacterial genome into another had to be developed. Oswald Avery's pioneering experiments in the 1940s showed that some bacteria could take up naked DNA, and with the advent of molecular cloning techniques DNA elements could be transformed into competent cells, typically cloning vectors, around 5-20 kbp long, and even bacterial artificial chromosomes can be maintained. In 2007, Venter's team reported that they had managed to transfer the chromosome of the species *Mycoplasma mycoides* to *Mycoplasma capricolum* by means of:

- isolating the genome of *M. mycoides*: gentle lysis of cells trapped in agar—molten agar mixed with cells and left to form a gel—followed by pulse field gel electrophoresis and the band of the correct size (circular 1.25Mbp) being isolated;

- making the recipient cells of *M. capricolum* competent: growth in rich media followed starvation in poor media where the nucleotide starvation results in inhibition of DNA replication and change of morphology; and

- polyethylene glycol-mediated transformation of the circular chromosome to the DNA-free cells followed by selection.

The term transformation is used to refer to insertion of a vector into a bacterial cell (by electroporation or heatshock). Here, transplantation is used akin to nuclear transplantation.

The switch from *M. genitalium* to *M. mycoides* was spurred due to the faster growth of the latter.

Bacterial Chromosome Synthesis

It is possible to create DNA sequences chemically (oligonucleotide synthesis) which is achieved by successive rounds of deprotection and coupling of protected phosphoramidite nucleotides with geometrically decreasing yields to length, making sequences longer than 1kb unfeasible. For longer sequences, DNA ligation is required. In 2008 Venter's group published a paper showing that they had managed to create a synthetic genome (a copy of *M. mycoides* sequence CP001621) by means of a hierarchical strategy:

- Synthesis → 1kbp: The genome sequence was synthesized by Blue Heron in 1078 1080bp cassettes with 80bp overlap and NotI restriction sites (inefficient but rare cutter).

- Ligation → 10kbp: 109 Groups of a series of 10 consecutive cassettes were ligated and cloned in E.coli on a plasmid and the correct permutation checked by sequencing, this would follow a geometric distribution with expected number of trials of 10.

- Multiplex PCR → 100kbp: 11 Groups of a series of 10 consecutive 10kbp assemblies (grown in yeast) were joined by multiplex PCR, using a primer pair for each 10kbp assembly.

- Isolation and recombination → secondary assemblies were isolated by means of the plug method above and joining and transformed into yeast spheroplasts without a vector sequence (present in assembly 811-900).

Synthetic Genome

In 2010, using the methods described above, Venter and colleagues created a strain of Mycoplasma mycoides called JCVI-syn1.0 with a synthetic genome. Initially the synthetic construct did not work, so to pin point the error—which caused a delay of 3 months in the whole project—a series of semi-synthetic constructs were created. Given the fact that the natural genome worked, the cause of the failed growth was an frameshift mutation in DnaA, a replication initiation factor, which, once corrected, worked and was verified.

The construction of a cell with a synthetic genome was done to test the methodology—allowing more modified genomes to be created in the future. To minimize sources of failure, the genome was created using a natural genome as a template. Due to the large size of a genome, apart from the elements required for propagation in yeast and residues from restriction sites, several differences are present in *Mycoplasma mycoides* JCVI-syn1.0 notably an *E.coli* transposon IS1 (an infection from the 10kb stage) and an 85bp duplication.

However, the project has received heavy criticism as it claims to have created a synthetic organism. This claim arises from the fact that the genome was synthesized chemically in many pieces (a synthetic method), joined together by means of molecular biological techniques (an artificial method), and transplanted into the cytoplasm of a natural cell (after a few generations, though, the original protein content is undetectable). The two species used as donor and recipient are of the same genus as the more distant two species are, the less the correct protein interactions are maintained, such as binding factors and binding sites, which mutate together (epistasis). Consequently, Paul Keim (a molecular geneticist at Northern Arizona University in Flagstaff) notes that "there are great challenges ahead before genetic engineers can mix match, and fully design an organism's genome from scratch" due to this issue. DNA is the template for protein construction and requires proteins as helper molecules to do so, a chicken-and-egg conundrum solved by the RNA world hypothesis, consequently synthetic naked DNA would require several proteins to create a viable cell. In 2000 and 2002 teams synthesized replicating hepatitis C virus (about 9600 nucleotides long) and poliovirus (about 7500 nucleotides long),Viruses, however, replicate by utilising host protein expression machinery. Furthermore, whereas DNA can easily be replicated (using DNA polymerase), transcribed (using RNA polymerase), and translated (using ribosomes and many other factors)—all *in vitro*, such reactions, so far, utilise cell extracts and most components have not been synthesized de novo—that is from inorganic or synthetically made organic chemicals only.

Watermarks

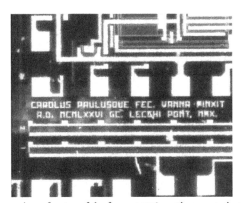

A hidden watermark on a semiconductor chip from 1976, acting as a signature of its creators. In an analogous way, JC Venter and his team added watermarks using stop codons to sign their creation.

A much publicised feature of the Mycoplasma laboratorium is the presence of watermark sequences as an ultimate proof of the achievement and as a publicity stunt—similar to the tradition of chip art, inscriptions on unused portions of microchips visible only by electron microscopy. The 4 watermarks (present in figure 1 in supplementary material of) are coded messages in the form of DNA base pairs, of 1246, 1081, 1109 and 1222 base pairs respectively, in natural peptides the 4 nucleotides encode in sets of 3 the 20 natural amino acids by means of the standard genetic code. Each amino acid *by convention* is represented by a letter, but in nature there is nothing which ties Alanine, a molecule, to the Latin letter A, a vowel, so this convention was disregarded in the latter watermarks. In the minimal genome organism the watermark were encoded as amino acids, with V as U, both in reference to Latin inscriptions and the lack of a standard amino acid for U containing the names of the researchers: (VENTERINSTITVTE, CRAIGVENTER, HAMSMITH, CINDIANDCLYDE, GLASSANDCLYDE). In the synthetic organism, instead the Latin alphabet—which in English has 26 letters, which is covered only in base 4 with 3 or more digits—was encoded by an undisclosed encoding. The encoding is fixed and 3 digits make an uppercase letter or Ascii symbol, possibly randomly allocated (not Ascii table, frequency or keyboard order). The content of the watermarks is as follows:

1. watermark 1 an HTML script which reads to a browser as text congratulating the decoder with an email link to click to prove the decoding.

2. watermark 2 contains a list of authors and a quote from James Joyce: "To live, to err, to fall, to triumph, to recreate life out of life".

3. watermark 3 contains more authors and a quote from Robert Oppenheimer (uncredited).

4. watermark 4 contains yet more authors and a quote from Richard Feynman: "What I cannot build, I cannot understand".

Concerns and Controversy

Press Coverage

The main controversy from the project is the undue amount of publicity it received from the press due to Venter's showmanship, to the degree that Jay Keasling, a pioneering synthetic biologist and founder of Amyris says "The only regulation we need is of my colleague's mouth".

Utility

Despite the funding for practical applications, as stressed by George M. Church, one of the main players in the field of synthetic biology, a few changes are required to obtain useful organisms now, such as biofuel production or bioremediation. However, speculation about the distant future's possible applications is rife. Venter himself is prone to such speculations, having asked for example, "What if we can make algae taste like beef?" If it were possible to create a synthetic cell without the use of preexisting recipient cells, however, many applications would become achievable which would be otherwise unattainable, such as a completely overhauled bacterium that works in a logically controlled way—removing what has been described as 'evolutionary messiness'—with lower mutation rates, categorical gene arrangement (colinearity), the possibility of adding novel nucleotides to increase encoding (a feat achieved in vitro (PCR)); or with a completely novel genetic code, such as has been achieved by experiments in which a few additional non-canonical amino acids were added.

Intellectual Property

The J. Craig Venter Institute filed patents for the Mycoplasma laboratorium genome (the "minimal bacterial genome") in the U.S. and internationally in 2006.This extension of the domain of biological patents is being challenged by the watchdog organization Action Group on Erosion, Technology and Concentration.

JCVI-syn3.0

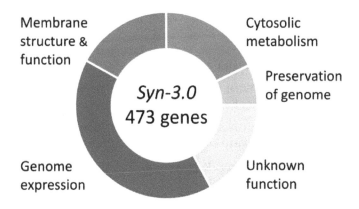

Gene functions in the minimal genome of the synthetic organism, *Syn 3*.

In 2016, the Venter Institute used genes from JCVI-syn1.0 to synthesize an even smaller genome they call JCVI-syn3.0, that contains 531,560 base pairs and 473 genes. Originally in 1996, after comparing *M. genitalium* with another small bacterium *Haemophilus influenza*, Arcady Mushegian and Eugene Koonin had proposed that there might be a common set of 256 genes which could be a minimal set of genes needed for viability. In this new organism, the number of genes can only be pared down to 473, 149 of which whose functions are completely unknown. The organism with the smallest known set of genes is *Nasuia deltocephalinicola* which has only 137 genes, but the minimal genome for any free-living organism would be different depending on its environment.

Similar Projects

From 2002 to 2010, a team at the Hungarian Academy of Science created a strain of *Escherichia coli* called MDS42, which is now sold by Scarab Genomics of Madison, WI under the name of "Clean Genome. E.coli", where 15% of the genome of the parental strain (E. coli K-12 MG1655) were removed to aid in molecular biology efficiency, removing IS elements, pseudogenes and phages, resulting in better maintenance of plasmid-encoded toxic genes, which are often inactivated by transposons. Biochemistry and replication machinery were not altered.

References

- Mount, David (2000). Bioinformatics, Sequence and Genome Analysis. Cold Spring Harbor Laboratory Press. pp. 2–3. ISBN 0-87969-597-8.

- Pevsner, Jonathan (2009). Bioinformatics and functional genomics (2nd ed.). Hoboken, N.J: Wiley-Blackwell. ISBN 9780470085851.

- Gagniuc, P; Ionescu-Tirgoviste, C (Sep 28, 2012). "Eukaryotic genomes may exhibit up to 10 generic classes of gene promoters.". BMC Genomics. 13: 512. doi:10.1186/1471-2164-13-512. PMC 3549790. PMID 23020586. |access-date= requires |url= (help)

- McClure, Max (19 July 2012). "Stanford researchers produce first complete computer model of an organism". Stanford University News. Retrieved 3 August 2012.

- Karr JR, Sanghvi JC, Macklin DN, et al. (July 2012). "A whole-cell computational model predicts phenotype from genotype". Cell. 150 (2): 389–401. doi:10.1016/j.cell.2012.05.044. PMC 3413483. PMID 22817898.

- John Markoff (20 July 2012). "In First, Software Emulates Lifespan of Entire Organism". The New York Times. Retrieved 3 August 2012.

- Yates, Diana (2009-04-23). "What makes a cow a cow? Genome sequence sheds light on ruminant evolution" (Press Release). EurekAlert!. Retrieved 2012-12-22.

- "Potential Benefits of Human Genome Project Research". Department of Energy, Human Genome Project Information. 2009-10-09. Retrieved 2010-06-18.

- Young L, Sung J, Stacey G, Masters JR. "Detection of Mycoplasma in cell cultures". Nat Protoc. 2010 5(5): 929–34. Epub 2010 Apr 22.

- Povolotskaya, IS; Kondrashov, FA (Jun 2010). "Sequence space and the ongoing expansion of the protein universe". Nature. 465 (7300): 922–6. doi:10.1038/nature09105.

- Tawfik, Dan S (2010). "Messy biology and the origins of evolutionary innovations". Nature Chemical Biology. 6: 692–696. doi:10.1038/nchembio.441.

Computational Neuroscience

Computational neuroscience is the study of brain functions; it links fields such as neuroscience, cognitive science and psychology. Topics such as neural coding, neural binding and neuroinformatics have elucidated in the following section and helps the readers in developing an in-depth understanding of computational neuroscience and its relation to computational biology.

Computational Neuroscience

Computational neuroscience (also theoretical neuroscience) studies brain function in terms of the information processing properties of the structures that make up the nervous system. It is an interdisciplinary computational science that links the diverse fields of neuroscience, cognitive science, and psychology with electrical engineering, computer science, mathematics, and physics.

Computational neuroscience is distinct from psychological connectionism and from learning theories of disciplines such as machine learning, neural networks, and computational learning theory in that it emphasizes descriptions of functional and biologically realistic neurons (and neural systems) and their physiology and dynamics. These models capture the essential features of the biological system at multiple spatial-temporal scales, from membrane currents, proteins, and chemical coupling to network oscillations, columnar and topographic architecture, and learning and memory.

These computational models are used to frame hypotheses that can be directly tested by biological or psychological experiments.

History

The term "computational neuroscience" was introduced by Eric L. Schwartz, who organized a conference, held in 1985 in Carmel, California, at the request of the Systems Development Foundation to provide a summary of the current status of a field which until that point was referred to by a variety of names, such as neural modeling, brain theory and neural networks. The proceedings of this definitional meeting were published in 1990 as the book *Computational Neuroscience*. The first open international meeting focused on Computational Neuroscience was organized by James M. Bower and John Miller in San Francisco, California in 1989 and has continued each year since as the annual CNS meeting The first graduate educational program in computational neuroscience was organized as the Computational and Neural Systems Ph.D. program at the California Institute of Technology in 1985.

The early historical roots of the field can be traced to the work of people such as Louis Lapicque, Hodgkin & Huxley, Hubel & Wiesel, and David Marr, to name a few. Lapicque introduced the integrate and fire model of the neuron in a seminal article published in 1907; this model is still one of the most popular models in computational neuroscience for both cellular and neural networks studies, as well as in mathematical neuroscience because of its simplicity. About 40 years later, Hodgkin & Huxley developed the voltage clamp and created the first biophysical model of the action potential. Hubel & Wiesel discovered that neurons in the primary visual cortex, the first cortical area to process information coming from the retina, have oriented receptive fields and are organized in columns. David Marr's work focused on the interactions between neurons, suggesting computational approaches to the study of how functional groups of neurons within the hippocampus and neocortex interact, store, process, and transmit information. Computational modeling of biophysically realistic neurons and dendrites began with the work of Wilfrid Rall, with the first multicompartmental model using cable theory.

Major Topics

Research in computational neuroscience can be roughly categorized into several lines of inquiry. Most computational neuroscientists collaborate closely with experimentalists in analyzing novel data and synthesizing new models of biological phenomena.

Single-neuron Modeling

Even single neurons have complex biophysical characteristics and can perform computations (e.g.). Hodgkin and Huxley's original model only employed two voltage-sensitive currents (Voltage sensitive ion channels are glycoprotein molecules which extend through the lipid bilayer, allowing ions to traverse under certain conditions through the axolemma), the fast-acting sodium and the inward-rectifying potassium. Though successful in predicting the timing and qualitative features of the action potential, it nevertheless failed to predict a number of important features such as adaptation and shunting. Scientists now believe that there are a wide variety of voltage-sensitive currents, and the implications of the differing dynamics, modulations, and sensitivity of these currents is an important topic of computational neuroscience.

The computational functions of complex dendrites are also under intense investigation. There is a large body of literature regarding how different currents interact with geometric properties of neurons.

Some models are also tracking biochemical pathways at very small scales such as spines or synaptic clefts.

There are many software packages, such as GENESIS and NEURON, that allow rapid and systematic *in silico* modeling of realistic neurons. Blue Brain, a project founded by Henry Markram from the École Polytechnique Fédérale de Lausanne, aims to construct a biophysically detailed simulation of a cortical column on the Blue Gene supercomputer.

A problem in the field is that detailed neuron descriptions are computationally expensive and this can handicap the pursuit of realistic network investigations, where many neurons need to be simulated. So, researchers that study large neural circuits typically represent each neuron and synapse simply, ignoring much of the biological detail. This is unfortunate as there is evidence that the richness of biophysical properties on the single neuron scale can supply mechanisms that serve as the building blocks for network dynamics. Hence there is a drive to produce simplified neuron models that can retain significant biological fidelity at a low computational overhead. Algorithms have been developed to produce faithful, faster running, simplified surrogate neuron models from computationally expensive, detailed neuron models.

Development, Axonal Patterning, and Guidance

How do axons and dendrites form during development? How do axons know where to target and how to reach these targets? How do neurons migrate to the proper position in the central and peripheral systems? How do synapses form? We know from molecular biology that distinct parts of the nervous system release distinct chemical cues, from growth factors to hormones that modulate and influence the growth and development of functional connections between neurons.

Theoretical investigations into the formation and patterning of synaptic connection and morphology are still nascent. One hypothesis that has recently garnered some attention is the *minimal wiring hypothesis*, which postulates that the formation of axons and dendrites effectively minimizes resource allocation while maintaining maximal information storage.

Sensory Processing

Early models of sensory processing understood within a theoretical framework are credited to Horace Barlow. Somewhat similar to the minimal wiring hypothesis described in the preceding section, Barlow understood the processing of the early sensory systems to be a form of efficient coding, where the neurons encoded information which minimized the number of spikes. Experimental and computational work have since supported this hypothesis in one form or another.

Current research in sensory processing is divided among a biophysical modelling of different subsystems and a more theoretical modelling of perception. Current models of perception have suggested that the brain performs some form of Bayesian inference and integration of different sensory information in generating our perception of the physical world.

Memory and Synaptic Plasticity

Earlier models of memory are primarily based on the postulates of Hebbian learning. Biologically relevant models such as Hopfield net have been developed to address the properties of associative, rather than content-addressable, style of memory that occur in biological systems. These attempts are primarily focusing on the formation of medium- and long-term memory, localizing in the hippocampus. Models of working memory, relying on theories of network oscillations and persistent activity, have been built to capture some features of the prefrontal cortex in context-related memory.

One of the major problems in neurophysiological memory is how it is maintained and changed through multiple time scales. Unstable synapses are easy to train but also prone to stochastic disruption. Stable synapses forget less easily, but they are also harder to consolidate. One recent computational hypothesis involves cascades of plasticity that allow synapses to function at multiple time scales. Stereochemically detailed models of the acetylcholine receptor-based synapse with the Monte Carlo method, working at the time scale of microseconds, have been built. It is likely that computational tools will contribute greatly to our understanding of how synapses function and change in relation to external stimulus in the coming decades.

Behaviors of Networks

Biological neurons are connected to each other in a complex, recurrent fashion. These connections are, unlike most artificial neural networks, sparse and usually specific. It is not known how information is transmitted through such sparsely connected networks. It is also unknown what the computational functions of these specific connectivity patterns are, if any.

The interactions of neurons in a small network can be often reduced to simple models such as the Ising model. The statistical mechanics of such simple systems are well-characterized theoretically. There has been some recent evidence that suggests that dynamics of arbitrary neuronal networks can be reduced to pairwise interactions. It is not known, however, whether such descriptive dynamics impart any important computational function. With the emergence of two-photon microscopy and calcium imaging, we now have powerful experimental methods with which to test the new theories regarding neuronal networks.

In some cases the complex interactions between *inhibitory* and *excitatory* neurons can be simplified using mean field theory, which gives rise to the population model of neural networks. While many neurotheorists prefer such models with reduced complexity, others argue that uncovering structural functional relations depends on including as much neuronal and network structure as possible. Models of this type are typically built in large simulation platforms like GENESIS or NEURON. There have been some attempts to provide unified methods that bridge and integrate these levels of complexity.

Cognition, Discrimination, and Learning

Computational modeling of higher cognitive functions has only recently begun. Experimental data comes primarily from single-unit recording in primates. The frontal lobe and parietal lobe function as integrators of information from multiple sensory modalities. There are some tentative ideas regarding how simple mutually inhibitory functional circuits in these areas may carry out biologically relevant computation.

The brain seems to be able to discriminate and adapt particularly well in certain contexts. For instance, human beings seem to have an enormous capacity for memorizing and recognizing faces. One of the key goals of computational neuroscience is to dissect how biological systems carry out these complex computations efficiently and potentially replicate these processes in building intelligent machines.

The brain's large-scale organizational principles are illuminated by many fields, including biology, psychology, and clinical practice. Integrative neuroscience attempts to consolidate these observations through unified descriptive models and databases of behavioral measures and recordings. These are the bases for some quantitative modeling of large-scale brain activity.

The Computational Representational Understanding of Mind (CRUM) is another attempt at modeling human cognition through simulated processes like acquired rule-based systems in decision making and the manipulation of visual representations in decision making.

Consciousness

One of the ultimate goals of psychology/neuroscience is to be able to explain the everyday experience of conscious life. Francis Crick and Christof Koch made some attempts to formulate a consistent framework for future work in neural correlates of consciousness (NCC), though much of the work in this field remains speculative.

Computational Clinical Neuroscience

It is a field that brings together experts in neuroscience, neurology, psychiatry, decision sciences and computational modeling to quantitatively define and investigate problems in neurological and psychiatric diseases, and to train scientists and clinicians that wish to apply these models to diagnosis and treatment.

Neural Coding

Neural coding is a neuroscience related field concerned with characterizing the relationship between the stimulus and the individual or ensemble neuronal responses and the relationship among the electrical activity of the neurons in the ensemble. Based on the theory that sensory and other information is represented in the brain by networks of neurons, it is thought that neurons can encode both digital and analog information.

Overview

Neurons are remarkable among the cells of the body in their ability to propagate signals rapidly over large distances. They do this by generating characteristic electrical pulses called action potentials: voltage spikes that can travel down nerve fibers. Sensory neurons change their activities by firing sequences of action potentials in various temporal patterns, with the presence of external sensory stimuli, such as light, sound, taste, smell and touch. It is known that information about the stimulus is encoded in this pattern of action potentials and transmitted into and around the brain.

Although action potentials can vary somewhat in duration, amplitude and shape, they are typically treated as identical stereotyped events in neural coding studies. If the brief duration of an action potential (about 1ms) is ignored, an action potential sequence, or spike train, can be characterized simply by a series of all-or-none point events in time. The lengths of interspike intervals (ISIs) between two successive spikes in a spike train often vary, apparently randomly. The study of neural coding involves measuring and characterizing how stimulus attributes, such as light or sound intensity, or motor actions, such as the direction of an arm movement, are represented by neuron action potentials or spikes. In order to describe and analyze neuronal firing, statistical methods and methods of probability theory and stochastic point processes have been widely applied.

With the development of large-scale neural recording and decoding technologies, researchers have begun to crack the neural code and already provided the first glimpse into the real-time neural code as memory is formed and recalled in the hippocampus, a brain region known to be central for memory formation. Neuroscientists have initiated several large-scale brain decoding projects.

Encoding and Decoding

The link between stimulus and response can be studied from two opposite points of view. Neural encoding refers to the map from stimulus to response. The main focus is to understand how neurons respond to a wide variety of stimuli, and to construct models that attempt to predict responses to other stimuli. Neural decoding refers to the reverse map, from response to stimulus, and the challenge is to reconstruct a stimulus, or certain aspects of that stimulus, from the spike sequences it evokes.

Coding Schemes

A sequence, or 'train', of spikes may contain information based on different coding schemes. In motor neurons, for example, the strength at which an innervated muscle is flexed depends solely on the 'firing rate', the average number of spikes per unit time (a 'rate code'). At the other end, a complex 'temporal code' is based on the precise timing of single spikes. They may be locked to an external stimulus such as in the visual and auditory system or be generated intrinsically by the neural circuitry.

Whether neurons use rate coding or temporal coding is a topic of intense debate within the neuroscience community, even though there is no clear definition of what these terms mean. In one theory, termed "neuroelectrodynamics", the following coding schemes are all considered to be epiphenomena, replaced instead by molecular changes reflecting the spatial distribution of electric fields within neurons as a result of the broad electromagnetic spectrum of action potentials, and manifested in information as spike directivity.

Rate Coding

The rate coding model of neuronal firing communication states that as the intensity of a stimulus increases, the frequency or rate of action potentials, or "spike firing", increases. Rate coding is sometimes called frequency coding.

Rate coding is a traditional coding scheme, assuming that most, if not all, information about the stimulus is contained in the firing rate of the neuron. Because the sequence of action potentials generated by a given stimulus varies from trial to trial, neuronal responses are typically treated statistically or probabilistically. They may be characterized by firing rates, rather than as specific spike sequences. In most sensory systems, the firing rate increases, generally non-linearly, with increasing stimulus intensity. Any information possibly encoded in the temporal structure of the spike train is ignored. Consequently, rate coding is inefficient but highly robust with respect to the ISI 'noise'.

During rate coding, precisely calculating firing rate is very important. In fact, the term "firing rate" has a few different definitions, which refer to different averaging procedures, such as an average over time or an average over several repetitions of experiment.

In rate coding, learning is based on activity-dependent synaptic weight modifications.

Rate coding was originally shown by ED Adrian and Y Zotterman in 1926. In this simple experiment different weights were hung from a muscle. As the weight of the stimulus increased, the number of spikes recorded from sensory nerves innervating the muscle also increased. From these original experiments, Adrian and Zotterman concluded that action potentials were unitary events, and that the frequency of events, and not individual event magnitude, was the basis for most inter-neuronal communication.

In the following decades, measurement of firing rates became a standard tool for describing the properties of all types of sensory or cortical neurons, partly due to the relative ease of measuring rates experimentally. However, this approach neglects all the information possibly contained in the exact timing of the spikes. During recent years, more and more experimental evidence has suggested that a straightforward firing rate concept based on temporal averaging may be too simplistic to describe brain activity.

Spike-count Rate

The Spike-count rate, also referred to as temporal average, is obtained by counting the number of spikes that appear during a trial and dividing by the duration of trial. The length T of the time window is set by experimenter and depends on the type of neuron recorded from and the stimulus. In practice, to get sensible averages, several spikes should occur within the time window. Typical values are T = 100 ms or T = 500 ms, but the duration may also be longer or shorter.

The spike-count rate can be determined from a single trial, but at the expense of losing all temporal resolution about variations in neural response during the course of the trial. Temporal averaging can work well in cases where the stimulus is constant or slowly varying and does not require a fast reaction of the organism — and this is the situation usually encountered in experimental protocols. Real-world input, however, is hardly stationary, but often changing on a fast time scale. For example, even when viewing a static image, humans perform saccades, rapid changes of the direction of gaze. The image projected onto the retinal photoreceptors changes therefore every few hundred milliseconds.

Despite its shortcomings, the concept of a spike-count rate code is widely used not only in experiments, but also in models of neural networks. It has led to the idea that a neuron transforms information about a single input variable (the stimulus strength) into a single continuous output variable (the firing rate).

There is a growing body of evidence that in Purkinje neurons, at least, information is not simply encoded in firing but also in the timing and duration of non-firing, quiescent periods.

Time-dependent Firing Rate

The time-dependent firing rate is defined as the average number of spikes (averaged over trials) appearing during a short interval between times t and t+Δt, divided by the duration of the interval. It works for stationary as well as for time-dependent stimuli. To experimentally measure the time-dependent firing rate, the experimenter records from a neuron while stimulating with some input sequence. The same stimulation sequence is repeated several times and the neuronal response is reported in a Peri-Stimulus-Time Histogram (PSTH). The time t is measured with respect to the start of the stimulation sequence. The Δt must be large enough (typically in the range of one or a few milliseconds) so there are sufficient number of spikes within the interval to obtain a reliable estimate of the average. The number of occurrences of spikes $n_K(t;t+\Delta t)$ summed over all repetitions of the experiment divided by the number K of repetitions is a measure of the typical activity of the neuron between time t and $t+\Delta t$. A further division by the interval length Δt yields time-dependent firing rate r(t) of the neuron, which is equivalent to the spike density of PSTH.

For sufficiently small Δt, $r(t)\Delta t$ is the average number of spikes occurring between times t and $t+\Delta t$ over multiple trials. If Δt is small, there will never be more than one spike within the interval between t and $t+\Delta t$ on any given trial. This means that $r(t)\Delta t$ is also the fraction of trials on which a spike occurred between those times. Equivalently, $r(t)$ Δt is the probability that a spike occurs during this time interval.

As an experimental procedure, the time-dependent firing rate measure is a useful method to evaluate neuronal activity, in particular in the case of time-dependent stimuli. The obvious problem with this approach is that it can not be the coding scheme used by neurons in the brain. Neurons can not wait for the stimuli to repeatedly present in an exactly same manner before generating response.

Nevertheless, the experimental time-dependent firing rate measure can make sense, if there are large populations of independent neurons that receive the same stimulus. Instead of recording from a population of N neurons in a single run, it is experimentally easier to record from a single neuron and average over N repeated runs. Thus, the time-dependent firing rate coding relies on the implicit assumption that there are always populations of neurons.

Temporal Coding

When precise spike timing or high-frequency firing-rate fluctuations are found to carry information, the neural code is often identified as a temporal code. A number of studies have found that the temporal resolution of the neural code is on a millisecond time scale, indicating that precise spike timing is a significant element in neural coding.

Neurons exhibit high-frequency fluctuations of firing-rates which could be noise or could carry information. Rate coding models suggest that these irregularities are noise, while temporal coding models suggest that they encode information. If the nervous system only used rate codes to convey information, a more consistent, regular firing rate would have been evolutionarily advantageous, and neurons would have utilized this code over other less robust options. Temporal coding supplies an alternate explanation for the "noise," suggesting that it actually encodes information and affects neural processing. To model this idea, binary symbols can be used to mark the spikes: 1 for a spike, 0 for no spike. Temporal coding allows the sequence 000111000111 to mean something different from 001100110011, even though the mean firing rate is the same for both sequences, at 6 spikes/10 ms. Until recently, scientists had put the most emphasis on rate encoding as an explanation for post-synaptic potential patterns. However, functions of the brain are more temporally precise than the use of only rate encoding seems to allow. In other words, essential information could be lost due to the inability of the rate code to capture all the available information of the spike train. In addition, responses are different enough between similar (but not identical) stimuli to suggest that the distinct patterns of spikes contain a higher volume of information than is possible to include in a rate code.

Temporal codes employ those features of the spiking activity that cannot be described by the firing rate. For example, time to first spike after the stimulus onset, characteristics based on the second and higher statistical moments of the ISI probability distribution, spike randomness, or precisely timed groups of spikes (temporal patterns) are candidates for temporal codes. As there is no absolute time reference in the nervous system, the information is carried either in terms of the relative timing of spikes in a population of neurons or with respect to an ongoing brain oscillation.

The temporal structure of a spike train or firing rate evoked by a stimulus is determined both by the dynamics of the stimulus and by the nature of the neural encoding process. Stimuli that change rapidly tend to generate precisely timed spikes and rapidly changing firing rates no matter what neural coding strategy is being used. Temporal coding refers to temporal precision in the response that does not arise solely from the dynamics of the stimulus, but that nevertheless relates to properties of the stimulus. The interplay between stimulus and encoding dynamics makes the identification of a temporal code difficult.

In temporal coding, learning can be explained by activity-dependent synaptic delay modifications. The modifications can themselves depend not only on spike rates (rate coding) but also on spike timing patterns (temporal coding), i.e., can be a special case of spike-timing-dependent plasticity.

The issue of temporal coding is distinct and independent from the issue of independent-spike coding. If each spike is independent of all the other spikes in the train, the temporal character of the neural code is determined by the behavior of time-dependent firing rate r(t). If r(t) varies slowly with time, the code is typically called a rate code, and if it varies rapidly, the code is called temporal.

Temporal Coding in Sensory Systems

For very brief stimuli, a neuron's maximum firing rate may not be fast enough to produce more than a single spike. Due to the density of information about the abbreviated stimulus contained in this single spike, it would seem that the timing of the spike itself would have to convey more information than simply the average frequency of action potentials over a given period of time. This model is especially important for sound localization, which occurs within the brain on the order of milliseconds. The brain must obtain a large quantity of information based on a relatively short neural response. Additionally, if low firing rates on the order of ten spikes per second must be distinguished from arbitrarily close rate coding for different stimuli, then a neuron trying to discriminate these two stimuli may need to wait for a second or more to accumulate enough information. This is not consistent with numerous organisms which are able to discriminate between stimuli in the time frame of milliseconds, suggesting that a rate code is not the only model at work.

To account for the fast encoding of visual stimuli, it has been suggested that neurons of the retina encode visual information in the latency time between stimulus onset and first action potential, also called latency to first spike. This type of temporal coding has been shown also in the auditory and somato-sensory system. The main drawback of such a coding scheme is its sensitivity to intrinsic neuronal fluctuations. In the primary visual cortex of macaques, the timing of the first spike relative to the start of the stimulus was found to provide more information than the interval between spikes. However, the interspike interval could be used to encode additional information, which is especially important when the spike rate reaches its limit, as in high-contrast situations. For this reason, temporal coding may play a part in coding defined edges rather than gradual transitions.

The mammalian gustatory system is useful for studying temporal coding because of its fairly distinct stimuli and the easily discernible responses of the organism. Temporally encoded information may help an organism discriminate between different tastants of the same category (sweet, bitter, sour, salty, umami) that elicit very similar responses in terms of spike count. The temporal component of the pattern elicited by each tastant may be used to determine its identity (e.g., the difference between two bitter tastants, such as quinine and denatonium). In this way, both rate coding and temporal coding may be used in the gustatory system – rate for basic tastant type, temporal for more specific differentiation. Research on mammalian gustatory system has shown that there is an abundance of information present in temporal patterns across populations of neurons, and this information is different from that which is determined by rate coding schemes. Groups of neurons may synchronize in response to a stimulus. In studies dealing with the front cortical portion of the brain in primates, precise patterns with short time scales only a few milliseconds in length were found across small populations of neurons which correlated with certain information processing behaviors. However, little information could be determined from the patterns; one possible theory is they represented the higher-order processing taking place in the brain.

As with the visual system, in mitral/tufted cells in the olfactory bulb of mice, first-spike latency relative to the start of a sniffing action seemed to encode much of the information about an odor. This strategy of using spike latency allows for rapid identification of and reaction to an odorant. In addition, some mitral/tufted cells have specific firing patterns for given odorants. This type of extra information could help in recognizing a certain odor, but is not completely necessary, as average spike count over the course of the animal's sniffing was also a good identifier. Along the same lines, experiments done with the olfactory system of rabbits showed distinct patterns which correlated with different subsets of odorants, and a similar result was obtained in experiments with the locust olfactory system.

Temporal Coding Applications

The specificity of temporal coding requires highly refined technology to measure informative, reliable, experimental data. Advances made in optogenetics allow neurologists to control spikes in individual neurons, offering electrical and spatial single-cell resolution. For example, blue light causes the light-gated ion channel channelrhodopsin to open, depolarizing the cell and producing a spike. When blue light is not sensed by the cell, the channel closes, and the neuron ceases to spike. The pattern of the spikes matches the pattern of the blue light stimuli. By inserting channelrhodopsin gene sequences into mouse DNA, researchers can control spikes and therefore certain behaviors of the mouse (e.g., making the mouse turn left). Researchers, through optogenetics, have the tools to effect different temporal codes in a neuron while maintaining the same mean firing rate, and thereby can test whether or not temporal coding occurs in specific neural circuits.

Optogenetic technology also has the potential to enable the correction of spike abnormalities at the root of several neurological and psychological disorders. If neurons do encode information in individual spike timing patterns, key signals could be missed by attempting to crack the code while looking only at mean firing rates. Understanding any temporally encoded aspects of the neural code and replicating these sequences in neurons could allow for greater control and treatment of neurological disorders such as depression, schizophrenia, and Parkinson's disease. Regulation of spike intervals in single cells more precisely controls brain activity than the addition of pharmacological agents intravenously.

Phase-of-firing Code

Phase-of-firing code is a neural coding scheme that combines the spike count code with a time reference based on oscillations. This type of code takes into account a time label for each spike according to a time reference based on phase of local ongoing oscillations at low or high frequencies. A feature of this code is that neurons adhere to a preferred order of spiking, resulting in firing sequence.

It has been shown that neurons in some cortical sensory areas encode rich naturalistic stimuli in terms of their spike times relative to the phase of ongoing network fluctuations, rather than only in terms of their spike count. Oscillations reflect local field potential signals. It is often categorized as a temporal code although the time label used for spikes is coarse grained. That is, four discrete values for phase are enough to represent all the information content in this kind of code with respect to the phase of oscillations in low frequencies. Phase-of-firing code is loosely based on the phase precession phenomena observed in place cells of the hippocampus.

Phase code has been shown in visual cortex to involve also high-frequency oscillations. Within a cycle of gamma oscillation, each neuron has its own preferred relative firing time. As a result, an entire population of neurons generates a firing sequence that has a duration of up to about 15 ms.

Population Coding

Population coding is a method to represent stimuli by using the joint activities of a number of neurons. In population coding, each neuron has a distribution of responses over some set of inputs, and the responses of many neurons may be combined to determine some value about the inputs.

From the theoretical point of view, population coding is one of a few mathematically well-formulated problems in neuroscience. It grasps the essential features of neural coding and yet is simple enough for theoretic analysis. Experimental studies have revealed that this coding paradigm is widely used in the sensor and motor areas of the brain. For example, in the visual area medial temporal (MT), neurons are tuned to the moving direction. In response to an object moving in a particular direction, many neurons in MT fire with a noise-corrupted and bell-shaped activity pattern across the population. The moving direction of the object is retrieved from the population activity, to be immune from the fluctuation existing in a single neuron's signal. In one classic example in the primary motor cortex, Apostolos Georgopoulos and colleagues trained monkeys to move a joystick towards a lit target. They found that a single neuron would fire for multiple target directions. However it would fire fastest for one direction and more slowly depending on how close the target was to the neuron's 'preferred' direction.

Kenneth Johnson originally derived that if each neuron represents movement in its preferred direction, and the vector sum of all neurons is calculated (each neuron has a firing rate and a preferred direction), the sum points in the direction of motion. In this manner, the population of neurons codes the signal for the motion. This particular population code is referred to as population vector coding. This particular study divided the field of motor physiologists between Evarts' "upper motor neuron" group, which followed the hypothesis that motor cortex neurons contributed to control of single muscles, and the Georgopoulos group studying the representation of movement directions in cortex.

The Johns Hopkins University Neural Encoding laboratory led by Murray Sachs and Eric Young developed place-time population codes, termed the Averaged-Localized-Synchronized-Response (ALSR) code for neural representation of auditory acoustic stimuli. This exploits both the place or tuning within the auditory nerve, as well as the phase-locking within each nerve fiber Auditory nerve. The first ALSR representation was for steady-state vowels; ALSR representations of pitch and formant frequencies in complex, non-steady state stimuli were demonstrated for voiced-pitch and formant representations in consonant-vowel syllables. The advantage of such representations is that global features such as pitch or formant transition profiles can be represented as global features across the entire nerve simultaneously via both rate and place coding.

Population coding has a number of other advantages as well, including reduction of uncertainty due to neuronal variability and the ability to represent a number of different stimulus attributes simultaneously. Population coding is also much faster than rate coding and can reflect changes in the stimulus conditions nearly instantaneously. Individual neurons in such a population typically have different but overlapping selectivities, so that many neurons, but not necessarily all, respond to a given stimulus.

Typically an encoding function has a peak value such that activity of the neuron is greatest if the perceptual value is close to the peak value, and becomes reduced accordingly for values less close to the peak value.

It follows that the actual perceived value can be reconstructed from the overall pattern of activity in the set of neurons. The Johnson/Georgopoulos vector coding is an example of simple averaging. A more sophisticated mathematical technique for performing such a reconstruction is the method of maximum likelihood based on a multivariate distribution of the neuronal responses. These models can assume independence, second order correlations, or even more detailed dependencies such as higher order maximum entropy models or copulas.

Correlation Coding

The correlation coding model of neuronal firing claims that correlations between action potentials, or "spikes", within a spike train may carry additional information above and beyond the simple timing of the spikes. Early work suggested that correlation between spike trains can only reduce, and never increase, the total mutual information present in the two spike trains about a stimulus feature. However, this was later demonstrated to be incorrect. Correlation structure can increase information content if noise and signal correlations are of opposite sign. Correlations can also carry information not present in the average firing rate of two pairs of neurons. A good example of this exists in the pentobarbital-anesthetized marmoset auditory cortex, in which a pure tone causes an increase in the number of correlated spikes, but not an increase in the mean firing rate, of pairs of neurons.

Independent-spike Coding

The independent-spike coding model of neuronal firing claims that each individual action potential, or "spike", is independent of each other spike within the spike train.

Position Coding

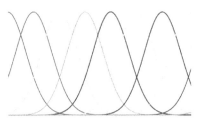

Plot of typical position coding

A typical population code involves neurons with a Gaussian tuning curve whose means vary linearly with the stimulus intensity, meaning that the neuron responds most strongly (in terms of spikes per second) to a stimulus near the mean. The actual intensity could be recovered as the stimulus level corresponding to the mean of the neuron with the greatest response. However, the noise inherent in neural responses means that a maximum likelihood estimation function is more accurate.

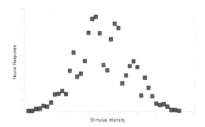

Neural responses are noisy and unreliable.

This type of code is used to encode continuous variables such as joint position, eye position, color, or sound frequency. Any individual neuron is too noisy to faithfully encode the variable using rate coding, but an entire population ensures greater fidelity and precision. For a population of unimodal tuning curves, i.e. with a single peak, the precision typically scales linearly with the number of neurons. Hence, for half the precision, half as many neurons are required. In contrast, when the tuning curves have multiple peaks, as in grid cells that represent space, the precision of the population can scale exponentially with the number of neurons. This greatly reduces the number of neurons required for the same precision.

Sparse Coding

The sparse code is when each item is encoded by the strong activation of a relatively small set of neurons. For each item to be encoded, this is a different subset of all available neurons.

As a consequence, sparseness may be focused on temporal sparseness ("a relatively small number of time periods are active") or on the sparseness in an activated population of neurons. In this latter case, this may be defined in one time period as the number of activated neurons relative to the total number of neurons in the population. This seems to be a hallmark of neural computations since compared to traditional computers, information is massively distributed across neurons. A major result in neural coding from Olshausen and Field is that sparse coding of natural images produces wavelet-like oriented filters that resemble the receptive fields of simple cells in the visual cortex. The capacity of sparse codes may be increased by simultaneous use of temporal coding, as found in the locust olfactory system.

Given a potentially large set of input patterns, sparse coding algorithms (e.g. Sparse Autoencoder) attempt to automatically find a small number of representative patterns which, when combined in the right proportions, reproduce the original input patterns. The sparse coding for the input then consists of those representative patterns. For example, the very large set of English sentences can be encoded by a small number of symbols (i.e. letters, numbers, punctuation, and spaces) combined in a particular order for a particular sentence, and so a sparse coding for English would be those symbols.

Linear Generative Model

Most models of sparse coding are based on the linear generative model. In this model, the symbols are combined in a linear fashion to approximate the input.

More formally, given a k-dimensional set of real-numbered input vectors $\vec{\xi} \in \mathbb{R}^k$ the goal of sparse coding is to determine n k-dimensional basis vectors $\vec{b_1}, \ldots, \vec{b_n} \in \mathbb{R}^k$ along with a sparse n-dimensional vector of weights or coefficients $\vec{s} \in \mathbb{R}^n$ for each input vector, so that a linear combination of the basis vectors with proportions given by the coefficients results in a close approximation to the input vector: $\vec{\xi} \approx \sum_{j=1}^{n} s_j \vec{b_j}$.

The codings generated by algorithms implementing a linear generative model can be classified into codings with *soft sparseness* and those with *hard sparseness*. These refer to the distribution of basis vector coefficients for typical inputs. A coding with soft sparseness has a smooth Gaussian-like distribution, but peakier than Gaussian, with many zero values, some small absolute values, fewer larger absolute values, and very few very large absolute values. Thus, many of the basis vectors are active. Hard sparseness, on the other hand, indicates that there are many zero values, *no* or *hardly any* small absolute values, fewer larger absolute values, and very few very large absolute values, and thus few of the basis vectors are active. This is appealing from a metabolic perspective: less energy is used when fewer neurons are firing.

Another measure of coding is whether it is *critically complete* or *overcomplete*. If the number of basis vectors n is equal to the dimensionality k of the input set, the coding is said to be critically complete. In this case, smooth changes in the input vector result in abrupt changes in the coefficients, and the coding is not able to gracefully handle small scalings, small translations, or noise in the inputs. If, however, the number of basis vectors is larger than the dimensionality of the input set, the coding is *overcomplete*. Overcomplete codings smoothly interpolate between input vectors and are robust under input noise. The human primary visual cortex is estimated to be overcomplete by a factor of 500, so that, for example, a 14 x 14 patch of input (a 196-dimensional space) is coded by roughly 100,000 neurons.

Biological Evidence

Sparse coding may be a general strategy of neural systems to augment memory capacity. To adapt to their environments, animals must learn which stimuli are associated with rewards or punishments and distinguish these reinforced stimuli from similar but irrelevant ones. Such task requires implementing stimulus-specific associative memories in which only a few neurons out of a population respond to any given stimulus and each neuron responds to only a few stimuli out of all possible stimuli.

Theoretical work on Sparse distributed memory has suggested that sparse coding increases the capacity of associative memory by reducing overlap between representations. Experimentally, sparse representations of sensory information have been observed in many systems, including vision, audition, touch, and olfaction. However, despite the accumulating evidence for widespread sparse coding and theoretical arguments for its importance, a demonstration that sparse coding improves the stimulus-specificity of associative memory has been lacking until recently.

Some progress has been made in 2014 by Gero Miesenböck's lab at the University of Oxford analyzing Drosophila Olfactory system. In Drosophila, sparse odor coding by the Kenyon cells of the mushroom body is thought to generate a large number of precisely addressable locations for the storage of odor-specific memories. Lin et al. demonstrated that sparseness is controlled by a negative feedback circuit between Kenyon cells and the GABAergic anterior paired lateral (APL) neuron. Systematic activation and blockade of each leg of this feedback circuit show that Kenyon cells activate APL and APL inhibits Kenyon cells. Disrupting the Kenyon cell-APL feedback loop decreases the sparseness of Kenyon cell odor responses, increases inter-odor correlations, and prevents flies from learning to discriminate similar, but not dissimilar, odors. These results suggest that feedback inhibition suppresses Kenyon cell activity to maintain sparse, decorrelated odor coding and thus the odor-specificity of memories.

Neural Binding

Neural binding refers to the neuroscientific aspect of what is commonly known as the binding problem. The Binding Problem is an interdisciplinary term, named for the difficulty of creating a comprehensive and verifiable model for the unity of consciousness. "Binding" refers to the integration of highly diverse neural information in the forming of one's cohesive experience. The neural binding hypothesis states that neural signals are paired through synchronized oscillations of neuronal activity that combine and recombine to allow for a wide variety of responses to context-dependent stimuli. These dynamic neural networks are thought to account for the flexibility and nuanced response of the brain to various situations. The coupling of these networks is transient, on the order of milliseconds, and allows for rapid activity.

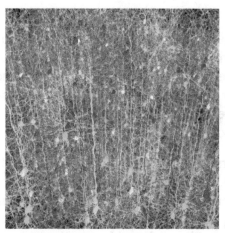

Neural binding involves the complex coordination of diverse neural circuits

A viable mechanism for this phenomenon must address (1) the difficulties of reconciling the global nature of the participating (exogenous) signals and their relevant (endogenous) associations, (2) the interface between lower perceptual processes and higher cognitive processes, (3) the identification of signals (sometimes referred to as "tagging") as they are processed and routed throughout the brain, and (4) the emergence of a unity of consciousness.

Proposed adaptive functions of neural binding have included the avoidance of hallucinatory phenomena generated by endogenous patterns alone as well as the avoidance of behavior driven by involuntary action alone.

There are several difficulties that must be addressed in this model. First, it must provide a mechanism for the integration of signals across different brain regions (both cortical and subcortical). It must also be able to explain the simultaneous processing of unrelated signals that are held separate from one another and integrated signals that must be viewed as a whole.

Interdisciplinary Correlates

The study of the binding problem in neuroscience stems from the much older psychological study of the binding phenomenon, which has its roots in the ancient philosophical study of the same problems. Today, there is a close interplay between neuroscience and psychology, which is especially relevant to neural binding.

Gestalt Psychology and Correlating Critiques

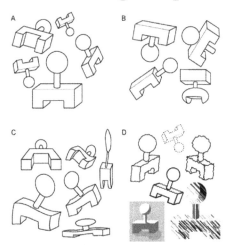

Representation of the multiple ways to perceive the same object

Gestalt psychology is a field that has been intertwined with neural binding due to its advances in conceptualizing how the brain views objects, reacts to stimuli, and then reacts on a global level. Since Gestalt Psychology has become so involved, "grouping" has become an important part of understanding neural binding. The scientists that supported this theory were solely focused on the idea that mechanisms in the brain operated preattentively.

"Grouping" has become especially important for neural binding due to studies in gamma wave activity in the brain. From single-unit recording scientists have been able to measure the oscillatory neuronal activity and have been able to better their understanding of the grouping or pairing of neurons. Thus, these pairings connect with Gestalt psychology and its theory that objects are seen independently of their separate pieces, in a more global manner. A study done by Gray, Konig, Engel and Singer in 1989 reported that when studying visual cortex cells, light moving in opposite directions had low relation to one another. Yet when the light rays were then pointed in the same direction, the correlative relationship was stronger. A paper addressing this idea states, "Thus, correlated activity was only obtained when cells responded to different aspects of the same 'Gestalt'". Other studies using EEGs from the human scalp also examined gamma wave activity, showing how stimuli seemed to be in accordance with preattentive binding.

To contrast this, another group of scientists (Treisman & Gelade) believed that the mechanisms did not work preattentively. They postulated that in order to make correct bindings there had to be attention. Hence, they called their theory "attentional binding." The idea of attentional binding is that, as someone places their attention on an object with multiple features, they develop over time a coherent representation of that object and the characteristics that it holds. These characteristics, after being processed through attention, can be stored in short-term memory or as episodic memories.

One more contrast to Gestalt psychological emphasis in neural binding was brought up by L. Chen. Chen asserts that the local-global idea of Gestalt does not suffice in explaining neural processing. Instead, Chen uses the idea that perception depends on "topological invariants that describe the geometrical potentiality of the entire stimulus configuration". The idea here is that looking at a certain object creates a stimulus which in turn fires a constellation of that object, and then the object becomes recognized.

The rebuttal to Chen's idea is that since each object has its own constellation, as well as its own particular set of neurons, there would not be enough space in the brain for all the appropriate neuronal pathways. This ratio of 1:1 simply could not support the many complex mechanisms of the human brain.

Later, more writings were produced regarding preattentive binding. Although they did not focus as much on Gestalt psychology, they were important to the idea of the pre-attentiveness of the brain. One such addition onto this theory was put out by Duncan and Humphreys. They said that some types of features, when trying to form the image, compete against one another for "the limited capacity object recognition stage". This means that certain parts of an object have multiple ways of being featured by the brain. Each different type of feature then competes with the others, trying to become the feature that is displayed to the individual. This can then account for the understanding of how each person views a whole object differently than another person. They also then see its global function on a very different scale.

This idea of differential grouping is also brought up by Aksentijevic, Elliott, and Barber. Their theory is based on different perceptions of geometrical space that can then supply a "starting point for a systematic exploration of the subjective properties of certain classes of visual and auditory grouping phenomena, such as apparent motion, grouping within static two-dimensional displays and auditory streaming." This idea shows how different people perceive geometrical space, which can lead to different auditory and visual streams.

Proposed Models

Temporal

The Temporal Binding Hypothesis has a history in neuroscience which spans back to at least the early 1980s. Christoph Von der Malsburg proposed that neurons carry two distinct signals, one of conventional rate code in relation to the 'effectiveness' of the feature it is encoding and another which is conveyed in terms of spike coordination between assemblies of neurons. A decade later Francis Crick & Christof Koch developed the model further by explaining the synchronization of distant neurons by transient gamma wave oscillations being guided by attention. By 1995, Francisco Varela had established the importance of the role of the oscillatory phase in the pairing of neuron assemblies.

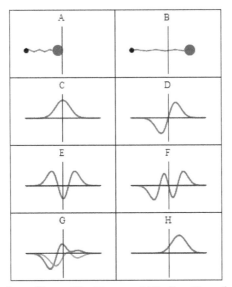

Some trajectories of a harmonic oscillator. The Temporal Binding Hypothesis and other areas of neural binding use this idea to describe the pairing of two oscillating waves, forming an image.

The Temporal Binding Hypothesis was first proposed as a way of addressing the combinatorial problem of neural binding, which emphasizes the impossibly large number of connections that would have to be made between neurons of overlapping function and association in order to achieve the degree of observable complexity in neural binding. Modern models that are currently being developed often retain the structure of temporal synchrony due to this significant advantage as well as the strong experimental support for the existence of global brain oscillations.

Gamma Band Activity

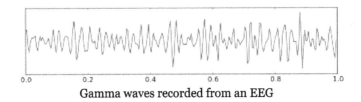

Gamma waves recorded from an EEG

It has been widely observed that distributed collections of neurons oscillate within the gamma band of frequencies (typically between 30–80 Hz).

Phasic Pairing Mechanisms

Varela's model describes the selection of cellular assemblies, sometimes referred to as resonant or reverberating (Lorente de Nó) circuits, as being integrated into a larger ensemble by transient spike phase locking. This addresses the explanatory difficulty of the simultaneous nature of binding because it allows many signals to be in transit in parallel within an overlapping frequency range without interference.

Criticism

The temporal binding models have been criticized by some for being unwarranted in their far-reaching speculative nature. This claim is usually made in favor of a more classical model of neural function.

Quantum Models

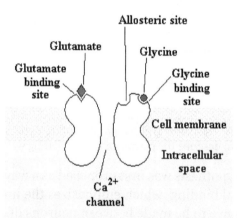

The NMDA channel acts as a coincidence detector, requiring multiple types of operators for activation

Some more recent models have incorporated quantum theory as a component of the underlying neural dynamics behind binding due to the strong explanatory power of quantum mechanics and their claim of the insufficiency of current models for explaining the complexity of the binding mechanism.

In 2001, da Rocha developed a model which utilized the basic structure of the Temporal Binding Hypothesis, with global phase synchronization being a primary mechanism of distributing information, but emphasized the importance of a quantum computation performed on a local level. His model depicts the NMDA receptor as the coincidence detector proposed in other theories. This is a physiological mechanism which has been criticized for being absent from a full theory of temporal binding previously.

Non-synchronous Models

Many non-temporal theories attempt to retain a more classical conception of neuron signaling based on hierarchical structures. This relies on the convergence of signals upon specific neural circuits as well as the dynamic routing of signaling pathways through specialized computational sub-assemblies.

These models can be vulnerable to the combinatorial and connectivity problems, which come as a natural consequence of depending solely on one-to-one communication of conventional information via spike rate coding. These models also require the seamless directing and combining of signals, which either assumes a controller (proposed to be the pulvinar nuclei) or a mechanism for the spontaneous self-assembly of neural ensembles.

Test Cases

Sensory

Much of the experimental evidence for neural binding has traditionally revolved around sensory awareness. Sensory awareness is accomplished by integrating things together by cognitively perceiving them and then segmenting them so that, in total, there is an image created. Since there can be an infinite number of possibilities in the perception of an object, this has been a unique area of study. The way the brain then collectively pieces certain things together via networking is important not only in the global way of perceiving but also in segmentation. Much of sensory awareness has to do with the taking of a single piece of an object's makeup and then binding its total characteristics so that the brain perceives the object in its final form. Much of the research for the understanding of segmentation and how the brain perceives an object has been done by studying cats. A major finding of this research has to do with the understanding of gamma waves oscillating at 40 Hz. The information was extracted from a study using the cat visual cortex. It was shown that the cortical neurons responded differently to spatially different objects. These firings of neurons ranged from 40–60 Hz in measure and when observed showed that they fired synchronously when observing different parts of the object. Such coherent responses point to the fact that brain is doing a kind of coding where it is piecing certain neurons together in the works of making the form of an object. Since the brain is putting these segmented pieces together unsupervised, a significant consonance is found with many philosophers (like Sigmund Freud) who theorize an underlying subconscious that helps to form every aspect of our conscious thought processes.

In order for these multiple firings from multiple areas to be combined into a specific extrinsic event, there must be help from the dorsal thalamus. It is not proven whether the dorsal thalamus is the primary organizer, but it does fit the specific profile for collecting neuronal activity and rapidly coordinating between what is happening in the brain and outside of it. The space in and around the dorsal thalamus, the thalomocortical area, is able to generate fast voltage-dependent membrane potential oscillations which allow it to react quickly to received messages. The types of channels that cover this area are presumed to be GABAergic. Since sensory awareness needs to be quick, the threshold for sodium and potassium in this area is quite low.

Cognitive

Francis Crick and Christof Koch proposed that specific neural activity can stimulate short-term memory, forming a continuous and dynamic consciousness.

Cognitive binding is associated with the different states of human consciousness. Two of the most studied states of consciousness are the wakefulness and REM sleep. There have been multiple studies showing, electrophysiologically, that these two states are quite similar in nature. This has led some neural binding theorists to study the modes of cognitive awareness in each state. Certain observations have even led these scientists to hypothesize that since there is little cognition going on during REM sleep, the increased thalamocortical responses show the action of processing in the waking preconscious.

The thalamus and cortex are important anatomical features in cognitive and sensory awareness. The understanding of how these neurons fire and relate to one other in each of these states (REM and Waking) is paramount to understanding awareness and its relation to neural binding.

In the waking state, neuronal activity in animals is subject to changes based on the current environment. Changes in environment act as a form of stress on the brain so that when sensory neurons are then fired synchronously, they acclimate to the new state. This new state can then be moved to the hippocampus where it can be stored for later use. In the words of James Newman and Anthony A. Grace in their article, "Binding Across Time" this idea is put forth: "The hippocampus is the primary recipient of inferotemporal outputs and is known to be the substrate for the consolidation of working memories to long term, episodic memories."

The logging of "episodes" is then used for "streaming", which can mediate by the selective gating of certain information reentering sensory awareness. Streaming and building of episodic memories would not be possible if neural binding did not unconsciously connect the two synchronous oscillations.

The pairing of these oscillations can then help input the correct sensory material. If these paired oscillations are not new, then cognitively these firings will be easily understood. If there are new firings, the brain will have to acclimate to the new understanding.

In REM sleep, the only extreme difference from the waking state is that the brain does not have the actual waking amount of sensory firings, so cognitively, there is not as much awareness here, although the activity of the "brain's eye" is still quite significant and very similar to the waking state. Studies have shown that during sleep there are still 40 Hz Oscillation firings. These firings are due to the perceived stimuli happening in dreams. "

Learning/Memory

Opitz argues that the binding of different brain areas is mediated by the hippocampus. Relational bindings, or relationships between separate objects, concepts, and memories, are very flexible because the targets can be combined in so many different ways to deal with the present situation, and the hippocampus ensures that these parts are arranged into a coherent whole. Particularly, the hippocampus has been implicated in binding that is involved with episodic memory, working memory, and language acquisition. According to Opitz, this is viable because the hippocampus meets all criteria to be suitable for the regulation relational binding and, based on its patterns of activity, it is likely that it is involved.

Clinical Implications

Autism

A young boy with autism who has arranged his toys in a row

Several researchers have suggested a clinical link between difficulties in neural binding and autism spectrum disorders. It has been postulated that there is a level of underconnectivity between certain areas of the autistic brain, specifically those areas that involve social cognition. They also hypothesize that there may be overconnectivity within certain neuronal cell assemblies. Researchers have suggested that these issues with coherence of neural networks give rise to the hallmark autistic symptoms, namely, impaired social cognition/interactions and repetitive behaviors.

There is one major piece of evidence suggesting that abnormal connectivity occurs in autism. Autistic brains are known to develop very rapidly early in life, and this could cause problems in the development of cortical connections. It has been suggested that this early overdevelopment may be a cause for the impaired connectivity in autism. Diffusion tensor imaging studies of autistic brains are consistent with this idea, as they show reduced myelination in the areas of the brain that deal with social cognition and theory of mind, or one's ability to comprehend what another person may be thinking. This provides further evidence for underconnectivity of the autistic brain.

Schizophrenia

It is also possible that problems with binding give way to the fractured mental state that is characteristic of schizophrenia. Schizophrenic patients experience a "disintegration of consciousness" which involves hallucinations, delusions, and generally disordered thinking. It is hypothesized that this mental disorganization is caused by underlying neural disorganization due to disordered binding, which is then further complicated by the occurrence of complex mental processes in this disordered state. This can essentially be viewed as a pathological rise in the neural complexity of the brain. The dissociative symptoms and disorganized speech associated with schizophrenia are consistent with this idea. It is also possible that disordered binding between the regulatory mechanisms of the brain gives rise to a lack of synchronized activation of its neural networks.

Self-portrait of a person with schizophrenia, representing that individual's perception of the distorted experience of reality in the disorder

Anesthesia

A deeper understanding of the mechanisms underlying consciousness on the biochemical level has practical implications which extend to the development of more effective and reliable anesthetics. This method is especially useful for the study of consciousness because of anesthetic's well-known ability to elicit unconsciousness. This often happens in a single moment, giving the impression of a collapse of conscious coherence. Stuart Hameroff is a notable anesthesiologist who promotes this method in the development of a science of consciousness.

Neuroinformatics

Neuroinformatics is a research field concerned with the organization of neuroscience data by the application of computational models and analytical tools. These areas of research are important for the integration and analysis of increasingly large-volume, high-dimensional, and fine-grain experimental data. Neuroinformaticians provide computational tools, mathematical models, and create interoperable databases for clinicians and research scientists. Neuroscience is a heterogeneous field, consisting of many and various sub-disciplines (e.g., cognitive Psychology, behavioral neuroscience, and behavioral genetics). In order for our understanding of the brain to continue to deepen, it is necessary that these sub-disciplines are able to share data and findings in a meaningful way; Neuroinformaticians facilitate this.

Neuroinformatics stands at the intersection of neuroscience and information science. Other fields, like genomics, have demonstrated the effectiveness of freely-distributed databases and the application of theoretical and computational models for solving complex problems. In Neuroinformatics, such facilities allow researchers to more easily quantitatively confirm their working theories by computational modeling. Additionally, neuroinformatics fosters collaborative research—an important fact that facilitates the field's interest in studying the multi-level complexity of the brain.

There are three main directions where neuroinformatics has to be applied:

- the development of tools and databases for management and sharing of neuroscience data at all levels of analysis,

- the development of tools for analyzing and modeling neuroscience data,

- the development of computational models of the nervous system and neural processes.

In the recent decade, as vast amounts of diverse data about the brain were gathered by many research groups, the problem was raised of how to integrate the data from thousands of publications in order to enable efficient tools for further research. The biological and neuroscience data are highly interconnected and complex, and by itself, integration represents a great challenge for scientists.

Combining informatics research and brain research provides benefits for both fields of science. On one hand, informatics facilitates brain data processing and data handling, by providing new electronic and software technologies for arranging databases, modeling and communication in brain research. On the other hand, enhanced discoveries in the field of neuroscience will invoke the development of new methods in information technologies (IT).

History

Starting in 1989, the United States National Institute of Mental Health (NIMH), the National Institute of Drug Abuse (NIDA) and the National Science Foundation (NSF) provided the National Academy of Sciences Institute of Medicine with funds to undertake a careful analysis and study of the need to create databases, share neuroscientific data and to examine how the field of information technology could create the tools needed for the increasing volume and modalities of neuroscientific data. The positive recommendations were reported in 1991 ("Mapping The Brain And Its Functions. Integrating Enabling Technologies Into Neuroscience Research." National Academy Press, Washington, D.C. ed. Pechura, C.M., and Martin, J.B.) This positive report enabled NIMH, now directed by Allan Leshner, to create the "Human Brain Project" (HBP), with the first grants awarded in 1993. The HBP was led by Koslow along with cooperative efforts of other NIH Institutes, the NSF, the National Aeronautics and Space Administration and the Department of Energy. The HPG and grant-funding initiative in this area slightly preceded the explosive expansion of the World Wide Web. From 1993 through 2004 this program grew to over 100 million dollars in funded grants.

Next, Koslow pursued the globalization of the HPG and neuroinformatics through the European Union and the Office for Economic Co-operation and Development (OECD), Paris, France. Two particular opportunities occurred in 1996.

- The first was the existence of the US/European Commission Biotechnology Task force co-chaired by Mary Clutter from NSF. Within the mandate of this committee, of which Koslow was a member the United States European Commission Committee on Neuroinformatics was established and co-chaired by Koslow from the United States. This committee resulted in the European Commission initiating support for neuroinformatics in Framework 5 and it has continued to support activities in neuroinformatics research and training.

- A second opportunity for globalization of neuroinformatics occurred when the participating governments of the Mega Science Forum (MSF) of the OECD were asked if they had any new scientific initiatives to bring forward for scientific cooperation around the globe. The White House Office of Science and Technology Policy requested that agencies in the federal government meet at NIH to decide if cooperation were needed that would be of global benefit. The NIH held a series of meetings in which proposals from different agencies were discussed. The proposal recommendation from the U.S. for the MSF was a combination of the NSF and NIH proposals. Jim Edwards of NSF supported databases and data-sharing in the area of biodiversity; Koslow proposed the HPG ? as a model for sharing neuroscientific data, with the new moniker of *neuroinformatics*.

The two related initiates were combined to form the United States proposal on "Biological Informatics". This initiative was supported by the White House Office of Science and Technology Policy and presented at the OECD MSF by Edwards and Koslow. An MSF committee was established on Biological Informatics with two subcommittees: 1. Biodiversity (Chair, James Edwards, NSF), and 2. Neuroinformatics (Chair, Stephen Koslow, NIH). At the end of two years the Neuroinformatics subcommittee of the Biological Working Group issued a report supporting a global neuroinformatics effort. Koslow, working with the NIH and the White House Office of Science and Technology Policy to establishing a new Neuroinformatics working group to develop specific recommendation to support the more general recommendations of the first report. The Global Science Forum (GSF; renamed from MSF) of the OECD supported this recommendation.

The International Neuroinformatics Coordinating Facility

This committee presented 3 recommendations to the member governments of GSF. These recommendations were:

1. National neuroinformatics programs should be continued or initiated in each country should have a national node to both provide research resources nationally and to serve as the contact for national and international coordination.

2. An International Neuroinformatics Coordinating Facility (INCF) should be established. The INCF will coordinate the implementation of a global neuroinformatics network through integration of national neuroinformatics nodes.

3. A new international funding scheme should be established. This scheme should eliminate national and disciplinary barriers and provide a most efficient approach to global collaborative research and data sharing. In this new scheme, each country will be expected to fund the participating researchers from their country.

The GSF neuroinformatics committee then developed a business plan for the operation, support and establishment of the INCF which was supported and approved by the GSF Science Ministers at its 2004 meeting. In 2006 the INCF was created and its central office established and set into operation at the Karolinska Institute, Stockholm, Sweden under the leadership of Sten Grillner. Sixteen countries (Australia, Canada, China, the Czech Republic, Denmark, Finland, France, Germany, India, Italy, Japan, the Netherlands, Norway, Sweden, Switzerland, the United Kingdom and the United States), and the EU Commission established the legal basis for the INCF and Programme in International Neuroinformatics (PIN). To date, fourteen countries (Czech Republic, Finland, France, Germany, Italy, Japan, Norway, Sweden, Switzerland, and the United States) are members of the INCF. Membership is pending for several other countries.

The goal of the INCF is to coordinate and promote international activities in neuroinformatics. The INCF contributes to the development and maintenance of database and computational infrastructure and support mechanisms for neuroscience applications. The system is expected to provide access to all freely accessible human brain data and resources to the international research community. The more general task of INCF is to provide conditions for developing convenient and flexible applications for neuroscience laboratories in order to improve our knowledge about the human brain and its disorders.

Society for Neuroscience Brain Information Group

On the foundation of all of these activities, Huda Akil, the 2003 President of the Society for Neuroscience (SfN) established the Brain Information Group (BIG) to evaluate the importance of neuroinformatics to neuroscience and specifically to the SfN. Following the report from BIG, SfN also established a neuroinformatics committee.

In 2004, SfN announced the Neuroscience Database Gateway (NDG) as a universal resource for neuroscientists through which almost any neuroscience databases and tools may be reached. The NDG was established with funding from NIDA, NINDS and NIMH. The Neuroscience Database Gateway has transitioned to a new enhanced platform, the Neuroscience Information Framework <http://www.neuinfo.org>. Funded by the NIH Neuroscience BLueprint, the NIF is a dynamic portal providing access to neuroscience-relevant resources (data, tools, materials) from a single search interface. The NIF builds upon the foundation of the NDG, but provides a unique set of tools tailored especially for neuroscientists: a more expansive catalog, the ability to search multiple databases directly from the NIF home page, a custom web index of neuroscience resources, and a neuroscience-focused literature search function.

Collaboration with other disciplines

Neuroinformatics is formed at the intersections of the following fields:

- neuroscience
- computer science
- biology
- experimental psychology
- medicine
- engineering
- physical sciences
- mathematics
- chemistry

Biology is concerned with molecular data (from genes to cell specific expression); medicine and anatomy with the structure of synapses and systems level anatomy; engineering – electrophysiology (from single channels to scalp surface EEG), brain imaging; computer science – databases, software tools, mathematical sciences – models, chemistry – neurotransmitters, etc. Neuroscience uses all aforementioned experimental and theoretical studies to learn about the brain through its various levels. Medical and biological specialists help to identify the unique cell types, and their elements and anatomical connections. Functions of complex organic molecules and structures, including a myriad of biochemical, molecular, and genetic mechanisms which regulate and control brain function, are determined by specialists in chemistry and cell biology. Brain imaging determines structural and functional information during mental and behavioral activity. Specialists in biophysics and physiology study physical processes within neural cells neuronal networks. The data from these fields of research is analyzed and arranged in databases and neural models in order to integrate various elements into a sophisticated system; this is the point where neuroinformatics meets other disciplines.

Neuroscience provides the following types of data and information on which neuroinformatics operates:

- Molecular and cellular data (ion channel, action potential, genetics, cytology of neurons, protein pathways),

- Data from organs and systems (visual cortex, perception, audition, sensory system, pain, taste, motor system, spinal cord),

- Cognitive data (language, emotion, motor learning, sexual behavior, decision making, social neuroscience),

- Developmental information (neuronal differentiation, cell survival, synaptic formation, motor differentiation, injury and regeneration, axon guidance, growth factors),

- Information about diseases and aging (autonomic nervous system, depression, anxiety, Parkinson's disease, addiction, memory loss),

- Neural engineering data (brain-computer interface), and

- Computational neuroscience data (computational models of various neuronal systems, from membrane currents, proteins to learning and memory).

Neuroinformatics uses databases, the Internet, and visualization in the storage and analysis of the mentioned neuroscience data.

Research Programs and Groups

Neuroscience Information Framework

The Neuroscience Information Framework (NIF) is an initiative of the NIH Blueprint for Neuroscience Research, which was established in 2004 by the National Institutes of Health. Unlike general search engines, NIF provides deeper access to a more focused set of resources that are relevant to neuroscience, search strategies tailored to neuroscience, and access to content that is traditionally "hidden" from web search engines. The NIF is a dynamic inventory of neuroscience databases, annotated and integrated with a unified system of biomedical terminology (i.e. NeuroLex). NIF supports concept-based queries across multiple scales of biological structure and multiple levels of biological function, making it easier to search for and understand the results. NIF will also provide a registry through which resources providers can disclose availability of resources relevant to neuroscience research. NIF is not intended to be a warehouse or repository itself, but a means for disclosing and locating resources elsewhere available via the web.

Genes to Cognition Project

A neuroscience research programme that studies genes, the brain and behaviour in an integrated manner. It is engaged in a large-scale investigation of the function of molecules found at the synapse. This is mainly focused on proteins that interact with the NMDA receptor, a receptor for the neurotransmitter, glutamate, which is required for processes of synaptic plasticity such as long-term potentiation (LTP). Many of the techniques used are high-throughput in nature, and integrating the various data sources, along with guiding the experiments has raised numerous informatics questions. The program is primarily run by Professor Seth Grant at the Wellcome Trust Sanger Institute, but there are many other teams of collaborators across the world.

Neurogenetics: GeneNetwork

Genenetwork started as component of the NIH Human Brain Project in 1999 with a focus on the genetic analysis of brain structure and function. This international program consists of tightly integrated genome and phenome data sets for human, mouse, and rat that are designed specifically for large-scale systems and network studies relating gene variants to differences in mRNA and protein expression and to differences in CNS structure and behavior. The great majority of data are open access. GeneNetwork has a companion neuroimaging web site—the Mouse Brain Library—that contains high resolution images for thousands of genetically defined strains of mice.

The Blue Brain Project

The Blue Brain Project was founded in May 2005, and uses an 8000 processor Blue Gene/L supercomputer developed by IBM. At the time, this was one of the fastest supercomputers in the world. The project involves:

- Databases: 3D reconstructed model neurons, synapses, synaptic pathways, microcircuit statistics, computer model neurons, virtual neurons.

- Visualization: microcircuit builder and simulation results visualizator, 2D, 3D and immersive visualization systems are being developed.

- Simulation: a simulation environment for large scale simulations of morphologically complex neurons on 8000 processors of IBM's Blue Gene supercomputer.

- Simulations and experiments: iterations between large scale simulations of neocortical microcircuits and experiments in order to verify the computational model and explore predictions.

The mission of the Blue Brain Project is to understand mammalian brain function and dysfunction through detailed simulations. The Blue Brain Project will invite researchers to build their own models of different brain regions in different species and at different levels of detail using Blue Brain Software for simulation on Blue Gene. These models will be deposited in an internet database from which Blue Brain software can extract and connect models together to build brain regions and begin the first whole brain simulations.

The Neuroinformatics Portal Pilot

The project is part of a larger effort to enhance the exchange of neuroscience data, data-analysis tools, and modeling software. The portal is supported from many members of the OECD Working Group on Neuroinformatics. The Portal Pilot is promoted by the German Ministry for Science and Education.

The Neuronal Time Series Analysis (NTSA)

NTSA Workbench is a set of tools, techniques and standards designed to meet the needs of neuroscientists who work with neuronal time series data. The goal of this project is to develop information system that will make the storage, organization, retrieval, analysis and sharing of experimental and simulated neuronal data easier. The ultimate aim is to develop a set of tools, techniques and standards in order to satisfy the needs of neuroscientists who work with neuronal data.

Japan National Neuroinformatics Resource

The Visiome Platform is the Neuroinformatics Search Service that provides access to mathematical models, experimental data, analysis libraries and related resources.

An online portal for neurophysiological data sharing is also available at BrainLiner.jp as part of the MEXT Strategic Research Program for Brain Sciences (SRPBS).

The CARMEN Project

The CARMEN project is a multi-site (11 universities in the United Kingdom) research project aimed at using GRID computing to enable experimental neuroscientists to archive their datasets in a structured database, making them widely accessible for further research, and for modellers and algorithm developers to exploit.

The Cognitive Atlas

The Cognitive Atlas is a project developing a shared knowledge base in cognitive science and neuroscience. This comprises two basic kinds of knowledge: tasks and concepts, providing definitions and properties thereof, and also relationships between them. An important feature of the site is ability to cite literature for assertions (e.g. "The Stroop task measures executive control") and to discuss their validity. It contributes to NeuroLex and the Neuroscience Information Framework, allows programmatic access to the database, and is built around semantic web technologies.

Research Groups

- *The Institute of Neuroinformatics* (INI) was established at the University of Zurich at the end of 1995. The mission of the Institute is to discover the key principles by which brains work and to implement these in artificial systems that interact intelligently with the real world.

- *The THOR Center for Neuroinformatics* was established April 1998 at the Department of Mathematical Modelling, Technical University of Denmark. Besides pursuing independent research goals, the THOR Center hosts a number of related projects concerning neural networks, functional neuroimaging, multimedia signal processing, and biomedical signal processing.

- *Netherlands state program* in neuroinformatics started in the light of the international OECD Global Science Forum which aim is to create a worldwide program in Neuroinformatics.

- Shun-ichi Amari, Laboratory for Mathematical Neuroscience, RIKEN Brain Science Institute Wako, Saitama, Japan. The target of Laboratory for Mathematical Neuroscience is to establish mathematical foundations of brain-style computations toward construction of a new type of information science.

- Gary Egan, Neuroimaging & Neuroinformatics, Howard Florey Institute, University of Melbourne, Melbourne, Australia. Institute scientists utilize brain imaging techniques, such as magnetic resonance imaging, to reveal the organization of brain networks involved in human thought.

- Andreas VM Herz Computational Neuroscience, ITB, Humboldt-University Berlin, Berlin Germany. This group focuses on computational neurobiology, in particular on the dynamics and signal processing capabilities of systems with spiking neurons.

- Nicolas Le Novère, EBI Computational Neurobiology, EMBL-EBI Hinxton, United Kingdom. The main goal of the group is to build realistic models of neuronal function at various levels, from the synapse to the micro-circuit, based on the precise knowledge of molecule functions and interactions (Systems Biology)

- *The Neuroinformatics Group in Bielefeld* has been active in the field of Artificial Neural Networks since 1989. Current research programmes within the group are focused on the improvement of man-machine-interfaces, robot-force-control, eye-tracking experiments, machine vision, virtual reality and distributed systems.

- Hanchuan Peng, Allen Institute for Brain Science, Seattle, USA. This group has focused on using large scale imaging computing and data analysis techniques to reconstruct single neuron models and mapping them in brains of different animals.

- Laboratory of Computational Embodied Neuroscience (LOCEN), Institute of Cognitive Sciences and Technologies, Italian National Research Council (ISTC-CNR), Rome, Italy. This group, founded in 2006 and currently led by Gianluca Baldassarre, has two objectives: (a) understanding the brain mechanisms underlying learning and expression of sensorimotor behaviour, and related motivations and higher-level cognition grounded on it, on the basis of embodied computational models; (b) transferring the acquired knowledge to building innovative controllers for autonomous humanoid robots capable of learning in an open-ended fashion on the basis of intrinsic and extrinsic motivations.

- NUST-SEECS Neuroinformatics Research Lab, Establishment of the Neuro-Informatics Lab at SEECS-NUST has enabled Pakistani researchers and members of the faculty to actively participate in such efforts, thereby becoming an active part of the above-mentioned experimentation, simulation, and visualization processes. The lab collaborates with the leading international institutions to develop highly skilled human resource in the related field. This lab facilitates neuroscientists and computer scientists in Pakistan to conduct their experiments and analysis on the data collected using state of the art research methodologies without investing in establishing the experimental neuroscience facilities. The key goal of this lab is to provide state of the art experimental and simulation facilities, to all beneficiaries including higher education institutes, medical researchers/practitioners, and technology industry.

Books in the Field

- Computing the Brain: A Guide to Neuroinformatics by Michael A. Arbib and Jeffrey S. Grethe (2001), ISBN 978-0123885432

- Electronic Collaboration in Science (Progress in Neuroinformatics Research Series) by Stephen H. Koslow and Michael F. Huerta (2000), ISBN 978-1138003187

- Databasing the Brain: From Data to Knowledge (Neuroinformatics) by Steven H. Koslow and Shankar Subramaniam, (2005), ISBN 978-0471309215

- Neuroinformatics: An Overview of the Human Brain Project (Progress in Neuroinformatics Research Series) by Stephen H. Koslow and Michael F. Huerta (1997),

- Neuroscience Databases: A Practical Guide by Rolf Kötter (2002),

- Biomedical Informatics: Computer Applications in Health Care and Biomedicine (Health Informatics) by James J. Cimino and Edward H. Shortliffe. (2006),

- Computational Neuroanatomy: Principles and Methods edited by Giorgio Ascoli (2002),

- Observed Brain Dynamics by Partha P. Mitra and Hemant Bokil (2007), ISBN 978-0195178081

- Neuroinformatics In: Methods in Molecular Biology. Ed. Chiquito J. Crasto, (2007),

- Principles of Computational Modelling in Neuroscience by David Steratt et al. (2011)

Technologies and Developments

The main technological tendencies in neuroinformatics are:

1. Application of computer science for building databases, tools, and networks in neuroscience;

2. Analysis and modeling of neuronal systems.

In order to organize and operate with neural data scientists need to use the standard terminology and atlases that precisely describe the brain structures and their relationships.

- Neuron Tracing and Reconstruction is an essential technique to establish digital models of the morphology of neurons. Such morphology is useful for neuron classification and simulation.

- BrainML is a system that provides a standard XML metaformat for exchanging neuroscience data.

- The Biomedical Informatics Research Network (BIRN) is an example of a grid system for neuroscience. BIRN is a geographically distributed virtual community of shared resources offering vast scope of services to advance the diagnosis and treatment of disease. BIRN allows combining databases, interfaces and tools into a single environment.

- Budapest Reference Connectome is a web based 3D visualization tool to browse connections in the human brain. Nodes, and connections are calculated from the MRI datasets of the Human Connectome Project.

- GeneWays is concerned with cellular morphology and circuits. GeneWays is a system for automatically extracting, analyzing, visualizing and integrating molecular pathway data from the research literature. The system focuses on interactions between molecular substances and actions, providing a graphical view on the collected information and allows researchers to review and correct the integrated information.

- Neocortical Microcircuit Database (NMDB). A database of versatile brain's data from cells to complex structures. Researchers are able not only to add data to the database but also to acquire and edit one.

- SenseLab. SenseLab is a long-term effort to build integrated, multidisciplinary models of neurons and neural systems. It was founded in 1993 as part of the original Human Brain Project. A collection of multilevel neuronal databases and tools. SenseLab contains six related databases that support experimental and theoretical research on the membrane properties that mediate information processing in nerve cells, using the olfactory pathway as a model system.

- BrainMaps.org is an interactive hig h-resolution digital brain atlas using a high-speed database and virtual microscope that is based on over 12 million megapixels of scanned images of several species, including human.

Another approach in the area of the brain mappings is the probabilistic atlases obtained from the real data from different group of people, formed by specific factors, like age, gender, diseased etc. Provides more flexible tools for brain research and allow obtaining more reliable and precise results, which cannot be achieved with the help of traditional brain atlases.

References

- Wu, Samuel Miao-sin; Johnston, Daniel (1995). Foundations of cellular neurophysiology. Cambridge, Mass: MIT Press. ISBN 0-262-10053-3.

- information processing in single neurons. Oxford [Oxfordshire]: Oxford University Press. ISBN 0-19-510491-9.

- Anderson, Charles H.; Eliasmith, Chris (2004). Neural Engineering: Computation, Representation, and Dynamics in Neurobiological Systems (Computational Neuroscience). Cambridge, Mass: The MIT Press. ISBN 0-262-55060-1.

- Gerstner, Wulfram; Kistler, Werner M. (2002). Spiking Neuron Models: Single Neurons, Populations, Plasticity. Cambridge University Press. ISBN 978-0-521-89079-3.

- Dayan, Peter; Abbott, L. F. (2001). Theoretical Neuroscience: Computational and Mathematical Modeling of Neural Systems. Massachusetts Institute of Technology Press. ISBN 978-0-262-04199-7.

- Geoffrois, E.; Edeline, J.M.; Vibert, J.F. (1994). "Learning by Delay Modifications". In Eeckman, Frank H. Computation in Neurons and Neural Systems. Springer. pp. 133–8. ISBN 978-0-7923-9465-5.

- Dayan P & Abbott LF. Theoretical Neuroscience: Computational and Mathematical Modeling of Neural Systems. Cambridge, Massachusetts: The MIT Press; 2001. ISBN 0-262-04199-5

- Rieke F, Warland D, de Ruyter van Steveninck R, Bialek W. Spikes: Exploring the Neural Code. Cambridge, Massachusetts: The MIT Press; 1999. ISBN 0-262-68108-0

Understanding Bioinformatics

Bioinformatics helps in the development of methods and tools for a better understanding of biology and biological data. Some of the features broadly explained in the text are sequence analysis, sequence assembly, sequence alignment, BLAST, multiple sequence alignment etc. This chapter is a compilation of the various aspects of bioinformatics that form an integral part of the broader subject matter.

Bioinformatics

Bioinformatics is an interdisciplinary field that develops methods and software tools for understanding biological data. As an interdisciplinary field of science, bioinformatics combines computer science, statistics, mathematics, and engineering to analyze and interpret biological data. Bioinformatics has been used for *in silico* analyses of biological queries using mathematical and statistical techniques.

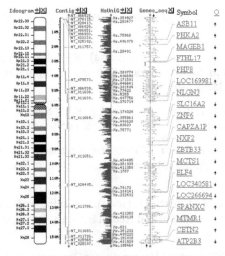

Map of the human X chromosome (from the National Center for Biotechnology Information website).

Bioinformatics is both an umbrella term for the body of biological studies that use computer programming as part of their methodology, as well as a reference to specific analysis "pipelines" that are repeatedly used, particularly in the field of genomics. Common uses of bioinformatics include the identification of candidate genes and nucleotides (SNPs). Often, such identification is made with the aim of better understanding the genetic basis of disease, unique adaptations, desirable properties (esp. in agricultural species), or differences between populations. In a less formal way, bioinformatics also tries to understand the organisational principles within nucleic acid and protein sequences, called proteomics.

Introduction

Bioinformatics has become an important part of many areas of biology. In experimental molecular biology, bioinformatics techniques such as image and signal processing allow extraction of useful results from large amounts of raw data. In the field of genetics and genomics, it aids in sequencing and annotating genomes and their observed mutations. It plays a role in the text mining of biological literature and the development of biological and gene ontologies to organize and query biological data. It also plays a role in the analysis of gene and protein expression and regulation. Bioinformatics tools aid in the comparison of genetic and genomic data and more generally in the understanding of evolutionary aspects of molecular biology. At a more integrative level, it helps analyze and catalogue the biological pathways and networks that are an important part of systems biology. In structural biology, it aids in the simulation and modeling of DNA, RNA, proteins as well as biomolecular interactions.

History

Historically, the term *bioinformatics* did not mean what it means today. Paulien Hogeweg and Ben Hesper coined it in 1970 to refer to the study of information processes in biotic systems. This definition placed bioinformatics as a field parallel to biophysics (the study of physical processes in biological systems) or biochemistry (the study of chemical processes in biological systems).

Sequences

```
5'ATGACGTGGGGA3'
3'TACTGCACCCCT5'
```

Sequences of genetic material are frequently used in bioinformatics and are easier to manage using computers than manually.

Computers became essential in molecular biology when protein sequences became available after Frederick Sanger determined the sequence of insulin in the early 1950s. Comparing multiple sequences manually turned out to be impractical. A pioneer in the field was Margaret Oakley Dayhoff, who has been hailed by David Lipman, director of the National Center for Biotechnology Information, as the "mother and father of bioinformatics." Dayhoff compiled one of the first protein sequence databases, initially published as books and pioneered methods of sequence alignment and molecular evolution. Another early contributor to bioinformatics was Elvin A. Kabat, who pioneered biological sequence analysis in 1970 with his comprehensive volumes of antibody sequences released with Tai Te Wu between 1980 and 1991.

Goals

To study how normal cellular activities are altered in different disease states, the biological data must be combined to form a comprehensive picture of these activities. Therefore, the field of bioinformatics has evolved such that the most pressing task now involves the analysis and interpretation of various types of data. This includes nucleotide and amino acid sequences, protein domains, and protein structures. The actual process of analyzing and interpreting data is referred to as computational biology. Important sub-disciplines within bioinformatics and computational biology include:

- Development and implementation of computer programs that enable efficient access to, use and management of, various types of information

- Development of new algorithms (mathematical formulas) and statistical measures that assess relationships among members of large data sets. For example, there are methods to locate a gene within a sequence, to predict protein structure and/or function, and to cluster protein sequences into families of related sequences.

The primary goal of bioinformatics is to increase the understanding of biological processes. What sets it apart from other approaches, however, is its focus on developing and applying computationally intensive techniques to achieve this goal. Examples include: pattern recognition, data mining, machine learning algorithms, and visualization. Major research efforts in the field include sequence alignment, gene finding, genome assembly, drug design, drug discovery, protein structure alignment, protein structure prediction, prediction of gene expression and protein–protein interactions, genome-wide association studies, the modeling of evolution and cell division/mitosis.

Bioinformatics now entails the creation and advancement of databases, algorithms, computational and statistical techniques, and theory to solve formal and practical problems arising from the management and analysis of biological data.

Over the past few decades, rapid developments in genomic and other molecular research technologies and developments in information technologies have combined to produce a tremendous amount of information related to molecular biology. Bioinformatics is the name given to these mathematical and computing approaches used to glean understanding of biological processes.

Common activities in bioinformatics include mapping and analyzing DNA and protein sequences, aligning DNA and protein sequences to compare them, and creating and viewing 3-D models of protein structures.

Relation to other Fields

Bioinformatics is a science field that is similar to but distinct from biological computation and computational biology. Biological computation uses bioengineering and biology to build biological computers, whereas bioinformatics uses computation to better understand biology. Bioinformatics and computational biology have similar aims and approaches, but they differ in scale: bioinformatics organizes and analyzes basic biological data, whereas computational biology builds theoretical models of biological systems, just as mathematical biology does with mathematical models.

Analyzing biological data to produce meaningful information involves writing and running software programs that use algorithms from graph theory, artificial intelligence, soft computing, data mining, image processing, and computer simulation. The algorithms in turn depend on theoretical foundations such as discrete mathematics, control theory, system theory, information theory, and statistics.

Sequence Analysis

```
A5ASC3.1    14 SIKLWPPSQTTRLLLVERMANNLST..PSIFTRK..YGSLSKEEARENAKQIEEVACSTANQ.....HYEKEPDGDGGSAVQLYAKECSKLILEVLK 101
B4F917.1    13 SIKLWPPSESTRIMLVDRMTNNLST..ESIFSRK..YRLLGKQEAHENAKTIEELCFALADE.....HFREEPDGDGSSAVQLYAKETSKMMLEVLK 100
A9S1V2.1    23 VFKLWPPSQGTREAVRQKMALKLSS..ACFESQS..FARIELADAQEHARAIEEVAFGAAQE.....ADSGGDKTGSAVVMVYAKHASKLMLETLR 109
B9GSN7.1    13 SVKLWPPGQSTRLMLVERMTKNFIT..PSFISRK..YGLLSKEEAEEDAKKIEEVAFAAANQ.....HYEKQPDGDGGSAVQIYAKESSRLMLEVLK 100
Q8HO56.1    30 SFSIWPPTQRTRDAVVRRLVDTLGG..DTILCKR..YGAVPAADAEPAARGIEAEAFDAAAA..SGEAAATASVEEGIKALQLYSKEVSRRLLDFVK 120
QOD4Z3.2    44 SLSIWPPSQRTRDAVVRRLVQTLVA..PSILSQR..YGAVPEAEAGRAAAAVEAERYAAVTES.SSAAAAPASVEDGIEVLQAYSKEVSRRLLELAK 135
B9MVW8.1    56 SFSIWPPTQRTRDAIISRLIETLST..TSVLSKR..YGTIPKEEASEASRRIEEEAFSGAST.......VASSEKDGLEVLQLYSKEISKRMLETVK 141
QOIYC5.1    29 SFAVWPPTRRTRDAVVRRLVAVLSGDTTTTALRKRYRYGAVPAADAERAARAVEAQAFDAASA....SSSSSSVEDGIETLQLYSREVSNRLLAFVR 121
A9NWJ46.1   13 SIKLWPPSESTRLMLVERMTDNLSS..VSFFSRK..YGLLSKEEAAENAKRIEETAFLAAND.....HEAKEPNLDDSSVVQFYAREASKLMLEALK 100
Q9C500.1    57 SLRIWPPTQKTRDAVLNRLIETLST..ESILSKR..YGTLKSDDATTVAKLIEEEAYGVASN.......AVSSDDDGIKILELYSKEISKRMLESVK 142
Q2HRI7.1    25 MYSIWPPKQRTRDAVKNRLIETLST..PSVLTKR..YGTMSADEASAAAIQIEDEAFSVANA.......SSSTSNDNVTILEVYSKEISKRMIETVK 110
Q9M7N3.1    28 SFKIWPPTQRTREAVVRRLVETLTS..QSVLSKR..YGVIPEEDATSAARIIEEEAFSVASV.ASAASTGGRPEDEWIEVLHIYSQEIXQRVVESAK 119
Q9M7N6.1    25 SFSIWPPTQRTRDAVINRLIESLST..PSILSKR..YGTLPQDEASETARLIEEEAFAAAGS.......TASDADDGIEILQVYSKEISKRMIDTVK 110
Q9LE82.1    14 SVKMWJPPSKSTRLMLVERMTKNITT..PSIFSRK..YGLLSVEEAEQDAKRIEDLAFATANK.....HFQNEPDGDGTSAVHVYAKESSKLMLDVIK 101
Q9M651.2    13 SIKLWPPSLPTRKALIERITNNFSS..KTIFTEK..YGSLTKDQATENAKRIEDIAFSTANQ.....QFEREPDGDGGSAVQLYAKECSKLILEVLK 100
B9R748.1    48 SLSIWPPTQRTRDAVITRLIETLSS..PSVLSKR..YGTISHDEAESAARRIEDEAFGVANT.......ATSAEDDGLEILQLYSKEISRRMLDTVK 133
```

The sequences of different genes or proteins may be aligned side-by-side to measure their similarity. This alignment compares protein sequences containing WPP domains.

Since the Phage Φ-X174 was sequenced in 1977, the DNA sequences of thousands of organisms have been decoded and stored in databases. This sequence information is analyzed to determine genes that encode proteins, RNA genes, regulatory sequences, structural motifs, and repetitive sequences. A comparison of genes within a species or between different species can show similarities between protein functions, or relations between species (the use of molecular systematics to construct phylogenetic trees). With the growing amount of data, it long ago became impractical to analyze DNA sequences manually. Today, computer programs such as BLAST are used daily to search sequences from more than 260 000 organisms, containing over 190 billion nucleotides. These programs can compensate for mutations (exchanged, deleted or inserted bases) in the DNA sequence, to identify sequences that are related, but not identical. A variant of this sequence alignment is used in the sequencing process itself.

DNA Sequencing

Before sequences can be analyzed they have to be obtained. DNA sequencing is still a non-trivial problem as the raw data may be noisy or afflicted by weak signals. Algorithms have been developed for base calling for the various experimental approaches to DNA sequencing.

Sequence Assembly

Most DNA sequencing techniques produce short fragments of sequence that need to be assembled to obtain complete gene or genome sequences. The so-called shotgun sequencing technique (which was used, for example, by The Institute for Genomic Research (TIGR) to sequence the first bacterial genome, *Haemophilus influenzae*) generates the sequences of many thousands of small DNA fragments (ranging from 35 to 900 nucleotides long, depending on the sequencing technology). The ends of these fragments overlap and, when aligned properly by a genome assembly program, can be used to reconstruct the complete genome. Shotgun sequencing yields sequence data quickly, but the task of assembling the fragments can be quite complicated for larger genomes. For a genome as large as the human genome, it may take many days of CPU time on large-memory, multiprocessor computers to assemble the fragments, and the resulting assembly usually contains numerous gaps that must be filled in later. Shotgun sequencing is the method of choice for virtually all genomes sequenced today, and genome assembly algorithms are a critical area of bioinformatics research.

Genome Annotation

In the context of genomics, annotation is the process of marking the genes and other biological features in a DNA sequence. This process needs to be automated because most genomes are too large to annotate by hand, not to mention the desire to annotate as many genomes as possible, as the rate of sequencing has ceased to pose a bottleneck. Annotation is made possible by the fact that genes have recognisable start and stop regions, although the exact sequence found in these regions can vary between genes.

The first genome annotation software system was designed in 1995 by Owen White, who was part of the team at The Institute for Genomic Research that sequenced and analyzed the first genome of a free-living organism to be decoded, the bacterium *Haemophilus influenzae*. White built a software system to find the genes (fragments of genomic sequence that encode proteins), the transfer RNAs, and to make initial assignments of function to those genes. Most current genome annotation systems work similarly, but the programs available for analysis of genomic DNA, such as the GeneMark program trained and used to find protein-coding genes in *Haemophilus influenzae*, are constantly changing and improving.

Following the goals that the Human Genome Project left to achieve after its closure in 2003, a new project developed by the National Human Genome Research Institute in the U.S appeared. The so-called ENCODE project is a collaborative data collection of the functional elements of the human genome that uses next-generation DNA-sequencing technologies and genomic tiling arrays, technologies able to generate automatically large amounts of data with lower research costs but with the same quality and viability.

Computational Evolutionary Biology

Evolutionary biology is the study of the origin and descent of species, as well as their change over time. Informatics has assisted evolutionary biologists by enabling researchers to:

- trace the evolution of a large number of organisms by measuring changes in their DNA, rather than through physical taxonomy or physiological observations alone,

- more recently, compare entire genomes, which permits the study of more complex evolutionary events, such as gene duplication, horizontal gene transfer, and the prediction of factors important in bacterial speciation,

- build complex computational population genetics models to predict the outcome of the system over time

- track and share information on an increasingly large number of species and organisms

Future work endeavours to reconstruct the now more complex tree of life.

The area of research within computer science that uses genetic algorithms is sometimes confused with computational evolutionary biology, but the two areas are not necessarily related.

Comparative Genomics

The core of comparative genome analysis is the establishment of the correspondence between genes (orthology analysis) or other genomic features in different organisms. It is these intergenomic maps that make it possible to trace the evolutionary processes responsible for the divergence of two genomes. A multitude of evolutionary events acting at various organizational levels shape genome evolution. At the lowest level, point mutations affect individual nucleotides. At a higher level, large chromosomal segments undergo duplication, lateral transfer, inversion, transposition, deletion and insertion. Ultimately, whole genomes are involved in processes of hybridization, polyploidization and endosymbiosis, often leading to rapid speciation. The complexity of genome evolution poses many exciting challenges to developers of mathematical models and algorithms, who have recourse to a spectra of algorithmic, statistical and mathematical techniques, ranging from exact, heuristics, fixed parameter and approximation algorithms for problems based on parsimony models to Markov Chain Monte Carlo algorithms for Bayesian analysis of problems based on probabilistic models.

Many of these studies are based on the homology detection and protein families computation.

Pan Genomics

Pan genomics is a concept introduced in 2005 by Tettelin and Medini which eventually took root in bioinformatics. Pan genome is the complete gene repertoire of a particular taxonomic group: although initially applied to closely related strains of a species, it can be applied to a larger context like genus, phylum etc. It is divided in two parts- The Core genome: Set of genes common to all the genomes under study (These are often house-keeping genes vital for survival) and The Dispensable/Flexible Genome: Set of genes not present in all but one or some genomes under study. a bioinformatics tool BPGA can be used to characterize the Pan Genome of bacterial species.

Genetics of Disease

With the advent of next-generation sequencing we are obtaining enough sequence data to map the genes of complex diseases such as diabetes, infertility, breast cancer or Alzheimer's Disease. Genome-wide association studies are a useful approach to pinpoint the mutations responsible for such complex diseases. Through these studies, thousands of DNA variants have been identified that are associated with similar diseases and traits. Furthermore, the possibility for genes to be used at prognosis, diagnosis or treatment is one of the most essential applications. Many studies are discussing both the promising ways to choose the genes to be used and the problems and pitfalls of using genes to predict disease presence or prognosis.

Analysis of Mutations in Cancer

In cancer, the genomes of affected cells are rearranged in complex or even unpredictable ways. Massive sequencing efforts are used to identify previously unknown point mutations in a variety of genes in cancer. Bioinformaticians continue to produce specialized automated systems to manage the sheer volume of sequence data produced, and they create new algorithms and software to compare the sequencing results to the growing collection of human genome sequences and germline polymorphisms. New physical detection technologies are employed, such as oligonucleotide microarrays to identify chromosomal gains and losses (called comparative genomic hybridization), and single-nucleotide polymorphism arrays to detect known *point mutations*. These detection methods simultaneously measure several hundred thousand sites throughout the genome, and when used in high-throughput to measure thousands of samples, generate terabytes of data per experiment. Again the massive amounts and new types of data generate new opportunities for bioinformaticians. The data is often found to contain considerable variability, or noise, and thus Hidden Markov model and change-point analysis methods are being developed to infer real copy number changes.

With the breakthroughs that this next-generation sequencing technology is providing to the field of Bioinformatics, cancer genomics could drastically change. These new methods and software allow bioinformaticians to sequence many cancer genomes quickly and affordably. This could create a more flexible process for classifying types of cancer by analysis of cancer driven mutations in the genome. Furthermore, tracking of patients while the disease progresses may be possible in the future with the sequence of cancer samples.

Another type of data that requires novel informatics development is the analysis of lesions found to be recurrent among many tumors.

Gene and Protein Expression

Analysis of Gene Expression

The expression of many genes can be determined by measuring mRNA levels with multiple techniques including microarrays, expressed cDNA sequence tag (EST) sequencing, serial analysis of gene expression (SAGE) tag sequencing, massively parallel signature sequencing (MPSS), RNA-Seq, also known as "Whole Transcriptome Shotgun Sequencing" (WTSS), or various applications of multiplexed in-situ hybridization. All of these techniques are extremely noise-prone and/or subject to bias in the biological measurement, and a major research area in computational biology involves developing statistical tools to separate signal from noise in high-throughput gene expression studies. Such studies are often used to determine the genes implicated in a disorder: one might compare microarray data from cancerous epithelial cells to data from non-cancerous cells to determine the transcripts that are up-regulated and down-regulated in a particular population of cancer cells.

Analysis of Protein Expression

Protein microarrays and high throughput (HT) mass spectrometry (MS) can provide a snapshot of the proteins present in a biological sample. Bioinformatics is very much involved in making sense of protein microarray and HT MS data; the former approach faces similar problems as with microarrays targeted at mRNA, the latter involves the problem of matching large amounts of mass data against predicted masses from protein sequence databases, and the complicated statistical analysis of samples where multiple, but incomplete peptides from each protein are detected.

Analysis of Regulation

Regulation is the complex orchestration of events by which a signal, potentially an extracellular signal such as a hormone, eventually leads to an increase or decrease in the activity of one or more proteins. Bioinformatics techniques have been applied to explore various steps in this process.

For example, gene expression can be regulated by nearby elements in the genome. Promoter analysis involves the identification and study of sequence motifs in the DNA surrounding the coding region of a gene. These motifs influence the extent to which that region is transcribed into mRNA. Enhancer elements far away from the promoter can also regulate gene expression, through three-dimensional looping interactions. These interactions can be determined by bioinformatic analysis of chromosome conformation capture experiments.

Expression data can be used to infer gene regulation: one might compare microarray data from a wide variety of states of an organism to form hypotheses about the genes involved in each state. In a single-cell organism, one might compare stages of the cell cycle, along with various stress conditions (heat shock, starvation, etc.). One can then apply clustering algorithms to that expression data to determine which genes are co-expressed. For example, the upstream regions (promoters) of co-expressed genes can be searched for over-represented regulatory elements. Examples of clustering algorithms applied in gene clustering are k-means clustering, self-organizing maps (SOMs), hierarchical clustering, and consensus clustering methods.

Analysis of Cellular Organization

Several approaches have been developed to analyze the location of organelles, genes, proteins, and other components within cells. This is relevant as the location of these components affects the events within a cell and thus helps us to predict the behavior of biological systems. A gene ontology category, *cellular compartment*, has been devised to capture subcellular localization in many biological databases.

Microscopy and Image Analysis

Microscopic pictures allow us to locate both organelles as well as molecules. It may also help us to distinguish between normal and abnormal cells, e.g. in cancer.

Protein Localization

The localization of proteins helps us to evaluate the role of a protein. For instance, if a protein is found in the nucleus it may be involved in gene regulation or splicing. By contrast, if a protein is found in mitochondria, it may be involved in respiration or other metabolic processes. Protein localization is thus an important component of protein function prediction.

Chromosome Topology

Data from high-throughput chromosome conformation capture experiments, such as Hi-C (experiment) and ChIA-PET, can provide information on the spatial proximity of DNA loci. Anaylsis of these experiments can determine the three-dimensional structure and nuclear organization of chromatin. Bioinformatic challenges in this field include partitioning the genome into domains, such as Topologically Associating Domains (TADs), that are organised together in three-dimensional space.

Structural Bioinformatics

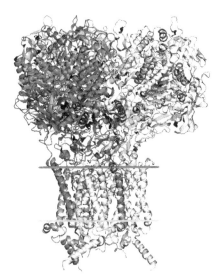

3-dimensional protein structures such as this one are common subjects in bioinformatic analyses.

Protein structure prediction is another important application of bioinformatics. The amino acid sequence of a protein, the so-called primary structure, can be easily determined from the sequence on the gene that codes for it. In the vast majority of cases, this primary structure uniquely determines a structure in its native environment. (Of course, there are exceptions, such as the bovine spongiform encephalopathy – a.k.a. Mad Cow Disease – prion.) Knowledge of this structure is vital in understanding the function of the protein. Structural information is usually classified as one of *secondary*, *tertiary* and *quaternary* structure. A viable general solution to such predictions remains an open problem. Most efforts have so far been directed towards heuristics that work most of the time.

One of the key ideas in bioinformatics is the notion of homology. In the genomic branch of bioinformatics, homology is used to predict the function of a gene: if the sequence of gene *A*, whose function is known, is homologous to the sequence of gene *B*, whose function is unknown, one could infer that B may share A's function. In the structural branch of bioinformatics, homology is used to determine which parts of a protein are important in structure formation and interaction with other proteins. In a technique called homology modeling, this information is used to predict the structure of a protein once the structure of a homologous protein is known. This currently remains the only way to predict protein structures reliably.

One example of this is the similar protein homology between hemoglobin in humans and the hemoglobin in legumes (leghemoglobin). Both serve the same purpose of transporting oxygen in the organism. Though both of these proteins have completely different amino acid sequences, their protein structures are virtually identical, which reflects their near identical purposes.

Other techniques for predicting protein structure include protein threading and *de novo* (from scratch) physics-based modeling.

Network and Systems Biology

Network analysis seeks to understand the relationships within biological networks such as metabolic or protein–protein interaction networks. Although biological networks can be constructed from a single type of molecule or entity (such as genes), network biology often attempts to integrate many different data types, such as proteins, small molecules, gene expression data, and others, which are all connected physically, functionally, or both.

Systems biology involves the use of computer simulations of cellular subsystems (such as the networks of metabolites and enzymes that comprise metabolism, signal transduction pathways and gene regulatory networks) to both analyze and visualize the complex connections of these cellular processes. Artificial life or virtual evolution attempts to understand evolutionary processes via the computer simulation of simple (artificial) life forms.

Molecular Interaction Networks

Interactions between proteins are frequently visualized and analyzed using networks. This network is made up of protein–protein interactions from *Treponema pallidum*, the causative agent of syphilis and other diseases.

Tens of thousands of three-dimensional protein structures have been determined by X-ray crystallography and protein nuclear magnetic resonance spectroscopy (protein NMR) and a central question in structural bioinformatics is whether it is practical to predict possible protein–protein interactions only based on these 3D shapes, without performing protein–protein interaction experiments. A variety of methods have been developed to tackle the protein–protein docking problem, though it seems that there is still much work to be done in this field.

Other interactions encountered in the field include Protein–ligand (including drug) and protein–peptide. Molecular dynamic simulation of movement of atoms about rotatable bonds is the fundamental principle behind computational algorithms, termed docking algorithms, for studying molecular interactions.

Others

Literature Analysis

The growth in the number of published literature makes it virtually impossible to read every paper, resulting in disjointed sub-fields of research. Literature analysis aims to employ computational and statistical linguistics to mine this growing library of text resources. For example:

- Abbreviation recognition – identify the long-form and abbreviation of biological terms

- Named entity recognition – recognizing biological terms such as gene names

- Protein–protein interaction – identify which proteins interact with which proteins from text

The area of research draws from statistics and computational linguistics.

High-throughput Image Analysis

Computational technologies are used to accelerate or fully automate the processing, quantification and analysis of large amounts of high-information-content biomedical imagery. Modern image analysis systems augment an observer's ability to make measurements from a large or complex set of images, by improving accuracy, objectivity, or speed. A fully developed analysis system may completely replace the observer. Although these systems are not unique to biomedical imagery, biomedical imaging is becoming more important for both diagnostics and research. Some examples are:

- high-throughput and high-fidelity quantification and sub-cellular localization (high-content screening, cytohistopathology, Bioimage informatics)

- morphometrics

- clinical image analysis and visualization

- determining the real-time air-flow patterns in breathing lungs of living animals

- quantifying occlusion size in real-time imagery from the development of and recovery during arterial injury

- making behavioral observations from extended video recordings of laboratory animals

- infrared measurements for metabolic activity determination

- inferring clone overlaps in DNA mapping, e.g. the Sulston score

High-throughput Single Cell Data Analysis

Computational techniques are used to analyse high-throughput, low-measurement single cell data, such as that obtained from flow cytometry. These methods typically involve finding populations of cells that are relevant to a particular disease state or experimental condition.

Biodiversity Informatics

Biodiversity informatics deals with the collection and analysis of biodiversity data, such as taxonomic databases, or microbiome data. Examples of such analyses include phylogenetics, niche modelling, species richness mapping, or species identification tools.

Databases

Databases are essential for bioinformatics research and applications. Many databases exist, covering various information types: for example, DNA and protein sequences, molecular structures, phenotypes and biodiversity. Databases may contain empirical data (obtained directly from experiments), predicted data (obtained from analysis), or, most commonly, both. They may be specific to a particular organism, pathway or molecule of interest. Alternatively, they can incorporate data compiled from multiple other databases. These databases vary in their format, way of accession and whether they are public or not.

Some of the most commonly used databases are listed below. For a more comprehensive list, please check the link at the beginning of the subsection.

- Used in Motif Finding: GenomeNet MOTIF Search
- Used in Gene Ontology: ToppGene FuncAssociate, Enrichr, GATHER
- Used in finding Protein Structures/Family: Pfam
- Used for Next Generation Sequencing: Sequence Read Archive
- Used in Gene Expression Analysis: GEO, ArrayExpress
- Used in Network Analysis: Interaction Analysis Databases(BioGRID, MINT, HPRD, Curated Human Signaling Network), Functional Networks (STRING, KEGG)
- Used in design of synthetic genetic circuits: GenoCAD

Software and Tools

Software tools for bioinformatics range from simple command-line tools, to more complex graphical programs and standalone web-services available from various bioinformatics companies or public institutions.

Open-source Bioinformatics Software

Many free and open-source software tools have existed and continued to grow since the 1980s. The combination of a continued need for new algorithms for the analysis of emerging types of biological readouts, the potential for innovative *in silico* experiments, and freely available open code bases have helped to create opportunities for all research groups to contribute to both bioinformatics and the range of open-source software available, regardless of their funding arrangements. The open source tools often act as incubators of ideas, or community-supported plug-ins in commercial applications. They may also provide *de facto* standards and shared object models for assisting with the challenge of bioinformation integration.

The range of open-source software packages includes titles such as Bioconductor, BioPerl, Biopython, BioJava, BioJS, BioRuby, Bioclipse, EMBOSS, .NET Bio, Orange with its bioinformatics add-on, Apache Taverna, UGENE and GenoCAD. To maintain this tradition and create further opportunities, the non-profit Open Bioinformatics Foundation have supported the annual Bioinformatics Open Source Conference (BOSC) since 2000.

An alternative method to build public bioinformatics databases is to use the MediaWiki engine with the *WikiOpener* extension. This system allows the database to be accessed and updated by all experts in the field.

Web Services in Bioinformatics

SOAP- and REST-based interfaces have been developed for a wide variety of bioinformatics applications allowing an application running on one computer in one part of the world to use algorithms, data and computing resources on servers in other parts of the world. The main advantages derive from the fact that end users do not have to deal with software and database maintenance overheads.

Basic bioinformatics services are classified by the EBI into three categories: SSS (Sequence Search Services), MSA (Multiple Sequence Alignment), and BSA (Biological Sequence Analysis). The availability of these service-oriented bioinformatics resources demonstrate the applicability of web-based bioinformatics solutions, and range from a collection of standalone tools with a common data format under a single, standalone or web-based interface, to integrative, distributed and extensible bioinformatics workflow management systems.

Bioinformatics Workflow Management Systems

A Bioinformatics workflow management system is a specialized form of a workflow management system designed specifically to compose and execute a series of computational or data manipulation steps, or a workflow, in a Bioinformatics application. Such systems are designed to

- provide an easy-to-use environment for individual application scientists themselves to create their own workflows

- provide interactive tools for the scientists enabling them to execute their workflows and view their results in real-time

- simplify the process of sharing and reusing workflows between the scientists.

- enable scientists to track the provenance of the workflow execution results and the workflow creation steps.

Some of the platforms giving this service: Galaxy, Kepler, Taverna, UGENE, Anduril.

Education Platforms

Software platforms designed to teach bioinformatics concepts and methods include Rosalind and online courses offered through the Swiss Institute of Bioinformatics Training Portal. The Canadian Bioinformatics Workshops provides videos and slides from training workshops on their website under a Creative Commons license. The 4273π project or 4273pi project also offers open source educational materials for free. The course runs on low cost raspberry pi computers and has been used to teach adults and school pupils. 4273π is actively developed by a consortium of academics and research staff who have run research level bioinformatics using raspberry pi computers and the 4273π operating system.

MOOC platforms also provide online certifications in bioinformatics and related disciplines, including Coursera's Bioinformatics Specialization (UC San Diego) and Genomic Data Science Specialization (Johns Hopkins) as well as EdX's Data Analysis for Life Sciences XSeries (Harvard).

Conferences

There are several large conferences that are concerned with bioinformatics. Some of the most notable examples are Intelligent Systems for Molecular Biology (ISMB), European Conference on Computational Biology (ECCB), and Research in Computational Molecular Biology (RECOMB).

Sequence Analysis

In bioinformatics, sequence analysis is the process of subjecting a DNA, RNA or peptide sequence to any of a wide range of analytical methods to understand its features, function, structure, or evolution. Methodologies used include sequence alignment, searches against biological databases, and others. Since the development of methods of high-throughput production of gene and protein sequences, the rate of addition of new sequences to the databases increased exponentially. Such a collection of sequences does not, by itself, increase the scientist's understanding of the biology of organisms. However, comparing these new sequences to those with known functions is a key way of understanding the biology of an organism from which the new sequence comes. Thus, sequence analysis can be used to assign function to genes and proteins by the study of the similarities between the compared sequences. Nowadays, there are many tools and techniques that provide the sequence comparisons (sequence alignment) and analyze the alignment product to understand its biology.

Sequence analysis in molecular biology includes a very wide range of relevant topics:

1. The comparison of sequences in order to find similarity, often to infer if they are related (homologous)

2. Identification of intrinsic features of the sequence such as active sites, post translational modification sites, gene-structures, reading frames, distributions of introns and exons and regulatory elements

3. Identification of sequence differences and variations such as point mutations and single nucleotide polymorphism (SNP) in order to get the genetic marker.

4. Revealing the evolution and genetic diversity of sequences and organisms

5. Identification of molecular structure from sequence alone

In chemistry, sequence analysis comprises techniques used to determine the sequence of a polymer formed of several monomers. In molecular biology and genetics, the same process is called simply "sequencing".

In marketing, sequence analysis is often used in analytical customer relationship management applications, such as NPTB models (Next Product to Buy).

In sociology, sequence methods are increasingly used to study life-course and career trajectories, patterns of organizational and national development, conversation and interaction structure, and the problem of work/family synchrony. This body of research has given rise to the emerging subfield of social sequence analysis.

History

Since the very first sequences of the insulin protein was characterised by Fred Sanger in 1951 biologists have been trying to use this knowledge to understand the function of molecules. According to Michael Levitt, sequence analysis was born in the period from 1969-1977. In 1969 the analysis of sequences of transfer RNAs were used to infer residuc interactions from correlated changes in the nucleotide sequences giving rise to a model of the tRNA secondary structure. In 1970, Saul B. Needleman and Christian D. Wunsch published the first computer algorithm for aligning two sequences. Over this time developments in obtaining nucleotide sequence greatly improved leading to the publication of the first complete genome of a bacteriophage in 1977.

Sequence Alignment

```
A5ASC3.1   14 SIKLWPPSQTTRLLLVERMANNLST..PSIFTRK..YGSLSKEEARENAKQIEEVACSTANQ.....HYEKEPDGDGGSAVQLYAKECSKLILEVLK 101
B4F917.1   13 SIKLWPPSESTRIMLVDRMTNNLST..ESIFSRK..YRLLGKQEAHENAKTIEELCFALADE.....HFREEPDGDGSSAVQLYAKETSKMMLEVLK 100
A9S1V2.1   23 VFKLWPPSQGTREAVRQKMALKLSS..ACFESQS..FARIELADAQEHARAIEEVAFGAAQE.....ADSGGDKTGSAVVMVYAKHASKLMLETLR 109
B9GSN7.1   13 SVKLWPPGQSTRLMLVERMTKNFIT..PSFISRK..YGLLSKEEAEEDAKKIEEVAFAAANQ.....HYEKQPDGDGSSAVQIYAKESSRLMLEVLK 100
Q8H056.1   30 SFSIWPPTQRTRDAVVRRLVDTLGG..DTILCKR..YGAVPAADAEPAARGIEAEAFDAAAA..SGEAAATASVEEGIKALQLYSKEVSRRLLDFVK 120
Q0D4Z3.2   44 SLSIWPPSQRTRDAVVRRLVQTLVA..PSILSQR..YGAVPEAEAGRAAAAVEAEAYAAVTES.SSAAAAPASVEDGIEVLQAYSKEVSRRLLELAK 135
B9MVW8.1   56 SFSIWPPTQRTRDAIISRLIETLST..TSVLSKR..YGTIPKEEASEASRRIEEEAFSGAST.......VASSEKDGLEVLQLYSKEISKRMLETVK 141
Q0IYC5.1   29 SFAVWPPTRRTRDAVVRRLVAVLSGDTTTALRKRYRYGAVPAADAERAARAVEAQAFDAASA....SSSSSSSVEDGIETLQLYSREVSNRLLAFVR 121
A9NWJ46.1  13 SIKLWPPSESTRLMLVERMTDNLSS..VSFFSRK..YGLLSKEEAAENAKRIEETAFLAAND....HEAKEPNLDDSSVVQFYAREASKLMLEALK 100
Q9C500.1   57 SLRIWPPTQKTRDAVLNRLIETLST..ESILSKR..YGTLKSDDATTVAKLIEEEAYGVASN......AVSSDDDGIKILELYSKEISKRMLESVK 142
Q2HRI7.1   25 MYSIWPPKQRTRDAVKNRLIETLST..PSVLTKR..YGTMSADEASAAAIQIEDEAFSVANA......SSSTSNDNVTILEVYSKEISKRMIETVK 110
Q9M7N3.1   28 SFKIWPPTQRTREAVVRRLVETLTS..QSVLSKR..YGVIPEEDATSAARIIEEEAFSVASV.ASAASTGGRPEDEWIEVLHIYSQEIXQRVVESAK 119
Q9M7N6.1   25 SFSIWPPTQRTRDAVINRLIESLST..PSILSKR..YGTLPQDEASETARLIEEEAFAAAGS......TASDADDGIEILQVYSKEISKRMIDTVK 110
Q9LE82.1   14 SVKMWPPSKSTRLMLVERMTKNITT..PSIFSRK..YGLLSVEEAEQDAKRIEDLAFATANK.....HFQNEPDGDGTSAVHVYAKESSKLMLDVIK 101
Q9M651.2   13 SIKLWPPSLPTRKALIERITNNFSS..KTIFTEK..YGSLTKDQATENAKRIEDIAFSTANQ.....QFEREPDGDGGSAVQLYAKECSKLILEVLK 100
B9R748.1   48 SLSIWPPTQRTRDAVITRLIETLSS..PSVLSKR..YGTISHDEAESAARRIEDEAFGVANT.......ATSAEDDGLEILQLYSKEISRRMLDTVK 133
```

Example multiple sequence alignment

There are millions of protein and nucleotide sequences known. These sequences fall into many groups of related sequences known as protein families or gene families. Relationships between these sequences are usually discovered by aligning them together and assigning this alignment a score. There are two main types of sequence alignment. Pair-wise sequence alignment only compares two sequences at a time and multiple sequence alignment compares many sequences in one go. Two important algorithms for aligning pairs of sequences are the Needleman-Wunsch algorithm and the Smith-Waterman algorithm. Popular tools for sequence alignment include:

- Pair-wise alignment - BLAST

- Multiple alignment - ClustalW, PROBCONS, MUSCLE, MAFFT, and T-Coffee.

A common use for pairwise sequence alignment is to take a sequence of interest and compare it to all known sequences in a database to identify homologous sequences. In general the matches in the database are ordered to show the most closely related sequences first followed by sequences with diminishing similarity. These matches are usually reported with a measure of statistical significance such as an Expectation value.

Profile Comparison

In 1987, Michael Gribskov, Andrew McLachlan, and David Eisenberg introduced the method of profile comparison for identifying distant similarities between proteins. Rather than using a single sequence, profile methods use a multiple sequence alignment to encode a profile which contains information about the conservation level of each residue. These profiles can then be used to search collections of sequences to find sequences that are related. Profiles are also known as Position Specific Scoring Matrices (PSSMs). In 1993, a probabilistic interpretation of profiles was introduced by David Haussler and colleagues using hidden Markov models. These models have become known as profile-HMMs.

In recent years, methods have been developed that allow the comparison of profiles directly to each other. These are known as profile-profile comparison methods.

Sequence Assembly

Sequence assembly refers to the reconstruction of a DNA sequence by aligning and merging small DNA fragments. It is an integral part of modern DNA sequencing. Since presently-available DNA sequencing technologies are ill-suited for reading long sequences, large pieces of DNA (such as genomes) are often sequenced by (1) cutting the DNA into small pieces, (2) reading the small fragments, and (3) reconstituting the original DNA by merging the information on various fragment.

Gene Prediction

Gene prediction or gene finding refers to the process of identifying the regions of genomic DNA that encode genes. This includes protein-coding genes as well as RNA genes, but may also include prediction of other functional elements such as regulatory regions. Gene finding is one of the first and most important steps in understanding the genome of a species once it has been sequenced. In general the prediction of bacterial genes is significantly simpler and more accurate than the prediction of genes in eukaryotic species that usually have complex intron/exon patterns.

Protein Structure Prediction

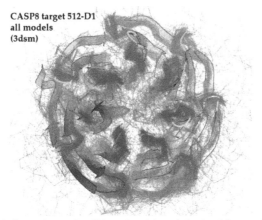

CASP8 target 512-D1
all models
(3dsm)

Target protein structure (3dsm, shown in ribbons), with Calpha backbones (in gray) of 354 predicted models for it submitted in the CASP8 structure-prediction experiment.

The 3D structures of molecules are of great importance to their functions in nature. Since structural prediction of large molecules at an atomic level is largely intractable problem, some biologists introduced ways to predict 3D structure at a primary sequence level. This includes biochemical or statistical analysis of amino acid residues in local regions and structural inference from homologs (or other potentially related proteins) with known 3D structures.

There have been a large number of diverse approaches to solve the structure prediction problem. In order to determine which methods were most effective a structure prediction competition was founded called CASP (Critical Assessment of Structure Prediction).

Methodology

The tasks that lie in the space of sequence analysis are often non-trivial to resolve and require the use of relatively complex approaches. Of the many types of methods used in practice, the most popular include:

- DNA patterns
- Dynamic programming
- Artificial Neural Network
- Hidden Markov Model
- Support Vector Machine
- Clustering
- Bayesian Network
- Regression Analysis
- Sequence mining
- Alignment-free sequence analysis

Sequence Assembly

In bioinformatics, sequence assembly refers to aligning and merging fragments from a longer DNA sequence in order to reconstruct the original sequence. This is needed as DNA sequencing technology cannot read whole genomes in one go, but rather reads small pieces of between 20 and 30000 bases, depending on the technology used. Typically the short fragments, called reads, result from shotgun sequencing genomic DNA, or gene transcript (ESTs).

The problem of sequence assembly can be compared to taking many copies of a book, passing each of them through a shredder with a different cutter, and piecing the text of the book back together just by looking at the shredded pieces. Besides the obvious difficulty of this task, there are some extra practical issues: the original may have many repeated paragraphs, and some shreds may be modified during shredding to have typos. Excerpts from another book may also be added in, and some shreds may be completely unrecognizable.

Genome Assemblers

The first sequence assemblers began to appear in the late 1980s and early 1990s as variants of simpler sequence alignment programs to piece together vast quantities of fragments generated by automated sequencing instruments called DNA sequencers. As the sequenced organisms grew in size and complexity (from small viruses over plasmids to bacteria and finally eukaryotes), the assembly programs used in these genome projects needed increasingly sophisticated strategies to handle:

- terabytes of sequencing data which need processing on computing clusters;

- identical and nearly identical sequences (known as *repeats*) which can, in the worst case, increase the time and space complexity of algorithms exponentially;

- errors in the fragments from the sequencing instruments, which can confound assembly.

Faced with the challenge of assembling the first larger eukaryotic genomes—the fruit fly Drosophila melanogaster in 2000 and the human genome just a year later,—scientists developed assemblers like Celera Assembler and Arachne able to handle genomes of 100-300 million base pairs. Subsequent to these efforts, several other groups, mostly at the major genome sequencing centers, built large-scale assemblers, and an open source effort known as AMOS was launched to bring together all the innovations in genome assembly technology under the open source framework.

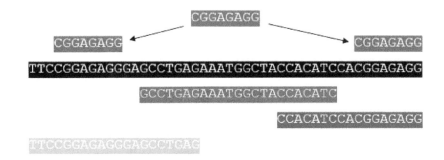

Sample sequence showing how a sequence assembler would take fragments and match by overlaps. Image also shows the potential problem of repeats in the sequence.

EST Assemblers

Expressed Sequence Tag or EST assembly differs from genome assembly in several ways. The sequences for EST assembly are the transcribed mRNA of a cell and represent only a subset of the whole genome. At a first glance, underlying algorithmical problems differ between genome and EST assembly. For instance, genomes often have large amounts of repetitive sequences, mainly in the inter-genic parts. Since ESTs represent gene transcripts, they will not contain these repeats. On the other hand, cells tend to have a certain number of genes that are constantly expressed in very high numbers (housekeeping genes), which again leads to the problem of similar sequences present in high numbers in the data set to be assembled.

Furthermore, genes sometimes overlap in the genome (sense-antisense transcription), and should ideally still be assembled separately. EST assembly is also complicated by features like (cis-) alternative splicing, trans-splicing, single-nucleotide polymorphism, and post-transcriptional modification.

De-novo vs. Mapping Assembly

In sequence assembly, two different types can be distinguished:

1. de-novo: assembling short reads to create full-length (sometimes novel) sequences

2. mapping: assembling reads against an existing backbone sequence, building a sequence that is similar but not necessarily identical to the backbone sequence

In terms of complexity and time requirements, de-novo assemblies are orders of magnitude slower and more memory intensive than mapping assemblies. This is mostly due to the fact that the assembly algorithm needs to compare every read with every other read (an operation that has a naive time complexity of $O(n^2)$; using a hash this can be reduced significantly). Referring to the comparison drawn to shredded books in the introduction: while for mapping assemblies one would have a very similar book as template (perhaps with the names of the main characters and a few locations changed), the de-novo assemblies are more hardcore in a sense as one would not know beforehand whether this would become a science book, a novel, a catalogue, or even several books. Also, every shred would be compared with every other shred.

Influence of Technological Changes

The complexity of sequence assembly is driven by two major factors: the number of fragments and their lengths. While more and longer fragments allow better identification of sequence overlaps, they also pose problems as the underlying algorithms show quadratic or even exponential complexity behaviour to both number of fragments and their length. And while shorter sequences are faster to align, they also complicate the layout phase of an assembly as shorter reads are more difficult to use with repeats or near identical repeats.

In the earliest days of DNA sequencing, scientists could only gain a few sequences of short length (some dozen bases) after weeks of work in laboratories. Hence, these sequences could be aligned in a few minutes by hand.

In 1975, the *Dideoxy termination* method (AKA *Sanger sequencing*) was invented and until shortly after 2000, the technology was improved up to a point where fully automated machines could churn out sequences in a highly parallelised mode 24 hours a day. Large genome centers around the world housed complete farms of these sequencing machines, which in turn led to the necessity of assemblers to be optimised for sequences from whole-genome shotgun sequencing projects where the reads

- are about 800–900 bases long

- contain sequencing artifacts like sequencing and cloning vectors

- have error rates between 0.5 and 10%

With the Sanger technology, bacterial projects with 20,000 to 200,000 reads could easily be assembled on one computer. Larger projects, like the human genome with approximately 35 million reads, needed large computing farms and distributed computing.

By 2004 / 2005, pyrosequencing had been brought to commercial viability by 454 Life Sciences. This new sequencing method generated reads much shorter than those of Sanger sequencing: initially about 100 bases, now 400-500 bases. Its much higher throughput and lower cost (compared to Sanger sequencing) pushed the adoption of this technology by genome centers, which in turn pushed development of sequence assemblers that could efficiently handle the read sets. The sheer amount of data coupled with technology-specific error patterns in the reads delayed development of assemblers; at the beginning in 2004 only the Newbler assembler from 454 was available. Released in mid-2007, the hybrid version of the MIRA assembler by Chevreux et al. was the first freely available assembler that could assemble 454 reads as well as mixtures of 454 reads and Sanger reads. Assembling sequences from different sequencing technologies was subsequently coined *hybrid assembly*.

From 2006, the Illumina (previously Solexa) technology has been available and can generate about 100 million reads per run on a single sequencing machine. Compare this to the 35 million reads of the human genome project which needed several years to be produced on hundreds of sequencing machines. Illumina was initially limited to a length of only 36 bases, making it less suitable for de novo assembly (such as de novo transcriptome assembly), but newer iterations of the technology achieve read lengths above 100 bases from both ends of a 3-400bp clone. Announced at the end of 2007, the SHARCGS assembler by Dohm et al. was the first published assembler that was used for an assembly with Solexa reads. It was quickly followed by a number of others.

Later, new technologies like SOLiD from Applied Biosystems, Ion Torrent and SMRT were released and new technologies (e.g. Nanopore sequencing) continue to emerge.

Greedy Algorithm

Given a set of sequence fragments the object is to find the shortest common supersequence.

1. Calculate pairwise alignments of all fragments.

2. Choose two fragments with the largest overlap.

3. Merge chosen fragments.

4. Repeat step 2 and 3 until only one fragment is left.

The result need not be an optimal solution to the problem.

Available Assemblers

The following table lists assemblers that have a de-novo assembly capability on at least one of the supported technologies.

Name	Type	Technologies	Author	Presented / Last updated	Licence*
ABySS	(large) genomes	Solexa, SOLiD	Simpson, J. et al.	2008 / 2014	NC-A
ALLPATHS-LG	(large) genomes	Solexa, SOLiD	Gnerre, S. et al.	2011	OS
AMOS	genomes	Sanger, 454	Salzberg, S. et al.	2002? / 2011	OS
Arapan-M	Medium Genomes (e.g. E.coli)	All	Sahli, M. & Shibuya, T.	2011 / 2012	OS
Arapan-S	Small Genomes (Viruses and Bacteria)	All	Sahli, M. & Shibuya, T.	2011 / 2012	OS
Celera WGA Assembler / CABOG	(large) genomes	Sanger, 454, Solexa	Myers, G. et al.; Miller G. et al.	2004 / 2015	OS
CLC Genomics Workbench & CLC Assembly Cell	genomes	Sanger, 454, Solexa, SOLiD	CLC bio	2008 / 2010 / 2014	C
Cortex	genomes	Solexa, SOLiD	Iqbal, Z. et al.	2011	OS
DBG2OLC	(large) genomes	Illumina, PacBio, Oxford Nanopore	Ye, C. et al	2014/2016	OS
DNA Baser Assembler	(small) genomes	Sanger, 454	Heracle Bio-Soft SRL	04.2016	C
DNA Dragon	genomes	Illumina, SOLiD, Complete Genomics, 454, Sanger	SequentiX	2011	C
DNAnexus	genomes	Illumina, SOLiD, Complete Genomics	DNAnexus	2011	C

DNASTAR Lasergene Genomics Suite	(large) genomes, exomes, transcriptomes, metagenomes, ESTs	Illumina, ABI SOLiD, Roche 454, Ion Torrent, Solexa, Sanger	DNASTAR	2007 / 2016	C
Edena	genomes	Illumina	D. Hernandez, P. François, L. Farinelli, M. Osteras, and J. Schrenzel.	2008/2013	OS
Euler	genomes	Sanger, 454 („Solexa ?)	Pevzner, P. et al.	2001 / 2006?	(C / NC-A?)
Euler-sr	genomes	454, Solexa	Chaisson, MJ. et al.	2008	NC-A
Fermi	(large) genomes	Illumina	Li, H.	2012	OS
Forge	(large) genomes, EST, metagenomes	454, Solexa, SOLiD, Sanger	Platt, DM, Evers, D.	2010	OS
Geneious	genomes	Sanger, 454, Solexa, Ion Torrent, Complete Genomics, PacBio, Oxford Nanopore, Illumina	Biomatters Ltd	2009 / 2013	C
Graph Constructor	(large) genomes	Sanger, 454, Solexa, SOLiD	Convey Computer Corporation	2011	C
HINGE	genomes	PacBio/Oxford Nanopore	Kamath, Shomorony, Xia et. al.	2016	OS
IDBA (Iterative De Bruijn graph short read Assembler)	(large) genomes	Sanger,454,Solexa	Yu Peng, Henry C. M. Leung, Siu-Ming Yiu, Francis Y. L. Chin	2010	(C / NC-A?)
LIGR Assembler (derived from TIGR Assembler)	genomic	Sanger	-	2009/ 2012	OS
MaSuRCA (Maryland Super Read - Celera Assembler)	(large) genomes	Sanger, Illumina, 454	Aleksey Zimin, Guillaume Marçais, Daniela Puiu, Michael Roberts, Steven L. Salzberg, James A. Yorke	2012 / 2013	OS

MIRA (Mimicking Intelligent Read Assembly)	genomes, ESTs	Sanger, 454, Solexa	Chevreux, B.	1998 / 2014	OS
NextGENe	(small genomes?)	454, Solexa, SOLiD	Softgenetics	2008	C
Newbler	genomes, ESTs	454, Sanger	454/Roche	2004/2012	C
PADENA	genomes	454, Sanger	454/Roche	2010	OS
PASHA	(large) genomes	Illumina	Liu, Schmidt, Maskell	2011	OS
Phrap	genomes	Sanger, 454, Solexa	Green, P.	1994 / 2008	C / NC-A
TIGR Assembler	genomic	Sanger	-	1995 / 2003	OS
Trinity	Transcriptomes	short reads (paired, oriented, mixed) Illumina, 454, Solid,...	Grabher, MG et al.	2011/2016	OS
Ray	genomes	Illumina, mix of Illumina and 454, paired or not	Sébastien Boisvert, François Laviolette & Jacques Corbeil.	2010	OS [GNU General Public License]
Sequencher	genomes	traditional and next generation sequence data	Gene Codes Corporation	1991 / 2009 / 2011	C
SGA	(large) genomes	Illumina, Sanger (Roche 454?, Ion Torrent?)	Simpson, J.T. et al.	2011 / 2012	OS
SHARCGS	(small) genomes	Solexa	Dohm et al.	2007 / 2007	OS
SOPRA	genomes	Illumina, SOLiD, Sanger, 454	Dayarian, A. et al.	2010 / 2011	OS
SparseAssembler	(large) genomes	Illumina, 454, Ion torrent	Ye, C. et al.	2012 / 2012	OS
SSAKE	(small) genomes	Solexa (SOLiD? Helicos?)	Warren, R. et al.	2007 / 2014	OS
SOAPdenovo	genomes	Solexa	Luo, R. et al.	2009 / 2013	OS
SPAdes	(small) genomes, single-cell	Illumina, Solexa, Sanger, 454, Ion Torrent, PacBio, Oxford Nanopore	Bankevich, A et al.	2012 / 2015	OS
Staden gap4 package	BACs (, small genomes?)	Sanger	Staden et al.	1991 / 2008	OS
Taipan	(small) genomes	Illumina	Schmidt, B. et al.	2009 / 2009	OS

VCAKE	(small) genomes	Solexa (SOLiD?, Helicos?)	Jeck, W. et al.	2007 / 2009	OS
Phusion assembler	(large) genomes	Sanger	Mullikin JC, et al.	2003 / 2006	OS
Quality Value Guided SRA (QSRA)	genomes	Sanger, Solexa	Bryant DW, et al.	2009 / 2009	OS
Velvet	(small) genomes	Sanger, 454, Solexa, SOLiD	Zerbino, D. et al.	2007 / 2011	OS
*Licences: OS = Open Source; C = Commercial; C / NC-A = Commercial but free for non-commercial and academics; Brackets = unclear, but most likely C / NC-A					

Alignment-free Sequence Analysis

On bioinformatics, alignment-free sequence analysis approaches to molecular sequence and structure data provide alternatives over alignment-based approaches.

The emergence and need for the analysis of different types of data generated through biological research has given rise to the field of bioinformatics. Molecular sequence and structure data of DNA, RNA, and proteins, gene expression profiles or microarray data, metabolic pathway data are some of the major types of data being analysed in bioinformatics. Among them sequence data is increasing at the exponential rate due to advent of next-generation sequencing technologies. Since the origin of bioinformatics, sequence analysis has remained the major area of research with wide range of applications in database searching, genome annotation, comparative genomics, molecular phylogeny and gene prediction. The pioneering approaches for sequence analysis were based on sequence alignment either global or local, pairwise or multiple sequence alignment. Alignment-based approaches generally give excellent results when the sequences under study are closely related and can be reliably aligned, but when the sequences are divergent, a reliable alignment cannot be obtained and hence the applications of sequence alignment are limited. Another limitation of alignment-based approaches is their computational complexity and are time-consuming and thus, are limited when dealing with large-scale sequence data. The advent of next-generation sequencing technologies has resulted in generation of voluminous sequencing data. The size of this sequence data poses challenges on alignment-based algorithms in their assembly, annotation and comparative studies.

Alignment-free Methods

Alignment-free methods can broadly be classified into four categories: a) methods based on k-mer/word frequency, b) methods based on substrings, c) methods based on information theory and d) methods based on graphical representation. Alignment-free approaches have been used in sequence similarity searches, clustering and classification of sequences, and more recently in phylogenetics (Figure 1).

Such molecular phylogeny analyses employing alignment-free approaches are said to be part of *next-generation phylogenomics*. A number of review articles provide in-depth review of alignment-free methods in sequence analysis.

Methods Based on k-mer/Word Frequency

The popular methods based on k-mer/word frequencies include feature frequency profile (FFP), Composition vector (CV), Return time distribution (RTD), frequency chaos game representation (FCGR). and Spaced Words

Feature Frequency Profile (Ffp)

The methodology involved in FFP based method starts by calculating the count of each possible k-mer (possible number of k-mers for nucleotide sequence: 4^k, while that for protein sequence: 20^k) in sequences. Each k-mer count in each sequence is then normalized by dividing it by total of all k-mers' count in that sequence. This leads to conversion of each sequence into its feature frequency profile. The pair wise distance between two sequences is then calculated Jensen–Shannon (JS) divergence between their respective FFPs. The distance matrix thus obtained can be used to construct phylogenetic tree using clustering algorithms like neighbor-joining, UPGMA etc.

Composition Vector (CV)

In this method frequency of appearance of each possible k-mer in a given sequence is calculated. The next characteristic step of this method is the subtraction of random background of these frequencies using Markov model to reduce the influence of random neutral mutations to highlight the role of selective evolution. The normalized frequencies are put a fixed order to form the composition vector (CV) of a given sequence. Cosine distance function is then used to compute pairwise distance between CVs of sequences. The distance matrix thus obtained can be used to construct phylogenetic tree using clustering algorithms like neighbor-joining, UPGMA etc. This method can be extended through resort to efficient pattern matching algorithms to include in the computation of the composition vectors: (i) all k-mers for any value of k, (ii) all substrings of any length up to an arbitrarily set maximum k value, (iii) all maximal substrings, where a substring is maximal if extending it by any character would cause a decrease in its occurrence count.

Return Time Distribution (RTD)

The RTD based method does not calculate the count of k-mers in sequences, instead it computes the time required for the reappearance of k-mers. The time refers to the number of residues in successive appearance of particular k-mer. Thus the occurrence of each k-mer in a sequence is calculated in the form of RTD, which is then summarised using two statistical parameters mean (μ) and standard deviation (σ). Thus each sequence is represented in the form of numeric vector of size $2 \cdot 4^k$ containing μ and σ of 4^k RTDs. The pair wise distance between sequences is calculated using Euclidean distance measure. The distance matrix thus obtained can be used to construct phylogenetic tree using clustering algorithms like neighbor-joining, UPGMA etc.

Frequency Chaos Game Representation (FCGR)

The FCGR methods have evolved from chaos game representation (CGR) technique, which provides scale independent representation for genomic sequences. The CGRs can be divided by grid lines where each grid square denotes the occurrence of oligonucleotides of a specific length in the sequence. Such representation of CGRs is termed as Frequency Chaos Game Representation (FCGR). This leads to representation of each sequence into FCGR. The pair wise distance between FCGRs of sequences can be calculated using the Pearson distance, the Hamming distance or the Euclidean distance.

Spaced-word Frequencies

While most alignment-free algorithms compare the word-composition of sequences, Spaced Words uses a pattern of care and don't care positions. The occurrence of a spaced word in a sequence is then defined by the characters at the match positions only, while the characters at the don't care positions are ignored. Instead of comparing the frequencies of contiguous words in the input sequences, this approach compares the frequencies of the spaced words according to the pre-defined pattern.

Methods Based on Substrings

The methods in this category employ the similarity and differences of substrings in a pair of sequences. These algorithms were mostly used for string processing in computer science.

Average Common Substring (ACS)

In this approach, for a chosen pair of sequences (A and B of lengths ℓ and m respectively), longest substring starting at some position is identified in one sequence (A) which exactly matches in the other sequence (B) at any position. In this way, lengths of longest substrings starting at different positions in sequence A and having exact matches at some positions in sequence B are calculated. All these lengths are averaged to derive a measure $L(A,B)$. Intuitively, larger the $L(A,B)$, the more similar the two sequences are. To account for the differences in the length of sequences, $L(A,B)$ is normalized [i.e. $L(A,B)>$]. This gives the similarity measure between the sequences.

In order to derive a distance measure, the inverse of similarity measure is taken and a correction term is subtracted from it to assure that $d(A,A)$ will be zero. Thus

$$d(A,B) = \left[\frac{\log m}{L(A,B)} \right] - \left[\frac{\log n}{L(A,A)} \right].$$

This measure $d(A,B)$ is not symmetric, so one has to compute $d_s(A,B) = d_s(B,A) = (d(A,B)+d(B,A))/2$, which gives final ACS measure between the two strings (A and B). The subsequence/substring search can be efficiently performed by using suffix trees.

K-Mismatch Average Common Substring Approach (kmacs)

This approach is a generalization of the ACS approach. To define the distance between two DNA or protein sequences, kmacs estimates for each position i of the first sequence the longest substring starting at i and matching a substring of the second sequence with up to k mismatches. It defines the average of these values as a measure of similarity between the sequences and turns this into a symmetric distance measure. Kmacs does not compute exact k-mismatch substrings, since this would be computational too costly, but approximates such substrings.

Mutation Distances (Kr)

This approach is closely related to the ACS, which calculates the number of substitutions per site between two DNA sequences using the shortest absent substring (termed as shustring).

Methods Based on Information Theory

Information Theory has provided successful methods for alignment-free sequence analysis and comparison. The existing applications of information theory include global and local characterization of DNA, RNA and proteins, estimating genome entropy to motif and region classification. It also holds promise in gene mapping, next-generation sequencing analysis and metagenomics.

Base–base Correlation (BBC)

Base–base correlation (BBC) converts the genome sequence into a unique 16-dimensional numeric vector using the following equation,

$$T_{ij}(K) = \sum_{\ell=1}^{K} P_{ij}(\ell) \cdot \log_2 \left(\frac{P_{ij}(\ell)}{P_i P_j} \right)$$

The P_i and P_j denotes the probabilities of bases i and j in the genome. The $P_{ij}(\ell)$ indicates the probability of bases i and j at distance ℓ in the genome. The parameter K indicates the maximum distance between the bases i and j. The variation in the values of 16 parameters reflect variation in the genome content and length.

Information Correlation and Partial Information Correlation (IC-PIC)

IC-PIC (information correlation and partial information correlation) based method employs the base correlation property of DNA sequence. IC and PIC were calculated using following formulas,

$$IC_\ell = -2\sum_i P_i \log_2 P_i + \sum_{ij} P_{ij}(\ell) \log_2 P_{ij}(\ell)$$

$$PIC_{ij}(\ell) = (P_{ij}(\ell) - P_i P_j(\ell))^2$$

The final vector is obtained as follows:

$$V = \frac{IC_\ell}{PIC_{ij}(\ell)} \text{ where } \ell \in \{\ell_0, \ell_0 + 1, \ldots, \ell_0 + n\},$$

which defines the range of distance between bases.

The pair wise distance between sequences is calculated using Euclidean distance measure. The distance matrix thus obtained can be used to construct phylogenetic tree using clustering algorithms like neighbor-joining, UPGMA etc.

Lempel–Ziv Compress

Lempel–Ziv complexity uses the relative information between the sequences. This complexity is measured by the number of steps required to generate a string given the prior knowledge of another string and a self-delimiting production process. This measure has a relation to measuring k-words in a sequence, as they can be easily used to generate the sequence. It is computational intensive method. Otu and Sayood (2003) used this method to construct five different distance measures for phylogenetic tree construction.

Context Modeling Compress

In the context modeling complexity the next-symbol predictions, of one or more statistical models, are combined or competing to yield a prediction that is based on events recorded in the past. The algorithmic information content derived from each symbol prediction can be used to compute algorithmic information profiles with a time proportional to the length of the sequence. The process has been applied to DNA sequence analysis.

Methods Based on Graphical Representation

Iterated Maps

The use of iterated maps for sequence analysis was first introduced by HJ Jefferey in 1990 when he proposed to apply the Chaos Game to map genomic sequences into a unit square. That report coined the procedure as Chaos Game Representation (CGR). However, only 3 years later this approach was first dismissed as a projection of a Markov transition table by N Goldman. This objection was overruled by the end of that decade when the opposite was found to be the case – that CGR bijectively maps Markov transition is into a fractal, order-free (degree-free) representation. The realization that iterated maps provide a bijective map between the symbolic space and numeric space led to the identification of a variety of alignment-free approaches to sequence comparison and characterization. These developments were reviewed in late 2013 by JS Almeida in. A number of web apps such as http://usm.github.com are available to demonstrate how to encode and compare arbitrary symbolic sequences.

Comparison of Alignment Based and Alignment-free Methods

Alignment-based methods	Alignment-free methods
These methods assume that homologous regions are contiguous (with gaps)	Does not assume such contiguity of homologous regions
Computes all possible pairwise comparisons of sequences; hence computationally expensive	Based on occurrences of sub-sequences; composition; computationally inexpensive, can be memory-intensive
Well-established approach in phylogenomics	Relatively recent and application in phylogenomics is limited; needs further testing for robustness and scalability
Requires substitution/evolutionary models	Less dependent on substitution/evolutionary models
Sensitive to stochastic sequence variation, recombination, horizontal (or lateral) genetic transfer, rate heterogeneity and sequences of varied lengths, especially when similarity lies in the "twilight zone"	Less sensitive to stochastic sequence variation, recombination, horizontal (or lateral) genetic transfer, rate heterogeneity and sequences of varied lengths
Best practice uses inference algorithms with complexity at least $O(n^2)$; less time-efficient	Inference algorithms typically $O(n^2)$ or less; more time-efficient

Heuristic in nature; statistical significance of how alignment scores relate to homology is difficult to assess	Exact solutions; statistical significance of the sequence distances (and degree of similarity) can be readily assessed

Applications of Alignment-free Methods

- Genomic rearrangements

- Molecular phylogenetics

- Metagenomics

- Next generation sequence data analysis

- Epigenomics

- Barcoding of species

- Population genetics

- Horizontal gene transfer

- Sero/genotyping of viruses

- Allergenicity prediction

- SNP discovery

- Recombination detection

List of Web Servers/Software for Alignment-free Methods

Name	Description	Availability
kmacs	k-mismatch average common substring approach	kmacs
Spaced words	Spaced-word frequencies	spaced-words
FFP	Feature frequency profile based phylogeny	FFP
CVTree	Composition vector based server for phylogeny	CVTree
RTD Phylogeny	Return time distribution based server for phylogeny	RTD Phylogeny
AGP	A multimethods web server for alignment-free genome phylogeny	AGP
Alfy	Alignment-free detection of local similarity among viral and bacterial genomes	Alfy
decaf+py	DistancE Calculation using Alignment-Free methods in PYthon	decaf+py
Dengue Subtyper	Genotyping of Dengue viruses based on RTD	Dengue Subtyper
WNV Typer	Genotyping of West nile viruses based on RTD	WNV Typer

AllergenFP	Allergenicity prediction by descriptor fingerprints	AllergenFP
kSNP v2	Alignment-Free SNP Discovery	kSNP v2
d2Tools	Comparison of Metatranscriptomic Samples Based on k-Tuple Frequencies	d2Tools
rush	Recombination detection Using SHustrings	rush
smash	Genomic rearrangements detection and visualisation	smash
GScompare	Oligonucleotide-based fast clustering of bacterial genomes	GScompare
COMET	Alignment-free subtyping of HIV-1, HIV-2 and HCV viral sequences	COMET

Sequence Alignment

In bioinformatics, a sequence alignment is a way of arranging the sequences of DNA, RNA, or protein to identify regions of similarity that may be a consequence of functional, structural, or evolutionary relationships between the sequences. Aligned sequences of nucleotide or amino acid residues are typically represented as rows within a matrix. Gaps are inserted between the residues so that identical or similar characters are aligned in successive columns. Sequence alignments are also used for non-biological sequences, such as calculating the edit distance cost between strings in a natural language or in financial data.

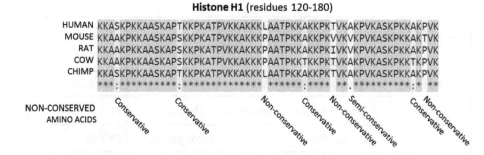

A sequence alignment, produced by ClustalO, of mammalian histone proteins.
Sequences are the amino acids for residues 120-180 of the proteins. Residues that are conserved across all sequences are highlighted in grey. Below the protein sequences is a key denoting conserved sequence (*), conservative mutations (:), semi-conservative mutations (.), and non-conservative mutations ( ).

Interpretation

If two sequences in an alignment share a common ancestor, mismatches can be interpreted as point mutations and gaps as indels (that is, insertion or deletion mutations) introduced in one or both lineages in the time since they diverged from one another.

In sequence alignments of proteins, the degree of similarity between amino acids occupying a particular position in the sequence can be interpreted as a rough measure of how conserved a particular region or sequence motif is among lineages. The absence of substitutions, or the presence of only very conservative substitutions (that is, the substitution of amino acids whose side chains have similar biochemical properties) in a particular region of the sequence, suggest that this region has structural or functional importance. Although DNA and RNA nucleotide bases are more similar to each other than are amino acids, the conservation of base pairs can indicate a similar functional or structural role.

Alignment Methods

Very short or very similar sequences can be aligned by hand. However, most interesting problems require the alignment of lengthy, highly variable or extremely numerous sequences that cannot be aligned solely by human effort. Instead, human knowledge is applied in constructing algorithms to produce high-quality sequence alignments, and occasionally in adjusting the final results to reflect patterns that are difficult to represent algorithmically (especially in the case of nucleotide sequences). Computational approaches to sequence alignment generally fall into two categories: *global alignments* and *local alignments*. Calculating a global alignment is a form of global optimization that "forces" the alignment to span the entire length of all query sequences. By contrast, local alignments identify regions of similarity within long sequences that are often widely divergent overall. Local alignments are often preferable, but can be more difficult to calculate because of the additional challenge of identifying the regions of similarity. A variety of computational algorithms have been applied to the sequence alignment problem. These include slow but formally correct methods like dynamic programming. These also include efficient, heuristic algorithms or probabilistic methods designed for large-scale database search, that do not guarantee to find best matches.

Representations

Alignments are commonly represented both graphically and in text format. In almost all sequence alignment representations, sequences are written in rows arranged so that aligned residues appear in successive columns. In text formats, aligned columns containing identical or similar characters are indicated with a system of conservation symbols. As in the image above, an asterisk or pipe symbol is used to show identity between two columns; other less common symbols include a colon for conservative substitutions and a period for semiconservative substitutions. Many sequence visualization programs also use color to display information about the properties of the individual sequence elements; in DNA and RNA sequences, this equates to assigning each nucleotide its own color. In protein alignments, such as the one in the image above, color is often used to indicate amino acid properties to aid in judging the conservation of a given amino acid substitution. For multiple sequences the last row in each column is often the consensus sequence determined by the alignment; the consensus sequence is also often represented in graphical format with a sequence logo in which the size of each nucleotide or amino acid letter corresponds to its degree of conservation.

Sequence alignments can be stored in a wide variety of text-based file formats, many of which were originally developed in conjunction with a specific alignment program or implementation. Most web-based tools allow a limited number of input and output formats, such as FASTA format and GenBank format and the output is not easily editable. Several conversion programs that provide graphical and/or command line interfaces are available, such as READSEQ and EMBOSS. There are also several programming packages which provide this conversion functionality, such as BioPython, BioRuby and BioPerl.

Global and Local Alignments

Global alignments, which attempt to align every residue in every sequence, are most useful when the sequences in the query set are similar and of roughly equal size. (This does not mean global alignments cannot start and/or end in gaps.) A general global alignment technique is the Needleman–Wunsch algorithm, which is based on dynamic programming. Local alignments are more useful for dissimilar sequences that are suspected to contain regions of similarity or similar sequence motifs within their larger sequence context. The Smith–Waterman algorithm is a general local alignment method also based on dynamic programming.

Hybrid methods, known as semiglobal or "glocal" (short for global-local) methods, attempt to find the best possible alignment that includes the start and end of one or the other sequence. This can be especially useful when the downstream part of one sequence overlaps with the upstream part of the other sequence. In this case, neither global nor local alignment is entirely appropriate: a global alignment would attempt to force the alignment to extend beyond the region of overlap, while a local alignment might not fully cover the region of overlap. Another case where semiglobal alignment is useful is when one sequence is short (for example a gene sequence) and the other is very long (for example a chromosome sequence). In that case, the short sequence should be globally aligned but only a local alignment is desired for the long sequence.

Pairwise Alignment

Pairwise sequence alignment methods are used to find the best-matching piecewise (local) or global alignments of two query sequences. Pairwise alignments can only be used between two sequences at a time, but they are efficient to calculate and are often used for methods that do not require extreme precision (such as searching a database for sequences with high similarity to a query). The three primary methods of producing pairwise alignments are dot-matrix methods, dynamic programming, and word methods; however, multiple sequence alignment techniques can also align pairs of sequences. Although each method has its individual strengths and weaknesses, all three pairwise methods have difficulty with highly repetitive sequences of low information content - especially where the number of repetitions differ in the two sequences to be aligned. One way of quantifying the utility of a given pairwise alignment is the 'maximum unique match' (MUM), or the longest subsequence that occurs in both query sequences. Longer MUM sequences typically reflect closer relatedness.

Dot-matrix Methods

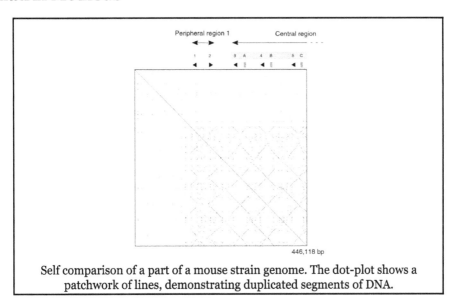

Self comparison of a part of a mouse strain genome. The dot-plot shows a patchwork of lines, demonstrating duplicated segments of DNA.

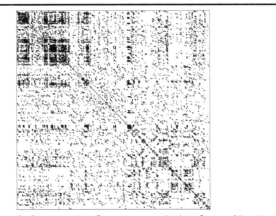

A DNA dot plot of a human zinc finger transcription factor (GenBank ID NM_002383), showing regional self-similarity. The main diagonal represents the sequence's alignment with itself; lines off the main diagonal represent similar or repetitive patterns within the sequence. This is a typical example of a recurrence plot.

The dot-matrix approach, which implicitly produces a family of alignments for individual sequence regions, is qualitative and conceptually simple, though time-consuming to analyze on a large scale. In the absence of noise, it can be easy to visually identify certain sequence features—such as insertions, deletions, repeats, or inverted repeats—from a dot-matrix plot. To construct a dot-matrix plot, the two sequences are written along the top row and leftmost column of a two-dimensional matrix and a dot is placed at any point where the characters in the appropriate columns match—this is a typical recurrence plot. Some implementations vary the size or intensity of the dot depending on the degree of similarity of the two characters, to accommodate conservative substitutions. The dot plots of very closely related sequences will appear as a single line along the matrix's main diagonal.

Problems with dot plots as an information display technique include: noise, lack of clarity, non-intuitiveness, difficulty extracting match summary statistics and match positions on the two sequences. There is also much wasted space where the match data is inherently duplicated across the diagonal and most of the actual area of the plot is taken up by either empty space or noise, and, finally, dot-plots are limited to two sequences. None of these limitations apply to Miropeats alignment diagrams but they have their own particular flaws.

Dot plots can also be used to assess repetitiveness in a single sequence. A sequence can be plotted against itself and regions that share significant similarities will appear as lines off the main diagonal. This effect can occur when a protein consists of multiple similar structural domains.

Dynamic Programming

The technique of dynamic programming can be applied to produce global alignments via the Needleman-Wunsch algorithm, and local alignments via the Smith-Waterman algorithm. In typical usage, protein alignments use a substitution matrix to assign scores to amino-acid matches or mismatches, and a gap penalty for matching an amino acid in one sequence to a gap in the other. DNA and RNA alignments may use a scoring matrix, but in practice often simply assign a positive match score, a negative mismatch score, and a negative gap penalty. (In standard dynamic programming, the score of each amino acid position is independent of the identity of its neighbors, and therefore base stacking effects are not taken into account. However, it is possible to account for such effects by modifying the algorithm.) A common extension to standard linear gap costs, is the usage of two different gap penalties for opening a gap and for extending a gap. Typically the former is much larger than the latter, e.g. -10 for gap open and -2 for gap extension. Thus, the number of gaps in an alignment is usually reduced and residues and gaps are kept together, which typically makes more biological sense. The Gotoh algorithm implements affine gap costs by using three matrices.

Dynamic programming can be useful in aligning nucleotide to protein sequences, a task complicated by the need to take into account frameshift mutations (usually insertions or deletions). The framesearch method produces a series of global or local pairwise alignments between a query nucleotide sequence and a search set of protein sequences, or vice versa. Its ability to evaluate frameshifts offset by an arbitrary number of nucleotides makes the method useful for sequences containing large numbers of indels, which can be very difficult to align with more efficient heuristic methods. In practice, the method requires large amounts of computing power or a system whose architecture is specialized for dynamic programming. The BLAST and EMBOSS suites provide basic tools for creating translated alignments (though some of these approaches take advantage of side-effects of sequence searching capabilities of the tools). More general methods are available from both commercial sources, such as *FrameSearch*, distributed as part of the Accelrys GCG package, and Open Source software such as Genewise.

The dynamic programming method is guaranteed to find an optimal alignment given a particular scoring function; however, identifying a good scoring function is often an empirical rather than a theoretical matter. Although dynamic programming is extensible to more than two sequences, it is prohibitively slow for large numbers of sequences or extremely long sequences.

Word Methods

Word methods, also known as k-tuple methods, are heuristic methods that are not guaranteed to find an optimal alignment solution, but are significantly more efficient than dynamic programming. These methods are especially useful in large-scale database searches where it is understood that a large proportion of the candidate sequences will have essentially no significant match with the query sequence. Word methods are best known for their implementation in the database search tools FASTA and the BLAST family. Word methods identify a series of short, nonoverlapping subsequences ("words") in the query sequence that are then matched to candidate database sequences. The relative positions of the word in the two sequences being compared are subtracted to obtain an offset; this will indicate a region of alignment if multiple distinct words produce the same offset. Only if this region is detected do these methods apply more sensitive alignment criteria; thus, many unnecessary comparisons with sequences of no appreciable similarity are eliminated.

In the FASTA method, the user defines a value k to use as the word length with which to search the database. The method is slower but more sensitive at lower values of k, which are also preferred for searches involving a very short query sequence. The BLAST family of search methods provides a number of algorithms optimized for particular types of queries, such as searching for distantly related sequence matches. BLAST was developed to provide a faster alternative to FASTA without sacrificing much accuracy; like FASTA, BLAST uses a word search of length k, but evaluates only the most significant word matches, rather than every word match as does FASTA. Most BLAST implementations use a fixed default word length that is optimized for the query and database type, and that is changed only under special circumstances, such as when searching with repetitive or very short query sequences. Implementations can be found via a number of web portals, such as EMBL FASTA and NCBI BLAST.

Multiple Sequence Alignment

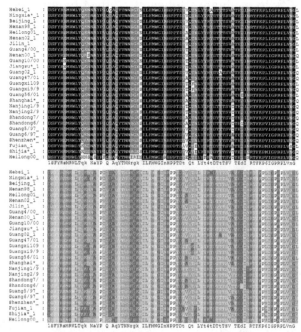

Alignment of 27 avian influenza hemagglutinin protein sequences colored by residue conservation (top) and residue properties (bottom)

Multiple sequence alignment is an extension of pairwise alignment to incorporate more than two sequences at a time. Multiple alignment methods try to align all of the sequences in a given query set. Multiple alignments are often used in identifying conserved sequence regions across a group of sequences hypothesized to be evolutionarily related. Such conserved sequence motifs can be used in conjunction with structural and mechanistic information to locate the catalytic active sites of enzymes. Alignments are also used to aid in establishing evolutionary relationships by constructing phylogenetic trees. Multiple sequence alignments are computationally difficult to produce and most formulations of the problem lead to NP-complete combinatorial optimization problems. Nevertheless, the utility of these alignments in bioinformatics has led to the development of a variety of methods suitable for aligning three or more sequences.

Dynamic Programming

The technique of dynamic programming is theoretically applicable to any number of sequences; however, because it is computationally expensive in both time and memory, it is rarely used for more than three or four sequences in its most basic form. This method requires constructing the n-dimensional equivalent of the sequence matrix formed from two sequences, where n is the number of sequences in the query. Standard dynamic programming is first used on all pairs of query sequences and then the "alignment space" is filled in by considering possible matches or gaps at intermediate positions, eventually constructing an alignment essentially between each two-sequence alignment. Although this technique is computationally expensive, its guarantee of a global optimum solution is useful in cases where only a few sequences need to be aligned accurately. One method for reducing the computational demands of dynamic programming, which relies on the "sum of pairs" objective function, has been implemented in the MSA software package.

Progressive Methods

Progressive, hierarchical, or tree methods generate a multiple sequence alignment by first aligning the most similar sequences and then adding successively less related sequences or groups to the alignment until the entire query set has been incorporated into the solution. The initial tree describing the sequence relatedness is based on pairwise comparisons that may include heuristic pairwise alignment methods similar to FASTA. Progressive alignment results are dependent on the choice of "most related" sequences and thus can be sensitive to inaccuracies in the initial pairwise alignments. Most progressive multiple sequence alignment methods additionally weight the sequences in the query set according to their relatedness, which reduces the likelihood of making a poor choice of initial sequences and thus improves alignment accuracy.

Many variations of the Clustal progressive implementation are used for multiple sequence alignment, phylogenetic tree construction, and as input for protein structure prediction. A slower but more accurate variant of the progressive method is known as T-Coffee.

Iterative Methods

Iterative methods attempt to improve on the heavy dependence on the accuracy of the initial pairwise alignments, which is the weak point of the progressive methods. Iterative methods optimize an objective function based on a selected alignment scoring method by assigning an initial global alignment and then realigning sequence subsets. The realigned subsets are then themselves aligned to produce the next iteration's multiple sequence alignment. Various ways of selecting the sequence subgroups and objective function are reviewed in.

Motif Finding

Motif finding, also known as profile analysis, constructs global multiple sequence alignments that attempt to align short conserved sequence motifs among the sequences in the query set. This is usually done by first constructing a general global multiple sequence alignment, after which the highly conserved regions are isolated and used to construct a set of profile matrices. The profile matrix for each conserved region is arranged like a scoring matrix but its frequency counts for each amino acid or nucleotide at each position are derived from the conserved region's character distribution rather than from a more general empirical distribution. The profile matrices are then used to search other sequences for occurrences of the motif they characterize. In cases where the original data set contained a small number of sequences, or only highly related sequences, pseudocounts are added to normalize the character distributions represented in the motif.

Techniques Inspired by Computer Science

A variety of general optimization algorithms commonly used in computer science have also been applied to the multiple sequence alignment problem. Hidden Markov models have been used to produce probability scores for a family of possible multiple sequence alignments for a given query set; although early HMM-based methods produced underwhelming performance, later applications have found them especially effective in detecting remotely related sequences because they are less susceptible to noise created by conservative or semiconservative substitutions. Genetic algorithms and simulated annealing have also been used in optimizing multiple sequence alignment scores as judged by a scoring function like the sum-of-pairs method. More complete details and software packages can be found in the main article multiple sequence alignment.

The Burrows–Wheeler transform has been successfully applied to fast short read alignment in popular tools such as Bowtie and BWA.

Structural Alignment

Structural alignments, which are usually specific to protein and sometimes RNA sequences, use information about the secondary and tertiary structure of the protein or RNA molecule to aid in aligning the sequences. These methods can be used for two or more sequences and typically produce local alignments; however, because they depend on the availability of structural information, they can only be used for sequences whose corresponding structures are known (usually through X-ray crystallography or NMR spectroscopy). Because both protein and RNA structure is more evolutionarily conserved than sequence, structural alignments can be more reliable between sequences that are very distantly related and that have diverged so extensively that sequence comparison cannot reliably detect their similarity.

Structural alignments are used as the "gold standard" in evaluating alignments for homology-based protein structure prediction because they explicitly align regions of the protein sequence that are structurally similar rather than relying exclusively on sequence information. However, clearly structural alignments cannot be used in structure prediction because at least one sequence in the query set is the target to be modeled, for which the structure is not known. It has been shown that, given the structural alignment between a target and a template sequence, highly accurate models of the target protein sequence can be produced; a major stumbling block in homology-based structure prediction is the production of structurally accurate alignments given only sequence information.

DALI

The DALI method, or distance matrix alignment, is a fragment-based method for constructing structural alignments based on contact similarity patterns between successive hexapeptides in the query sequences. It can generate pairwise or multiple alignments and identify a query sequence's structural neighbors in the Protein Data Bank (PDB). It has been used to construct the FSSP structural alignment database (Fold classification based on Structure-Structure alignment of Proteins, or Families of Structurally Similar Proteins). A DALI webserver can be accessed at DALI and the FSSP is located at The Dali Database.

SSAP

SSAP (sequential structure alignment program) is a dynamic programming-based method of structural alignment that uses atom-to-atom vectors in structure space as comparison points. It has been extended since its original description to include multiple as well as pairwise alignments, and has been used in the construction of the CATH (Class, Architecture, Topology, Homology) hierarchical database classification of protein folds. The CATH database can be accessed at CATH Protein Structure Classification.

Combinatorial Extension

The combinatorial extension method of structural alignment generates a pairwise structural alignment by using local geometry to align short fragments of the two proteins being analyzed and then assembles these fragments into a larger alignment. Based on measures such as rigid-body root mean square distance, residue distances, local secondary structure, and surrounding environmental features such as residue neighbor hydrophobicity, local alignments called "aligned fragment pairs" are generated and used to build a similarity matrix representing all possible structural alignments within predefined cutoff criteria. A path from one protein structure state to the other is then traced through the matrix by extending the growing alignment one fragment at a time. The optimal such path defines the combinatorial-extension alignment. A web-based server implementing the method and providing a database of pairwise alignments of structures in the Protein Data Bank is located at the Combinatorial Extension website.

Phylogenetic Analysis

Phylogenetics and sequence alignment are closely related fields due to the shared necessity of evaluating sequence relatedness. The field of phylogenetics makes extensive use of sequence alignments in the construction and interpretation of phylogenetic trees, which are used to classify the evolutionary relationships between homologous genes represented in the genomes of divergent species. The degree to which sequences in a query set differ is qualitatively related to the sequences' evolutionary distance from one another. Roughly speaking, high sequence identity suggests that the sequences in question have a comparatively young most recent common ancestor, while low identity suggests that the divergence is more ancient. This approximation, which reflects the "molecular clock" hypothesis that a roughly constant rate of evolutionary change can be used to extrapolate the elapsed time since two genes first diverged (that is, the co-alescence time), assumes that the effects of mutation and selection are constant across sequence lineages. Therefore, it does not account for possible difference among organisms or species in the rates of DNA repair or the possible functional conservation of specific regions in a sequence. (In the case of nucleotide sequences, the molecular clock hypothesis in its most basic form also discounts the difference in acceptance rates between silent mutations that do not alter the meaning of a given codon and other mutations that result in a different amino acid being incorporated into the protein.) More statistically accurate methods allow the evolutionary rate on each branch of the phylogenetic tree to vary, thus producing better estimates of coalescence times for genes.

Progressive multiple alignment techniques produce a phylogenetic tree by necessity because they incorporate sequences into the growing alignment in order of relatedness. Other techniques that assemble multiple sequence alignments and phylogenetic trees score and sort trees first and calculate a multiple sequence alignment from the highest-scoring tree. Commonly used methods of phylogenetic tree construction are mainly heuristic because the problem of selecting the optimal tree, like the problem of selecting the optimal multiple sequence alignment, is NP-hard.

Assessment of Significance

Sequence alignments are useful in bioinformatics for identifying sequence similarity, producing phylogenetic trees, and developing homology models of protein structures. However, the biological relevance of sequence alignments is not always clear. Alignments are often assumed to reflect a degree of evolutionary change between sequences descended from a common ancestor; however, it is formally possible that convergent evolution can occur to produce apparent similarity between proteins that are evolutionarily unrelated but perform similar functions and have similar structures.

In database searches such as BLAST, statistical methods can determine the likelihood of a particular alignment between sequences or sequence regions arising by chance given the size and composition of the database being searched. These values can vary significantly depending on the search space. In particular, the likelihood of finding a given alignment by chance increases if the database consists only of sequences from the same organism as the query sequence. Repetitive sequences in the database or query can also distort both the search results and the assessment of statistical significance; BLAST automatically filters such repetitive sequences in the query to avoid apparent hits that are statistical artifacts.

Methods of statistical significance estimation for gapped sequence alignments are available in the literature.

Assessment of Credibility

Statistical significance indicates the probability that an alignment of a given quality could arise by chance, but does not indicate how much superior a given alignment is to alternative alignments of the same sequences. Measures of alignment credibility indicate the extent to which the best scoring alignments for a given pair of sequences are substantially similar. Methods of alignment credibility estimation for gapped sequence alignments are available in the literature.

Scoring Functions

The choice of a scoring function that reflects biological or statistical observations about known sequences is important to producing good alignments. Protein sequences are frequently aligned using substitution matrices that reflect the probabilities of given character-to-character substitutions. A series of matrices called PAM matrices (Point Accepted Mutation matrices, originally defined by Margaret Dayhoff and sometimes referred to as "Dayhoff matrices") explicitly encode evolutionary approximations regarding the rates and probabilities of particular amino acid mutations. Another common series of scoring matrices, known as BLOSUM (Blocks Substitution Matrix), encodes empirically derived substitution probabilities. Variants of both types of matrices are used to detect sequences with differing levels of divergence, thus allowing users of BLAST or FASTA to restrict searches to more closely related matches or expand to detect more divergent sequences. Gap penalties account for the introduction of a gap - on the evolutionary model, an insertion or deletion mutation - in both nucleotide and protein sequences, and therefore the penalty values should be proportional to the expected rate of such mutations. The quality of the alignments produced therefore depends on the quality of the scoring function.

It can be very useful and instructive to try the same alignment several times with different choices for scoring matrix and/or gap penalty values and compare the results. Regions where the solution is weak or non-unique can often be identified by observing which regions of the alignment are robust to variations in alignment parameters.

Other Biological Uses

Sequenced RNA, such as expressed sequence tags and full-length mRNAs, can be aligned to a sequenced genome to find where there are genes and get information about alternative splicing and RNA editing. Sequence alignment is also a part of genome assembly, where sequences are aligned to find overlap so that *contigs* (long stretches of sequence) can be formed. Another use is SNP analysis, where sequences from different individuals are aligned to find single basepairs that are often different in a population.

Non-biological Uses

The methods used for biological sequence alignment have also found applications in other fields, most notably in natural language processing and in social sciences, where the Needleman-Wunsch algorithm is usually referred to as Optimal matching. Techniques that generate the set of elements from which words will be selected in natural-language generation algorithms have borrowed multiple sequence alignment techniques from bioinformatics to produce linguistic versions of computer-generated mathematical proofs. In the field of historical and comparative linguistics, sequence alignment has been used to partially automate the comparative method by which linguists traditionally reconstruct languages. Business and marketing research has also applied multiple sequence alignment techniques in analyzing series of purchases over time.

Software

A more complete list of available software categorized by algorithm and alignment type is available at sequence alignment software, but common software tools used for general sequence alignment tasks include ClustalW2 and T-coffee for alignment, and BLAST and FASTA3x for database searching. Commercial tools such as Geneious and Pattern-Hunter are also available.

Alignment algorithms and software can be directly compared to one another using a standardized set of benchmark reference multiple sequence alignments known as BAliBASE. The data set consists of structural alignments, which can be considered a standard against which purely sequence-based methods are compared. The relative performance of many common alignment methods on frequently encountered alignment problems has been tabulated and selected results published online at BAliBASE. A comprehensive list of BAliBASE scores for many (currently 12) different alignment tools can be computed within the protein workbench STRAP.

BLAST

In bioinformatics, BLAST for Basic Local Alignment Search Tool is an algorithm for comparing primary biological sequence information, such as the amino-acid sequences of proteins or the nucleotides of DNA sequences. A BLAST search enables a researcher to compare a query sequence with a library or database of sequences, and identify library sequences that resemble the query sequence above a certain threshold.

Different types of BLASTs are available according to the query sequences. For example, following the discovery of a previously unknown gene in the mouse, a scientist will typically perform a BLAST search of the human genome to see if humans carry a similar gene; BLAST will identify sequences in the human genome that resemble the mouse gene based on similarity of sequence. The BLAST algorithm and program were designed by Stephen Altschul, Warren Gish, Webb Miller, Eugene Myers, and David J. Lipman at the National Institutes of Health and was published in the *Journal of Molecular Biology* in 1990 and cited over 50,000 times.

Background

BLAST is one of the most widely used bioinformatics programs for sequence searching. It addresses a fundamental problem in bioinformatics research. The heuristic algorithm it uses is much faster than other approaches, such as calculating an optimal alignment. This emphasis on speed is vital to making the algorithm practical on the huge genome databases currently available, although subsequent algorithms can be even faster.

Before BLAST, FASTA was developed by David J. Lipman and William R. Pearson in 1985.

Before fast algorithms such as BLAST and FASTA were developed, doing database searches for protein or nucleic sequences was very time consuming because a full alignment procedure (e.g., the Smith–Waterman algorithm) was used.

While BLAST is faster than any Smith-Waterman implementation for most cases, it cannot "guarantee the optimal alignments of the query and database sequences" as Smith-Waterman algorithm does. The optimality of Smith-Waterman "ensured the best performance on accuracy and the most precise results" at the expense of time and computer power.

BLAST is more time-efficient than FASTA by searching only for the more significant patterns in the sequences, yet with comparative sensitivity. This could be further realized by understanding the algorithm of BLAST introduced below.

Examples of other questions that researchers use BLAST to answer are:

- Which bacterial species have a protein that is related in lineage to a certain protein with known amino-acid sequence

- What other genes encode proteins that exhibit structures or motifs such as ones that have just been determined

BLAST is also often used as part of other algorithms that require approximate sequence matching.

The BLAST algorithm and the computer program that implements it were developed by Stephen Altschul, Warren Gish, and David Lipman at the U.S. National Center for Biotechnology Information (NCBI), Webb Miller at the Pennsylvania State University, and Gene Myers at the University of Arizona. It is available on the web on the NCBI website. Alternative implementations include AB-BLAST (formerly known as WU-BLAST), FSA-BLAST (last updated in 2006), and ScalaBLAST.

The original paper by Altschul, *et al.* was the most highly cited paper published in the 1990s.

Input

Input sequences (in FASTA or Genbank format) and weight matrix.

Output

BLAST output can be delivered in a variety of formats. These formats include HTML, plain text, and XML formatting. For NCBI's web-page, the default format for output is HTML. When performing a BLAST on NCBI, the results are given in a graphical format showing the hits found, a table showing sequence identifiers for the hits with scoring related data, as well as alignments for the sequence of interest and the hits received with corresponding BLAST scores for these. The easiest to read and most informative of these is probably the table.

If one is attempting to search for a proprietary sequence or simply one that is unavailable in databases available to the general public through sources such as NCBI, there is a BLAST program available for download to any computer, at no cost. This can be found at BLAST+ executables. There are also commercial programs available for purchase. Databases can be found from the NCBI site, as well as from Index of BLAST databases (FTP).

Process

Using a heuristic method, BLAST finds similar sequences, by locating short matches between the two sequences. This process of finding similar sequences is called seeding. It is after this first match that BLAST begins to make local alignments. While attempting to find similarity in sequences, sets of common letters, known as words, are very important. For example, suppose that the sequence contains the following stretch of letters, GLKFA. If a BLAST was being conducted under normal conditions, the word size would be 3 letters. In this case, using the given stretch of letters, the searched words would be GLK, LKF, KFA. The heuristic algorithm of BLAST locates all common three-letter words between the sequence of interest and the hit sequence or sequences from the database. This result will then be used to build an alignment. After making words for the sequence of interest, the rest of the words are also assembled. These words must satisfy a requirement of having a score of at least the threshold T, when compared by using a scoring matrix. One commonly used scoring matrix for BLAST searches is BLOSUM62, although the optimal scoring matrix depends on sequence similarity. Once both words and neighborhood words are assembled and compiled, they are compared to the sequences in the database in order to find matches. The threshold score T determines whether or not a particular word will be included in the alignment. Once seeding has been conducted, the alignment which is only 3 residues long, is extended in both directions by the algorithm used by BLAST. Each extension impacts the score of the alignment by either increasing or decreasing it. If this score is higher than a pre-determined T, the alignment will be included in the results given by BLAST. However, if this score is lower than this pre-determined T, the alignment will cease to extend, preventing the areas of poor alignment from being included in the BLAST results. Note that increasing the T score limits the amount of space available to search, decreasing the number of neighborhood words, while at the same time speeding up the process of BLAST.

Algorithm

To run the software, BLAST requires a query sequence to search for, and a sequence to search against (also called the target sequence) or a sequence database containing multiple such sequences. BLAST will find sub-sequences in the database which are similar to sub sequences in the query. In typical usage, the query sequence is much smaller than the database, e.g., the query may be one thousand nucleotides while the database is several billion nucleotides.

The main idea of BLAST is that there are often High-scoring Segment Pairs (HSP) contained in a statistically significant alignment. BLAST searches for high scoring sequence alignments between the query sequence and the existing sequences in the database using a heuristic approach that approximates the Smith-Waterman algorithm. However, the exhaustive Smith-Waterman approach is too slow for searching large genomic databases such as GenBank. Therefore, the BLAST algorithm uses a heuristic approach that is less accurate than the Smith-Waterman algorithm but over 50 times faster. The speed and relatively good accuracy of BLAST are among the key technical innovations of the BLAST programs.

An overview of the BLAST algorithm (a protein to protein search) is as follows: and CTGA2016

1. Remove low-complexity region or sequence repeats in the query sequence.

"Low-complexity region" means a region of a sequence composed of few kinds of elements. These regions might give high scores that confuse the program to find the actual significant sequences in the database, so they should be filtered out. The regions will be marked with an X (protein sequences) or N (nucleic acid sequences) and then be ignored by the BLAST program. To filter out the low-complexity regions, the SEG program is used for protein sequences and the program DUST is used for DNA sequences. On the other hand, the program XNU is used to mask off the tandem repeats in protein sequences.

2. Make a k-letter word list of the query sequence.

Take k=3 for example, we list the words of length 3 in the query protein sequence (k is usually 11 for a DNA sequence) "sequentially", until the last letter of the query sequence is included. The method is illustrated in figure 1.

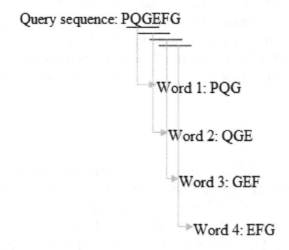

Query sequence: PQGEFG

Word 1: PQG

Word 2: QGE

Word 3: GEF

Word 4: EFG

The method to establish the k-letter query word list. Adapted from Biological Sequence Analysis I, Current Topics in Genome Analysis .

3   List the possible matching words.

This step is one of the main differences between BLAST and FASTA. FASTA cares about all of the common words in the database and query sequences that are listed in step 2; however, BLAST only cares about the high-scoring words. The scores are created by comparing the word in the list in step 2 with all the 3-letter words. By using the scoring matrix (substitution matrix) to score the comparison of each residue pair, there are 20^3 possible match scores for a 3-letter word. For example, the score obtained by comparing PQG with PEG and PQA is 15 and 12, respectively. For DNA words, a match is scored as +5 and a mismatch as -4, or as +2 and -3. After that, a neighborhood word score threshold T is used to reduce the number of possible matching words. The words whose scores are greater than the threshold T will remain in the possible matching words list, while those with lower scores will be discarded. For example, PEG is kept, but PQA is abandoned when T is 13.

4   Organize the remaining high-scoring words into an efficient search tree.

This allows the program to rapidly compare the high-scoring words to the database sequences.

5   Repeat step 3 to 4 for each k-letter word in the query sequence.

6   Scan the database sequences for exact matches with the remaining high-scoring words.

The BLAST program scans the database sequences for the remaining high-scoring word, such as PEG, of each position. If an exact match is found, this match is used to seed a possible un-gapped alignment between the query and database sequences.

7. Extend the exact matches to high-scoring segment pair (HSP).

- The original version of BLAST stretches a longer alignment between the query and the database sequence in the left and right directions, from the position where the exact match occurred. The extension does not stop until the accumulated total score of the HSP begins to decrease. A simplified example is presented in figure 2.

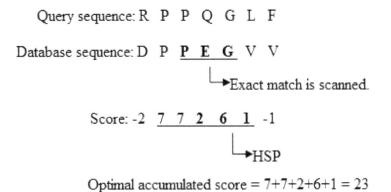

Fig. 2 The process to extend the exact match. Adapted from Biological Sequence Analysis I, Current Topics in Genome Analysis .

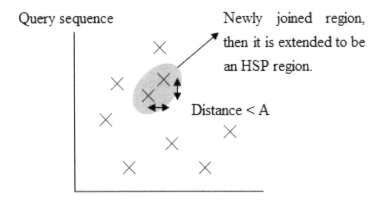

Database sequence

The positions of the exact matches.

- To save more time, a newer version of BLAST, called BLAST2 or gapped BLAST, has been developed. BLAST2 adopts a lower neighborhood word score threshold to maintain the same level of sensitivity for detecting sequence similarity. Therefore, the possible matching words list in step 3 becomes longer. Next, the exact matched regions, within distance A from each other on the same diagonal in figure 3, will be joined as a longer new region. Finally, the new regions are then extended by the same method as in the original version of BLAST, and the HSPs' (High-scoring segment pair) scores of the extended regions are then created by using a substitution matrix as before.

8   List all of the HSPs in the database whose score is high enough to be considered.

We list the HSPs whose scores are greater than the empirically determined cutoff score S. By examining the distribution of the alignment scores modeled by comparing random sequences, a cutoff score S can be determined such that its value is large enough to guarantee the significance of the remaining HSPs.

9   Evaluate the significance of the HSP score.

BLAST next assesses the statistical significance of each HSP score by exploiting the Gumbel extreme value distribution (EVD). (It is proved that the distribution of Smith-Waterman local alignment scores between two random sequences follows the Gumbel EVD. For local alignments containing gaps it is not proved.). In accordance with the Gumbel EVD, the probability p of observing a score S equal to or greater than x is given by the equation

$$p(S \geq x) = 1 - \exp\left(-e^{-\lambda(x-\mu)}\right)$$

where

$$\mu = \left[\log(Km'n')\right] \Big/ \lambda$$

The statistical parameters λ and K are estimated by fitting the distribution of the ungapped local alignment scores, of the query sequence and a lot of shuffled versions (Global or local shuffling) of a database sequence, to the Gumbel extreme value distribution. Note that λ and K depend upon the substitution matrix, gap penalties, and sequence composition (the letter frequencies). m' and n' are the effective lengths of the query and database sequences, respectively. The original sequence length is shortened to the effective length to compensate for the edge effect (an alignment start near the end of one of the query or database sequence is likely not to have enough sequence to build an optimal alignment). They can be calculated as

$$m' \approx m - (\ln Kmn) \Big/ H$$

$$n' \approx n - (\ln Kmn) \Big/ H$$

where H is the average expected score per aligned pair of residues in an alignment of two random sequences. Altschul and Gish gave the typical values, $\lambda = 0.318$, $K = 0.13$, and $H = 0.40$, for un-gapped local alignment using BLOSUM62 as the substitution matrix. Using the typical values for assessing the significance is called the lookup table method; it is not accurate. The expect score E of a database match is the number of times that an unrelated database sequence would obtain a score S higher than x by chance. The expectation E obtained in a search for a database of D sequences is given by

$$E \approx 1 - e^{-p(s>x)D}$$

Furthermore, when $p < 0.1$, E could be approximated by the Poisson distribution as

$$E \approx pD$$

This expectation or expect value "E" (often called an E score or E-value or e-value) assessing the significance of the HSP score for un-gapped local alignment is reported in the BLAST results. The calculation shown here is modified if individual HSPs are combined, such as when producing gapped alignments (described below), due to the variation of the statistical parameters.

10 Make two or more HSP regions into a longer alignment.

Sometimes, we find two or more HSP regions in one database sequence that can be made into a longer alignment. This provides additional evidence of the relation be-tween the query and database sequence. There are two methods, the Poisson method and the sum-of-scores method, to compare the significance of the newly combined HSP regions. Suppose that there are two combined HSP regions with the pairs of scores (65, 40) and (52, 45), respectively. The Poisson method gives more significance to the set with the maximal lower score (45>40). However, the sum-of-scores method prefers the first set, because 65+40 (105) is greater than 52+45(97). The original BLAST uses the Poisson method; gapped BLAST and the WU-BLAST uses the sum-of scores method.

11 Show the gapped Smith-Waterman local alignments of the query and each of the matched database sequences.

- The original BLAST only generates un-gapped alignments including the initially found HSPs individually, even when there is more than one HSP found in one database sequence.

- BLAST2 produces a single alignment with gaps that can include all of the initially found HSP regions. Note that the computation of the score and its corresponding E-value involves use of adequate gap penalties.

12 Report every match whose expect score is lower than a threshold parameter E.

Parallel BLAST

Parallel BLAST versions of split databases are implemented using MPI and Pthreads, and have been ported to various platforms including Windows, Linux, Solaris, Mac OS X, and AIX. Popular approaches to parallelize BLAST include query distribution, hash table segmentation, computation parallelization, and database segmentation (partition). Databases are split into equal sized pieces and stored locally on each node. Each query is run on all nodes in parallel and the resultant BLAST output files from all nodes merged to yield the final output.

Program

The BLAST program can either be downloaded and run as a command-line utility "blastall" or accessed for free over the web. The BLAST web server, hosted by the NCBI, allows anyone with a web browser to perform similarity searches against constantly updated databases of proteins and DNA that include most of the newly sequenced organisms.

The BLAST program is based on an open-source format, giving everyone access to it and enabling them to have the ability to change the program code. This has led to the creation of several BLAST "spin-offs".

There are now a handful of different BLAST programs available, which can be used depending on what one is attempting to do and what they are working with. These different programs vary in query sequence input, the database being searched, and what is being compared. These programs and their details are listed below:

BLAST is actually a family of programs (all included in the blastall executable). These include:

Nucleotide-nucleotide BLAST (blastn)

> This program, given a DNA query, returns the most similar DNA sequences from the DNA database that the user specifies.

Protein-protein BLAST (blastp)

> This program, given a protein query, returns the most similar protein sequences from the protein database that the user specifies.

Position-Specific Iterative BLAST (PSI-BLAST) (blastpgp)

> This program is used to find distant relatives of a protein. First, a list of all closely related proteins is created. These proteins are combined into a general "profile" sequence, which summarises significant features present in these sequences. A query against the protein database is then run using this profile, and a larger group of proteins is found. This larger group is used to construct another profile, and the process is repeated.

> By including related proteins in the search, PSI-BLAST is much more sensitive in picking up distant evolutionary relationships than a standard protein-protein BLAST.

Nucleotide 6-frame translation-protein (blastx)

> This program compares the six-frame conceptual translation products of a nucleotide query sequence (both strands) against a protein sequence database.

Nucleotide 6-frame translation-nucleotide 6-frame translation (tblastx)

> This program is the slowest of the BLAST family. It translates the query nucleotide sequence in all six possible frames and compares it against the six-frame translations of a nucleotide sequence database. The purpose of tblastx is to find very distant relationships between nucleotide sequences.

Protein-nucleotide 6-frame translation (tblastn)

> This program compares a protein query against the all six reading frames of a nucleotide sequence database.

Large numbers of query sequences (megablast)

> When comparing large numbers of input sequences via the command-line BLAST, "megablast" is much faster than running BLAST multiple times. It concatenates many input sequences together to form a large sequence before searching the BLAST database, then post-analyzes the search results to glean individual alignments and statistical values.

Of these programs, BLASTn and BLASTp are the most commonly used because they use direct comparisons, and do not require translations. However, since protein sequences are better conserved evolutionarily than nucleotide sequences, tBLASTn, tBLASTx, and BLASTx, produce more reliable and accurate results when dealing with coding DNA. They also enable one to be able to directly see the function of the protein sequence, since by translating the sequence of interest before searching often gives you annotated protein hits.

Alternative Versions

A version designed for comparing large genomes or DNA is BLASTZ.

CS-BLAST (ContSxt-Specific BLAST) is an extended version of BLAST for searching protein sequences that finds twice as many remotely related sequences as BLAST at the same speed and error rate. In CS-BLAST, the mutation probabilities between amino acids depend not only on the single amino acid, as in BLAST, but also on its local sequence context. Washington University produced an alternative version of NCBI BLAST, called WU-BLAST. The rights have since been acquired to Advanced Biocomputing, LLC.

In 2009, NCBI has released a new set of BLAST executables, the C++ based BLAST+, and has released parallel versions until 2.2.26. Starting with version 2.2.27 (April

2013), only BLAST+ executables are available. Among the changes is the replacement of the blastall executable with separate executables for the different BLAST programs, and changes in option handling. The formatdb utility (C based) has been replaced by makeblastdb (C++ based) and databases formatted by either one should be compatible for identical blast releases. The algorithms remain similar, however, the number of hits found and their order can vary significantly between the older and the newer version.

Accelerated Versions

- CLC bio and SciEngines GmbH collaborate on an FPGA accelerator they claim will give 188x acceleration of BLAST.

- TimeLogic offers another FPGA-accelerated implementation of the BLAST algorithm called Tera-BLAST.

- The Mitrion-C Open Bio Project is an ongoing effort to port BLAST to run on Mitrion FPGAs.

- The GPU-Blast is an accelerated version of NCBI BLASTP for CUDA which is 3x~4x faster than NCBI Blast.

- The CUDA-BLASTP is a version of BLASTP that is GPU-accelerated and is claimed to run up to 10x faster than NCBI BLAST.

- G-BLASTN is an accelerated version of NCBI blastn and megablast, whose speedup varies from 4x to 14x (compared to the same runs with 4 CPU threads). Its current limitation is that the database must fit into the GPU memory.

- MPIBlast is a parallel implementation of NCBI BLAST using Message Passing Interface. By efficiently utilizing distributed computational resources through database fragmentation, query segmentation, intelligent scheduling, and parallel I/O, mpiBLAST improves NCBI BLAST performance by several orders of magnitude while scaling to hundreds of processors.

- Paracel BLAST is a commercial parallel implementation of NCBI BLAST, supporting hundreds of processors.

- CaBLAST makes search on large databases orders of magnitude faster by exploiting redundancy in data.

Alternatives to BLAST

An extremely fast but considerably less sensitive alternative to BLAST is BLAT (Blast Like Alignment Tool). While BLAST does a linear search, BLAT relies on k-mer indexing the database, and can thus often find seeds faster. Another software alternative similar to BLAT is PatternHunter.

Advances in sequencing technology in the late 2000s has made searching for very similar nucleotide matches an important problem. New alignment programs tailored for this use typically use BWT-indexing of the target database (typically a genome). Input sequences can then be mapped very quickly, and output is typically in the form of a BAM file. Example alignment programs are BWA, SOAP, and Bowtie.

For protein identification, searching for known domains (for instance from Pfam) by matching with Hidden Markov Models is a popular alternative, such as HMMER.

An alternative to BLAST for comparing two banks of sequences is PLAST. PLAST provides a high-performance general purpose bank to bank sequence similarity search tool relying on the PLAST and ORIS algorithms. Results of PLAST are very similar to BLAST, but KLAST is significantly faster and capable of comparing large sets of sequences with a small memory (i.e. RAM) footprint.

For applications in metagenomics, where the task is to compare billions of short DNA reads against tens of millions of protein references, DIAMOND runs at up to 20,000 times as fast as BLASTX, while maintaining a high level of sensitivity.

Uses of BLAST

BLAST can be used for several purposes. These include identifying species, locating domains, establishing phylogeny, DNA mapping, and comparison.

Identifying species

> With the use of BLAST, you can possibly correctly identify a species or find homologous species. This can be useful, for example, when you are working with a DNA sequence from an unknown species.

Locating domains

> When working with a protein sequence you can input it into BLAST, to locate known domains within the sequence of interest.

Establishing phylogeny

> Using the results received through BLAST you can create a phylogenetic tree using the BLAST web-page. Phylogenies based on BLAST alone are less reliable than other purpose-built computational phylogenetic methods, so should only be relied upon for "first pass" phylogenetic analyses.

DNA mapping

> When working with a known species, and looking to sequence a gene at an unknown location, BLAST can compare the chromosomal position of the sequence of interest, to relevant sequences in the database(s).

Comparison

When working with genes, BLAST can locate common genes in two related species, and can be used to map annotations from one organism to another.

Comparing BLAST and the Smith-Waterman Process

While both Smith-Waterman and BLAST are used to find homologous sequences by searching and comparing a query sequence with those in the databases, they do have their differences.

Due to the fact that BLAST is based on a heuristic algorithm, the results received through BLAST, in terms of the hits found, may not be the best possible results, as it will not provide you with all the hits within the database. BLAST misses hard to find matches.

A better alternative in order to find the best possible results would be to use the Smith-Waterman algorithm. This method varies from the BLAST method in two areas, accuracy and speed. The Smith-Waterman option provides better accuracy, in that it finds matches that BLAST cannot, because it does not miss any information. Therefore, it is necessary for remote homology. However, when compared to BLAST, it is more time consuming, not to mention that it requires large amounts of computer usage and space. However, technologies to speed up the Smith-Waterman process have been found to improve the time necessary to perform a search dramatically. These technologies include FPGA chips and SIMD technology.

In order to receive better results from BLAST, the settings can be changed from their default settings. However, there is no given or set way of changing these settings in order to receive the best results for a given sequence. The settings available for change are E-Value, gap costs, filters, word size, and substitution matrix. Note, that the algorithm used for BLAST was developed from the algorithm used for Smith-Waterman. BLAST employs an alignment which finds "local alignments between sequences by finding short matches and from these initial matches (local) alignments are created".

Multiple Sequence Alignment

A multiple sequence alignment (MSA) is a sequence alignment of three or more biological sequences, generally protein, DNA, or RNA. In many cases, the input set of query sequences are assumed to have an evolutionary relationship by which they share a lineage and are descended from a common ancestor. From the resulting MSA, sequence homology can be inferred and phylogenetic analysis can be conducted to assess the sequences' shared evolutionary origins. Visual depictions of the alignment as in the image at right illustrate mutation events such as point mutations (single amino acid or nucleotide changes) that appear as differing characters in a single alignment column, and insertion or deletion mutations (indels or gaps) that appear as hyphens in one or more of the sequences in the alignment. Multiple sequence alignment is often used to assess sequence conservation of protein domains, tertiary and secondary structures, and even individual amino acids or nucleotides.

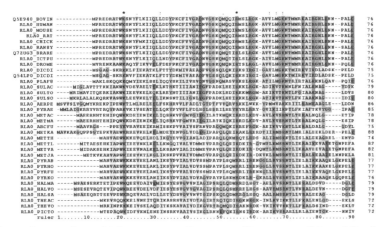

First 90 positions of a protein multiple sequence alignment of instances of the acidic ribosomal protein Po (L10E) from several organisms. Generated with ClustalX.

Multiple sequence alignment also refers to the process of aligning such a sequence set. Because three or more sequences of biologically relevant length can be difficult and are almost always time-consuming to align by hand, computational algorithms are used to produce and analyze the alignments. MSAs require more sophisticated methodologies than pairwise alignment because they are more computationally complex. Most multiple sequence alignment programs use heuristic methods rather than global optimization because identifying the optimal alignment between more than a few sequences of moderate length is prohibitively computationally expensive.

Dynamic Programming and Computational Complexity

A direct method for producing an MSA uses the dynamic programming technique to identify the globally optimal alignment solution. For proteins, this method usually involves two sets of parameters: a gap penalty and a substitution matrix assigning scores or probabilities to the alignment of each possible pair of amino acids based on the similarity of the amino acids' chemical properties and the evolutionary probability of the mutation. For nucleotide sequences a similar gap penalty is used, but a much simpler substitution matrix, wherein only identical matches and mismatches are considered, is typical. The scores in the substitution matrix may be either all positive or a mix of positive and negative in the case of a global alignment, but must be both positive and negative, in the case of a local alignment.

For n individual sequences, the naive method requires constructing the n-dimensional equivalent of the matrix formed in standard pairwise sequence alignment. The search space thus increases exponentially with increasing n and is also strongly dependent on sequence length. Expressed with the big O notation commonly used to measure computational complexity, a naïve MSA takes $O(Length)$ time to produce. To find the global optimum for n sequences this way has been shown to be an NP-complete problem. In 1989, based on Carrillo-Lipman Algorithm, Altschul introduced a practical method that uses pairwise alignments to constrain the n-dimensional search space. In this approach pairwise dynamic programming alignments are performed on each pair of sequences in the query set, and only the space near the n-dimensional intersection of these alignments is searched for the n-way alignment. The MSA program optimizes the sum of all of the pairs of characters at each position in the alignment (the so-called *sum of pair* score) and has been implemented in a software program for constructing multiple sequence alignments.

Progressive Alignment Construction

The most widely used approach to multiple sequence alignments uses a heuristic search known as progressive technique (also known as the hierarchical or tree method) developed by Paulien Hogeweg and Ben Hesper in 1984. Progressive alignment builds up a final MSA by combining pairwise alignments beginning with the most similar pair and progressing to the most distantly related. All progressive alignment methods require two stages: a first stage in which the relationships between the sequences are represented as a tree, called a *guide tree*, and a second step in which the MSA is built by adding the sequences sequentially to the growing MSA according to the guide tree. The initial *guide tree* is determined by an efficient clustering method such as neighbor-joining or UPGMA, and may use distances based on the number of identical two letter sub-sequences (as in FASTA rather than a dynamic programming alignment).

Progressive alignments are not guaranteed to be globally optimal. The primary problem is that when errors are made at any stage in growing the MSA, these errors are then propagated through to the final result. Performance is also particularly bad when all of the sequences in the set are rather distantly related. Most modern progressive methods modify their scoring function with a secondary weighting function that assigns scaling factors to individual members of the query set in a nonlinear fashion based on their phylogenetic distance from their nearest neighbors. This corrects for non-random selection of the sequences given to the alignment program.

Progressive alignment methods are efficient enough to implement on a large scale for many (100s to 1000s) sequences. Progressive alignment services are commonly available on publicly accessible web servers so users need not locally install the applications of interest. The most popular progressive alignment method has been the Clustal family, especially the weighted variant ClustalW to which access is provided by a large number of web portals including GenomeNet, EBI, and EMBNet. Different portals or implementations can vary in user interface and make different parameters accessible to the user. ClustalW is used extensively for phylogenetic tree construction, in spite of the author's explicit warnings that unedited alignments should not be used in such studies and as input for protein structure prediction by homology modeling. Current version of Clustal family is ClustalW2. EMBL-EBI announced that CLustalW2 will be expired in August 2015. They recommend Clustal Omega which performs based on seeded guide trees and HMM profile-profile techniques for protein alignments. They offer different MSA tools for progressive DNA alignments. One of them is MAFFT (Multiple Alignment using Fast Fourier Transform).

Another common progressive alignment method called T-Coffee is slower than Clustal and its derivatives but generally produces more accurate alignments for distantly related sequence sets. T-Coffee calculates pairwise alignments by combining the direct alignment of the pair with indirect alignments that aligns each sequence of the pair to a third sequence. It uses the output from Clustal as well as another local alignment program LALIGN, which finds multiple regions of local alignment between two sequences. The resulting alignment and phylogenetic tree are used as a guide to produce new and more accurate weighting factors.

Because progressive methods are heuristics that are not guaranteed to converge to a global optimum, alignment quality can be difficult to evaluate and their true biological significance can be obscure. A semi-progressive method that improves alignment quality and does not use a lossy heuristic while still running in polynomial time has been implemented in the program PSAlign.

Iterative Methods

A set of methods to produce MSAs while reducing the errors inherent in progressive methods are classified as "iterative" because they work similarly to progressive methods but repeatedly realign the initial sequences as well as adding new sequences to the growing MSA. One reason progressive methods are so strongly dependent on a high-quality initial alignment is the fact that these alignments are always incorporated into the final result — that is, once a sequence has been aligned into the MSA, its alignment is not considered further. This approximation improves efficiency at the cost of accuracy. By contrast, iterative methods can return to previously calculated pairwise alignments or sub-MSAs incorporating subsets of the query sequence as a means of optimizing a general objective function such as finding a high-quality alignment score.

A variety of subtly different iteration methods have been implemented and made available in software packages; reviews and comparisons have been useful but generally refrain from choosing a "best" technique. The software package PRRN/PRRP uses a hill-climbing algorithm to optimize its MSA alignment score and iteratively corrects both alignment weights and locally divergent or "gappy" regions of the growing MSA. PRRP performs best when refining an alignment previously constructed by a faster method.

Another iterative program, DIALIGN, takes an unusual approach of focusing narrowly on local alignments between sub-segments or sequence motifs without introducing a gap penalty. The alignment of individual motifs is then achieved with a matrix representation similar to a dot-matrix plot in a pairwise alignment. An alternative method that uses fast local alignments as anchor points or "seeds" for a slower global-alignment procedure is implemented in the CHAOS/DIALIGN suite.

A third popular iteration-based method called MUSCLE (multiple sequence alignment by log-expectation) improves on progressive methods with a more accurate distance measure to assess the relatedness of two sequences. The distance measure is updated between iteration stages (although, in its original form, MUSCLE contained only 2-3 iterations depending on whether refinement was enabled).

Consensus Methods

Consensus methods attempt to find the optimal multiple sequence alignment given multiple different alignments of the same set of sequences. There are two commonly used consensus methods, M-COFFEE and MergeAlign. M-COFFEE uses multiple sequence alignments generated by seven different methods to generate consensus alignments. MergeAlign is capable of generating consensus alignments from any number of input alignments generated using different models of sequence evolution or different methods of multiple sequence alignment. The default option for MergeAlign is to infer a consensus alignment using alignments generated using 91 different models of protein sequence evolution.

Hidden Markov Models

Hidden Markov models are probabilistic models that can assign likelihoods to all possible combinations of gaps, matches, and mismatches to determine the most likely MSA or set of possible MSAs. HMMs can produce a single highest-scoring output but can also generate a family of possible alignments that can then be evaluated for biological significance. HMMs can produce both global and local alignments. Although HMM-based methods have been developed relatively recently, they offer significant improvements in computational speed, especially for sequences that contain overlapping regions.

Typical HMM-based methods work by representing an MSA as a form of directed acyclic graph known as a partial-order graph, which consists of a series of nodes representing possible entries in the columns of an MSA. In this representation a column that is absolutely conserved (that is, that all the sequences in the MSA share a particular character at a particular position) is coded as a single node with as many outgoing connections as there are possible characters in the next column of the alignment. In the terms of a typical hidden Markov model, the observed states are the individual alignment columns and the "hidden" states represent the presumed ancestral sequence from which the sequences in the query set are hypothesized to have descended. An efficient search variant of the dynamic programming method, known as the Viterbi algorithm, is generally used to successively align the growing MSA to the next sequence in the query set to produce a new MSA. This is distinct from progressive alignment methods because the alignment of prior sequences is updated at each new sequence addition. However, like progressive methods, this technique can be influenced by the order in which the sequences in the query set are integrated into the alignment, especially when the sequences are distantly related.

Several software programs are available in which variants of HMM-based methods have been implemented and which are noted for their scalability and efficiency, although properly using an HMM method is more complex than using more common progressive methods. The simplest is POA (Partial-Order Alignment); a similar but more generalized method is implemented in the packages SAM (Sequence Alignment and Modeling System). and HMMER. SAM has been used as a source of alignments for protein structure prediction to participate in the CASP structure prediction experiment and to develop a database of predicted proteins in the yeast species *S. cerevisiae*. HHsearch is a software package for the detection of remotely related protein sequences based on the pairwise comparison of HMMs. A server running HHsearch (HHpred) was by far the fastest of the 10 best automatic structure prediction servers in the CASP7 and CASP8 structure prediction competitions.

Genetic Algorithms and Simulated Annealing

Standard optimization techniques in computer science — both of which were inspired by, but do not directly reproduce, physical processes — have also been used in an attempt to more efficiently produce quality MSAs. One such technique, genetic algorithms, has been used for MSA production in an attempt to broadly simulate the hypothesized evolutionary process that gave rise to the divergence in the query set. The method works by breaking a series of possible MSAs into fragments and repeatedly rearranging those fragments with the introduction of gaps at varying positions. A general objective function is optimized during the simulation, most generally the "sum of pairs" maximization function introduced in dynamic programming-based MSA methods. A technique for protein sequences has been implemented in the software program SAGA (Sequence Alignment by Genetic Algorithm) and its equivalent in RNA is called RAGA.

The technique of simulated annealing, by which an existing MSA produced by another method is refined by a series of rearrangements designed to find better regions of alignment space than the one the input alignment already occupies. Like the genetic algorithm method, simulated annealing maximizes an objective function like the sum-of-pairs function. Simulated annealing uses a metaphorical "temperature factor" that determines the rate at which rearrangements proceed and the likelihood of each rearrangement; typical usage alternates periods of high rearrangement rates with relatively low likelihood (to explore more distant regions of alignment space) with periods of lower rates and higher likelihoods to more thoroughly explore local minima near the newly "colonized" regions. This approach has been implemented in the program MSA-SA (Multiple Sequence Alignment by Simulated Annealing).

Phylogeny-aware Methods

Non-homologous exon alignment by an iterative method (a), and by a phylogeny-aware method (b)

Most multiple sequence alignment methods try to minimize the number of insertions/deletions (gaps) and, as a consequence, produce compact alignments. This causes several problems if the sequences to be aligned contain non-homologous regions, if gaps are informative in a phylogeny analysis. These problems are common in newly produced sequences that are poorly annotated and may contain frame-shifts, wrong domains or non-homologous spliced exons.

The first such method was developed in 2005 by Löytynoja and Goldman. The same authors released a software package called *PRANK* in 2008. PRANK improves alignments when insertions are present. Nevertheless, it runs slowly compared to progressive and/or iterative methods which have been developed for several years.

In 2012, two new phylogeny-aware tools appeared. One is called *PAGAN* that was developed by the same team as PRANK. The other is *ProGraphMSA* developed by Szalkowski. Both software packages were developed independently but share common features, notably the use of graph algorithms to improve the recognition of non-homologous regions, and an improvement in code making these software faster than PRANK.

Motif Finding

```
DAMMfly2R_ : MYLPERTEHQKIERLY-----------------------------------------DSNRVN-------------AEPGQGL----
DCP1fly2R_ : ---------------MTD-----------------ECVTRNYGVGIRSPNGSENRGS-FIMADNTDAK-------------GCTPESLVVGG
DRICEfly3R : MDATNNGESADQVGIRVGN----------------PEQPNDHTDALGSV-GSGGAGSSGLVAGSSHPY-------------GSGAIGQLANG
DECAYfly3R : MDDTDFSLFGQKNKHK-----------------------------------------KDKADATKIA-------------HTPTSEL----
DRONCfly3L : MQPPELEIGMPKRHREHIRKNLNILVEWTNYERLAMECVQQGILTVQMLRNTQDLNGK-PFNMDEKDVRVEQHRRLLLKITQRGPTAYNLLINA
STRICAfly2 : MGWWSKKSETDRSQPSQELVAQDPRTRVQTTSAATETTNTAVQNSTITDNNKQTVTEI-TTRQTVTHTQRALITETTTRRTPSQAELEALFAKI
DREDDPAfly : MSASAIYRPFPKVKHFCIFPIAMAGSNLLIHLDTIDQNDLIYVERDMNFAQKVGLGFL-LYGDDHSDATYILQKLLAMTRSDFPQSDLLIKFAK
DREDDPBfly : MSASAIYRPFPKVKHFCIFPIAMAGSNLLIHLDTIDQNDLIYVERDMNFAQKVGLGFL-LYGDDHSDATYILQKLLAMTRSDFPQSDLLIKFAK
DREDDPCfly : MSASAIYRPFPKVKHFCIFPIAMAGSNLLIHLDTIDQNDLIYVERDMNFAQKVGLGFL-LYGDDHSDATYILQKLLAMTRSDFPQSDLLIKFAK
```

Alignment of the seven Drosophila caspases colored by motifs as identified by MEME. When motif positions and sequence alignments are generated independently, they often correlate well but not perfectly, as in this example.

Motif finding, also known as profile analysis, is a method of locating sequence motifs in global MSAs that is both a means of producing a better MSA and a means of producing a scoring matrix for use in searching other sequences for similar motifs. A variety of methods for isolating the motifs have been developed, but all are based on identifying short highly conserved patterns within the larger alignment and constructing a matrix similar to a substitution matrix that reflects the amino acid or nucleotide composition of each position in the putative motif. The alignment can then be refined using these matrices. In standard profile analysis, the matrix includes entries for each possible character as well as entries for gaps. Alternatively, statistical pattern-finding algorithms can identify motifs as a precursor to an MSA rather than as a derivation. In many cases when the query set contains only a small number of sequences or contains only highly related sequences, pseudocounts are added to normalize the distribution reflected in the scoring matrix. In particular, this corrects zero-probability entries in the matrix to values that are small but nonzero.

Blocks analysis is a method of motif finding that restricts motifs to ungapped regions in the alignment. Blocks can be generated from an MSA or they can be extracted from unaligned sequences using a precalculated set of common motifs previously generated from known gene families. Block scoring generally relies on the spacing of high-frequency characters rather than on the calculation of an explicit substitution matrix. The BLOCKS server provides an interactive method to locate such motifs in unaligned sequences.

Statistical pattern-matching has been implemented using both the expectation-maximization algorithm and the Gibbs sampler. One of the most common motif-finding tools, known as MEME, uses expectation maximization and hidden Markov methods to generate motifs that are then used as search tools by its companion MAST in the combined suite MEME/MAST.

Non-Coding Multiple Sequence Alignment

Non-coding DNA regions, especially TFBSs, are rather more conserved and not necessarily evolutionarily related, and may have converged from non-common ancestors. Thus, the assumptions used to align protein sequences and DNA coding regions are inherently different from those that hold for TFBS sequences. Although it is meaningful to align DNA coding regions for homologous sequences using mutation operators, alignment of binding site sequences for the same transcription factor cannot rely on evolutionary related mutation operations. Similarly, the evolutionary operator of point mutations can be used to define an edit distance for coding sequences, but this has little meaning for TFBS sequences because any sequence variation has to maintain a certain level of specificity for the binding site to function. This becomes specifically important when trying to align known TFBS sequences to build supervised models to predict unknown locations of the same TFBS. Hence, Multiple Sequence Alignment methods need to adjust the underlying evolutionary hypothesis and the operators used as in the work published incorporating neighbouring base thermodynamic information to align the binding sites searching for the lowest thermodynamic alignment conserving specificity of the binding site, EDNA .

Alignment Visualization and Quality Control

The necessary use of heuristics for multiple alignment means that for an arbitrary set of proteins, there is always a good chance that an alignment will contain errors. For example, an evaluation of several leading alignment programs using the BAliBase benchmark found that at least 24% of all pairs of aligned amino acids were incorrectly aligned. These errors can arise because of unique insertions into one or more regions of sequences, or through some more complex evolutionary process leading to proteins that do not align easily by sequence alone. As the number of sequence and their divergence increases many more errors will be made simply because of the heuristic nature of MSA algorithms. Multiple sequence alignment viewers enable alignments to be visually reviewed, often by inspecting the quality of alignment for annotated functional sites on two or more sequences. Many also enable the alignment to be edited to correct these (usually minor) errors, in order to obtain an optimal 'curated' alignment suitable for use in phylogenetic analysis or comparative modeling.

However, as the number of sequences increases and especially in genome-wide studies that involve many MSAs it is impossible to manually curate all alignments. Furthermore, manual curation is subjective. And finally, even the best expert cannot confidently align the more ambiguous cases of highly diverged sequences. In such cases it is common practice to use automatic procedures to exclude unreliably aligned regions from the MSA. For the purpose of phylogeny reconstruction the Gblocks program is widely used to remove alignment blocks suspect of low quality, according to various cutoffs on the number of gapped sequences in alignment columns. However, these criteria may excessively filter out regions with insertion/deletion events that may still be aligned reliably, and these regions might be desirable for other purposes such as detection of positive selection. A few alignment algorithms output site-specific scores that allow the selection of high-confidence regions. Such a service was first offered by the SOAP program, which tests the robustness of each column to perturbation in the parameters of the popular alignment program CLUSTALW. The T-Coffee program uses a library of alignments in the construction of the final MSA, and its output MSA is colored according to confidence scores that reflect the agreement between different alignments in the library regarding each aligned residue. Its extension, TCS : (Transitive Consistency Score), uses T-Coffee libraries of pairwise alignments to evaluate any third party MSA. Pairwise projections can be produced using fast or slow methods, thus allowing a trade-off between speed and accuracy. Another alignment program that can output an MSA with confidence scores is FSA, which uses a statistical model that allows calculation of the uncertainty in the alignment. The HoT (Heads-Or-Tails) score can be used as a measure of site-specific alignment uncertainty due to the existence of multiple co-optimal solutions. The GUIDANCE program calculates a similar site-specific confidence measure based on the robustness of the alignment to uncertainty in the guide tree that is used in progressive alignment programs. An alternative, more statistically justified approach to assess alignment uncertainty is the use of probabilistic evolutionary models for joint estimation of phylogeny and alignment. A Bayesian approach allows calculation of posterior probabilities of estimated phylogeny and alignment, which is a measure of the confidence in these estimates. In this case, a posterior probability can be calculated for each site in the alignment. Such an approach was implemented in the program BAli-Phy.

There free available programs for visualization of multiple sequence alignments: JalView, UGENE.

Use in Phylogenetics

Multiple sequence alignments can be used to create a phylogenetic tree. This is made possible by two reasons. The first is because functional domains that are known in annotated sequences can be used for alignment in non-annotated sequences. The other is that conserved regions known to be functionally important can be found. This makes it possible for multiple sequence alignments to be used to analyze and find evolutionary relationships through homology between sequences. Point mutations and insertion or deletion events (called indels) can be detected.

Multiple sequence alignments can also be used to identify functionally important sites, such as binding sites, active sites, or sites corresponding to other key functions, by locating conserved domains. When looking at multiple sequence alignments, it is useful to consider different aspects of the sequences when comparing sequences. These aspects include identity, similarity, and homology. Identity means that the sequences have identical residues at their respective positions. On the other hand, similarity has to do with the sequences being compared having similar residues quantitatively. For example, in terms of nucleotide sequences, pyrimidines are considered similar to each other, as are purines. Similarity ultimately leads to homology, in that the more similar sequences are, the closer they are to being homologous. This similarity in sequences can then go on to help find common ancestry.

References

- Kim N; Lee C (2008). "Bioinformatics detection of alternative splicing". Methods Mol. Biol. Methods in Molecular Biology™. 452: 179–97. doi:10.1007/978-1-60327-159-2_9. ISBN 978-1-58829-707-5. PMID 18566765.

- Mount, D. W. (2004). Bioinformatics: Sequence and Genome Analysis (2nd ed.). Cold Spring Harbor Press. ISBN 978-0-87969-712-9.

- Wong, KC (2016). Computational Biology and Bioinformatics: Gene Regulation. CRC Press (Taylor & Francis Group). ISBN 9781498724975.

- Moody, Glyn (2004). Digital Code of Life: How Bioinformatics is Revolutionizing Science, Medicine, and Business. ISBN 978-0-471-32788-2.

- Gusfield, Dan (1997). Algorithms on strings, trees, and sequences : computer science and computational biology (Reprinted (with corr.) ed.). Cambridge [u.a.]: Cambridge Univ. Press. ISBN 9780521585194.

- Mount DM. (2004). Bioinformatics: Sequence and Genome Analysis (2nd ed.). Cold Spring Harbor Laboratory Press: Cold Spring Harbor, NY. ISBN 0-87969-608-7.

- Altschul SF; Gish W (1996). "Local Alignment Statistics". Meth.Enz. Methods in Enzymology. 266: 460–480. doi:10.1016/S0076-6879(96)66029-7. ISBN 9780121821678.

- Brohée, Sylvain; Barriot, Roland; Moreau, Yves. "Biological knowledge bases using Wikis: combining the flexibility of Wikis with the structure of databases". Bioinformatics. Oxford Journals. Retrieved 5 May 2015.

Biological Networks: An Overview

Biological networks are networks that relate to biological systems. Biological networks offer mathematical illustrations that are found in ecological or physiological studies. The following section is an overview of the subject matter incorporating all the major characteristics of biological networks.

Biological Network

A biological network is any network that applies to biological systems. A network is any system with sub-units that are linked into a whole, such as species units linked into a whole food web. Biological networks provide a mathematical representation of connections found in ecological, evolutionary, and physiological studies, such as neural networks. The analysis of biological networks with respect to human diseases has led to the field of network medicine.

Network Biology and Bioinformatics

Complex biological systems may be represented and analyzed as computable networks. For example, ecosystems can be modeled as networks of interacting species or a protein can be modeled as a network of amino acids. Breaking a protein down farther, amino acids can be represented as a network of connected atoms, such as carbon, nitrogen, and oxygen. Nodes and edges are the basic components of a network. Nodes represent units in the network, while edges represent the interactions between the units. Nodes can represent a wide-array of biological units, from individual organisms to individual neurons in the brain. Two important properties of a network are degree and betweenness centrality. Degree (or connectivity, a distinct usage from that used in graph theory) is the number of edges that connect a node, while betweenness is a measure of how central a node is in a network. Nodes with high betweenness essentially serve as bridges between different portions of the network (i.e. interactions must pass through this node to reach other portions of the network). In social networks, nodes with high degree or high betweenness may play important roles in the overall composition of a network.

As early as the 1980s, researchers started viewing DNA or genomes as the dynamic storage of a language system with precise computable finite states represented as a finite state machine. Recent complex systems research has also suggested some far-reaching commonality in the organization of information in problems from biology, computer science, and physics, such as the Bose–Einstein condensate (a special state of matter).

Bioinformatics has increasingly shifted its focus from individual genes, proteins, and search algorithms to large-scale networks often denoted as -omes such as biome, interactome, genome and proteome. Such theoretical studies have revealed that biological networks share many features with other networks such as the Internet or social networks, e.g. their network topology.

Networks in Biology

Protein–protein Interaction Networks

Many protein–protein interactions (PPIs) in a cell form *protein interaction networks* (PINs) where proteins are *nodes* and their interactions are *edges*. PINs are the most intensely analyzed networks in biology. There are dozens of PPI detection methods to identify such interactions. The yeast two-hybrid system is a commonly used experimental technique for the study of binary interactions.

Recent studies have indicated conservation of molecular networks through deep evolutionary time. Moreover, it has been discovered that proteins with high degrees of connectedness are more likely to be essential for survival than proteins with lesser degrees. This suggests that the overall composition of the network (not simply interactions between protein pairs) is important for the overall functioning of an organism.

Gene Regulatory Networks (DNA–Protein Interaction Networks)

The activity of genes is regulated by transcription factors, proteins that typically bind to DNA. Most transcription factors bind to multiple binding sites in a genome. As a result, all cells have complex gene regulatory networks. For instance, the human genome encodes on the order of 1,400 DNA-binding transcription factors that regulate the expression of more than 20,000 human genes. Technologies to study gene regulatory networks include ChIP-chip, ChIP-seq, CliP-seq, and others.

Gene Co-expression Networks (Transcript–transcript Association Networks)

Gene co-expression networks can be interpreted as association networks between variables that measure transcript abundances. These networks have been used to provide a systems biologic analysis of DNA microarray data, RNA-seq data, miRNA data etc. weighted gene co-expression network analysis is widely used to identify co-expression modules and intramodular hub genes. Co-expression modules may correspond to cell types or pathways. Highly connected intramodular hubs can be interpreted as representatives of their respective module.

Metabolic Networks

The chemical compounds of a living cell are connected by biochemical reactions which convert one compound into another. The reactions are catalyzed by enzymes. Thus, all compounds in a cell are parts of an intricate biochemical network of reactions which is called metabolic network. It is possible to use network analyses to infer how selection acts on metabolic pathways.

Signaling Networks

Signals are transduced within cells or in between cells and thus form complex signaling networks. For instance, in the MAPK/ERK pathway is transduced from the cell surface to the cell nucleus by a series of protein–protein interactions, phosphorylation reactions, and other events. Signaling networks typically integrate protein–protein interaction networks, gene regulatory networks, and metabolic networks.

Neuronal Networks

The complex interactions in the brain make it a perfect candidate to apply network theory. Neurons in the brain are deeply connected with one another and this results in complex networks being present in the structural and functional aspects of the brain. For instance, small-world network properties have been demonstrated in connections between cortical areas of the primate brain. This suggests that cortical areas of the brain are not directly interacting with each other, but most areas can be reached from all others through only a few interactions.

Food Webs

All organisms are connected to each other through feeding interactions. That is, if a species eats or is eaten by another species, they are connected in an intricate food web of predator and prey interactions. The stability of these interactions has been a long-standing question in ecology. That is to say, if certain individuals are removed, what happens to the network (i.e. does it collapse or adapt)? Network analysis can be used to explore food web stability and determine if certain network properties result in more stable networks. Moreover, network analysis can be used to determine how selective removals of species will influence the food web as a whole. This is especially important considering the potential species loss due to global climate change.

Between-species Interaction Networks

In biology, pairwise interactions have historically been the focus of intense study. With the recent advances in network science, it has become possible to scale up pairwise interactions to include individuals of many species involved in many sets of interactions to understand the structure and function of larger ecological networks. The use of network analysis can allow for both the discovery and understanding how these complex interactions link together within the system's network, a property which has previously been overlooked. This powerful tool allows for the study of various types of interactions (from competitive to cooperative) using the same general framework. For example, plant-pollinator interactions are mutually beneficial and often involve many different species of pollinators as well as many different species of plants. These interactions are critical to plant reproduction and thus the accumulation of resources at the base of the food chain for primary consumers, yet these interaction networks are threatened by anthropogenic change. The use of network analysis can illuminate how pollination networks work and may in turn inform conservation efforts. Within pollination networks, nestedness (i.e., specialists interact with a subset of species that generalists interact with), redundancy (i.e., most plants are pollinated by many pollinators), and modularity play a large role in network stability. These network properties may actually work to slow the spread of disturbance effects through the system and potentially buffer the pollination network from anthropogenic changes somewhat. More generally, the structure of species interactions within an ecological network can tell us something about the diversity, richness, and robustness of the network. Researchers can even compare current constructions of species interactions networks with historical reconstructions of ancient networks to determine how networks have changed over time. Recent research into these complex species interactions networks is highly concerned with understanding what factors (e.g., diversity) lead to network stability.

Within-species Interaction Networks

Network analysis provides the ability to quantify associations between individuals, which makes it possible to infer details about the network as a whole at the species and/or population level. Researchers interested in animal behavior across a multitude of taxa, from insects to primates, are starting to incorporate network analysis into their research. Researchers interested in social insects (e.g., ants and bees) have used network analyses to better understand division of labor, task allocation, and foraging optimization within colonies; Other researchers are interested in how certain network properties at the group and/or population level can explain individual level behaviors. For instance, a study on wire-tailed manakins (a small passerine bird) found that a male's degree in the network largely predicted the ability of the male to rise in the social hierarchy (i.e. eventually obtain a territory and matings). In bottlenose dolphin groups, an individual's degree and betweenness centrality values may predict whether or not that individual will exhibit certain behaviors, like the use of side flopping and upside-down lobtailing to lead group traveling efforts; individuals with high betweenness values are more connected and can obtain more information, and thus are better suited to lead group travel and therefore tend to exhibit these signaling behaviors more than other group members. Network analysis can also be used to describe the social organization within a species more generally, which frequently reveals important proximate mechanisms promoting the use of certain behavioral strategies. These descriptions are frequently linked to ecological properties (e.g., resource distribution). For example, network analyses revealed subtle differences in the group dynamics of two related equid fission-fusion species, Grevy's zebra and onagers, living in variable environments; Grevy's zebras show distinct preferences in their association choices when they fission into smaller groups, whereas onagers do not. Similarly, researchers interested in primates have also utilized network analyses to compare social organizations across the diverse primate order, suggesting that using network measures (such as centrality, assortativity, modularity, and betweenness) may be useful in terms of explaining the types of social behaviors we see within certain groups and not others. Finally, social network analysis can also reveal important fluctuations in animal behaviors across changing environments. For example, network analyses in female chacma baboons (*Papio hamadryas ursinus*) revealed important dynamic changes across seasons which were previously unknown; instead of creating stable, long-lasting social bonds with friends, baboons were found to exhibit more variable relationships which were dependent on short-term contingencies related to group level dynamics as well as environmental variability. This is a very small set of broad examples of how researchers can use network analysis to study animal behavior. Research in this area is currently expanding very rapidly. Social network analysis is a valuable tool for studying animal behavior across all animal species, and has the potential to uncover new information about animal behavior and social ecology that was previously poorly understood.

Interactome

In molecular biology, an interactome is the whole set of molecular interactions in a particular cell. The term specifically refers to physical interactions among molecules (such as those among proteins, also known as protein–protein interactions, PPIs) but can also describe sets of indirect interactions among genes (genetic interactions). The interactomes based on PPIs should be associated to the proteome of the corresponding specie in order to provide a global view ("omic") of all the possible molecular interactions that a protein can present. A recent compendium of interactomes can be obtained in the resource: APID interactomes.

Part of the DISC1 interactome with genes represented by text in boxes and interactions noted by lines between the genes. From Hennah and Porteous, 2009.

The word "interactome" was originally coined in 1999 by a group of French scientists headed by Bernard Jacq. Mathematically, interactomes are generally displayed as graphs. Though interactomes may be described as biological networks, they should not be confused with other networks such as neural networks or food webs.

Molecular Interaction Networks

Molecular interactions can occur between molecules belonging to different biochemical families (proteins, nucleic acids, lipids, carbohydrates, etc.) and also within a given family. Whenever such molecules are connected by physical interactions, they form molecular interaction networks that are generally classified by the nature of the compounds involved. Most commonly, *interactome* refers to *protein–protein interaction* (PPI) network (PIN) or subsets thereof. For instance, the Sirt-1 protein interactome and Sirt family second order interactome is the network involving Sirt-1 and its directly interacting proteins where as second order interactome illustrates interactions up to second order of neighbors (Neighbors of neighbors). Another extensively studied type of interactome is the protein–DNA interactome, also called a *gene-regulatory network*, a network formed by transcription factors, chromatin regulatory proteins, and their target genes. Even *metabolic networks* can be considered as molecular interaction networks: metabolites, i.e. chemical compounds in a cell, are converted into each other by enzymes, which have to bind their substrates physically.

In fact, all interactome types are interconnected. For instance, protein interactomes contain many enzymes which in turn form biochemical networks. Similarly, gene regulatory networks overlap substantially with protein interaction networks and signaling networks.

Size of Interactomes

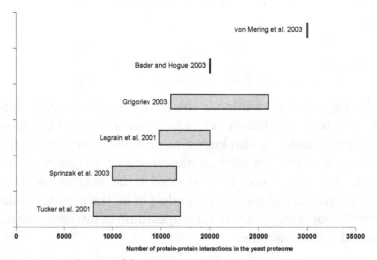

Estimates of the yeast protein interactome. From

It has been suggested that the size of an organism's interactome correlates better than genome size with the biological complexity of the organism. Although protein–protein interaction maps containing several thousand binary interactions are now available for several species, none of them is presently complete and the size of interactomes is still a matter of debate.

Yeast

The yeast interactome, i.e. all protein–protein interactions among proteins of *Saccharomyces cerevisiae*, has been estimated to contain between 10,000 and 30,000 interactions. A reasonable estimate may be on the order of 20,000 interactions. Larger estimates often include indirect or predicted interactions, often from affinity purification/mass spectrometry (AP/MS) studies.

Genetic Interaction Networks

Genes interact in the sense that they affect each other's function. For instance, a mutation may be harmless, but when it is combined with another mutation, the combination may turn out to be lethal. Such genes are said to "interact genetically". Genes that are connected in such a way form *genetic interaction networks*. Some of the goals of these networks are: develop a functional map of a cell's processes, drug target identification, and to predict the function of uncharacterized genes.

In 2010, the most "complete" gene interactome produced to date was compiled from about 5.4 million two-gene comparisons to describe "the interaction profiles for ~75% of all genes in the budding yeast," with ~170,000 gene interactions. The genes were grouped based on similar function so as to build a functional map of the cell's processes. Using this method the study was able to predict known gene functions better than any other genome-scale data set as well as adding functional information for genes that hadn't been previously described. From this model genetic interactions can be observed at multiple scales which will assist in the study of concepts such as gene conservation. Some of the observations made from this study are that there were twice as many negative as positive interactions, negative interactions were more informative than positive interactions, and genes with more connections were more likely to result in lethality when disrupted.

Interactomics

Interactomics is a discipline at the intersection of bioinformatics and biology that deals with studying both the interactions and the consequences of those interactions between and among proteins, and other molecules within a cell. Interactomics thus aims to compare such networks of interactions (i.e., interactomes) between and within species in order to find how the traits of such networks are either preserved or varied.

Interactomics is an example of "top-down" systems biology, which takes an overhead, as well as overall, view of a biosystem or organism. Large sets of genome-wide and proteomic data are collected, and correlations between different molecules are inferred. From the data new hypotheses are formulated about feedbacks between these molecules. These hypotheses can then be tested by new experiments.

Experimental Methods to Map Interactomes

The study of interactomes is called interactomics. The basic unit of a protein network is the protein–protein interaction (PPI). While there are numerous methods to study PPIs, there are relatively few that have been used on a large scale to map whole interactomes.

The yeast two hybrid system (Y2H) is suited to explore the binary interactions among two proteins at a time. Affinity purification and subsequent mass spectrometry is suited to identify a protein complex. Both methods can be used in a high-throughput (HTP) fashion. Yeast two hybrid screens allow include false positive interactions between proteins that are never expressed in the same time and place; affinity capture mass spectrometry does not have this drawback, and is the current gold standard. Yeast two-hybrid data better indicates non-specific tendencies towards sticky interactions rather while affinity capture mass spectrometry better indicates functional in vivo protein–protein interactions.

Computational Methods to Study Interactomes

Once an interactome has been created, there are numerous ways to analyze its properties. However, there are two important goals of such analyses. First, scientists try to elucidate the systems properties of interactomes, e.g. the topology of its interactions. Second, studies may focus on individual proteins and their role in the network. Such analyses are mainly carried out using bioinformatics methods and include the following, among many others:

Validation

First, the coverage and quality of an interactome has to be evaluated. Interactomes are never complete, given the limitations of experimental methods. For instance, it has been estimated that typical Y2H screens detect only 25% or so of all interactions in an interactome. The coverage of an interactome can be assessed by comparing it to benchmarks of well-known interactions that have been found and validated by independent assays. Other methods filter out false positives calculating the similarity of known annotations of the proteins involved or define a likelyhood of interaction using the subcellular localization of these proteins.

Predicting PPIs

Using experimental data as a starting point, *homology transfer* is one way to predict interactomes. Here, PPIs from one organism are used to predict interactions among homologous proteins in another organism ("*interologs*"). However, this approach has certain limitations, primarily because the source data may not be reliable (e.g. contain false positives and false negatives). In addition, proteins and their interactions change

during evolution and thus may have been lost or gained. Nevertheless, numerous interactomes have been predicted, e.g. that of *Bacillus licheniformis.*

Schziophrenia PPI.

Some algorithms use experimental evidence on structural complexes, the atomic details of binding interfaces and produce detailed atomic models of protein–protein complexes as well as other protein–molecule interactions. Other algorithms use only sequence information, thereby creating unbiased complete networks of interaction with
many mistakes.

Some methods use machine learning to distinguish how interacting protein pairs differ from non-interacting protein pairs in terms of pairwise features such as cellular
colocalization, gene co-expression, how closely located on a DNA are the genes that
encode the two proteins, and so on. Random Forest has been found to be most-effec-
tive machine learning method for protein interaction prediction. Such methods have
been applied for discovering protein interactions on human interactome, specifically
the interactome of Membrane proteins and the interactome of Schizophrenia-associat-
ed proteins.

Text Mining of PPIs

Some efforts have been made to extract systematically interaction networks directly
from the scientific literature. Such approaches range in terms of complexity from simple co-occurrence statistics of entities that are mentioned together in the same context (e.g. sentence) to sophisticated natural language processing and machine learning
methods for detecting interaction relationships.

Protein Function Prediction

Protein interaction networks have been used to predict the function of proteins of unknown functions. This is usually based on the assumption that uncharacterized pro-

teins have similar functions as their interacting proteins (*guilt by association*). For example, YbeB, a protein of unknown function was found to interact with ribosomal proteins and later shown to be involved in translation. Although such predictions may be based on single interactions, usually several interactions are found. Thus, the whole network of interactions can be used to predict protein functions, given that certain functions are usually enriched among the interactors.

Perturbations and Disease

The *topology* of an interactome makes certain predictions how a network reacts to the perturbation (e.g. removal) of nodes (proteins) or edges (interactions). Such perturbations can be caused by mutations of genes, and thus their proteins, and a network reaction can manifest as a disease. A network analysis can identified drug targets and biomarkers of diseases.

Network Structure and Topology

Interaction networks can be analyzed using the tools of graph theory. Network properties include the degree distribution, clustering coefficients, betweenness centrality, and many others. The distribution of properties among the proteins of an interactome has revealed that the interactome networks often have scale-free topology where functional modules within a network indicate specialized subnetworks. Such modules can be functional, as in a signaling pathway, or structural, as in a protein complex. In fact, it is a formidable task to identify protein complexes in an interactome, given that a network on its own does not directly reveal the presence of a stable complex.

Studied Interactomes

Viral Interactomes

Viral protein interactomes consist of interactions among viral or phage proteins. They were among the first interactome projects as their genomes are small and all proteins can be analyzed with limited resources. Viral interactomes are connected to their host interactomes, forming virus-host interaction networks. Some published virus interactomes include

Bacteriophage

- *Escherichia coli* bacteriophage lambda
- *Escherichia coli* bacteriophage T7
- *Streptococcus pneumoniae* bacteriophage Dp-1
- *Streptococcus pneumoniae* bacteriophage Cp-1

The lambda and VZV interactomes are not only relevant for the biology of these viruses but also for technical reasons: they were the first interactomes that were mapped with multiple Y2H vectors, proving an improved strategy to investigate interactomes more completely than previous attempts have shown.

Human (Mammalian) Viruses

- Human varicella zoster virus (VZV)
- Chandipura virus
- Epstein-Barr virus (EBV)
- Hepatitis C virus (HPC), Human-HCV interactions
- Hepatitis E virus (HEV)
- Herpes simplex virus 1 (HSV-1)
- Kaposi's sarcoma-associated herpesvirus (KSHV)
- Murine cytomegalovirus (mCMV)

Bacterial Interactomes

Relatively few bacteria have been comprehensively studied for their protein–protein interactions. However, none of these interactomes are complete in the sense that they captured all interactions. In fact, it has been estimated that none of them covers more than 20% or 30% of all interactions, primarily because most of these studies have only employed a single method, all of which discover only a subset of interactions. Among the published bacterial interactomes (including partial ones) are

Species	proteins total	interactions	type
Helicobacter pylori	1,553	~3,004	Y2H
Campylobacter jejuni	1,623	11,687	Y2H
Treponema pallidum	1,040	3,649	Y2H
Escherichia coli	4,288	(5,993)	AP/MS
Escherichia coli	4,288	2,234	Y2H
Mesorhizobium loti	6,752	3,121	Y2H
Mycobacterium tuberculosis	3,959	>8000	B2H
Mycoplasma genitalium	482		AP/MS
Synechocystis sp. PCC6803	3,264	3,236	Y2H
Staphylococcus aureus (MRSA)	2,656	13,219	AP/MS

The *E. coli* and *Mycoplasma* interactomes have been analyzed using large-scale protein complex affinity purification and mass spectrometry (AP/MS), hence it is not easily possible to infer direct interactions. The others have used extensive yeast two-hybrid (Y2H) screens. The *Mycobacterium tuberculosis* interactome has been analyzed using a bacterial two-hybrid screen (B2H).

Note that numerous additional interactomes have been predicted using computational methods.

Eukaryotic Interactomes

There have been several efforts to map eukaryotic interactomes through HTP methods. While no biological interactomes have been fully characterized, over 90% of proteins in *Saccharomyces cerevisiae* have been screened and their interactions characterized, making it the best-characterized interactome. Species whose interactomes have been studied in some detail include

- *Schizosaccharomyces pombe*
- *Caenorhabditis elegans*
- *Drosophila melanogaster*
- *Homo sapiens*

Recently, the pathogen-host interactomes of Hepatitis C Virus/Human (2008), Epstein Barr virus/Human (2008), Influenza virus/Human (2009) were delineated through HTP to identify essential molecular components for pathogens and for their host's immune system.

Predicted Interactomes

As described above, PPIs and thus whole interactomes can be predicted. While the reliability of these predictions is debatable, they are providing hypotheses that can be tested experimentally. Interactomes have been predicted for a number of species, e.g.

- Human (*Homo sapiens*)
- Rice (*Oryza sativa*)
- *Xanthomonas oryzae*
- *Arabidopsis thaliana*
- Tomato
- *Brassica rapa*
- Maize, corn (*Zea mays*)
- *Populus trichocarpa*

Network Properties of Interactomes

Protein interaction networks can be analyzed with the same tool as other networks. In fact, they share many properties with biological or social networks. Some of the main characteristics are as follows.

The *Treponema pallidum* protein interactome.

Degree Distribution

The degree distribution describes the number of proteins that have a certain number of connections. Most protein interaction networks show a scale-free (power law) degree distribution where the connectivity distribution $P(k) \sim k^{-\gamma}$ with k being the degree. This relationship can also be seen as a straight line on a log-log plot since, the above equation is equal to $\log(P(k)) \sim -\gamma \cdot \log(k)$. One characteristic of such distributions is that there are many proteins with few interactions and few proteins that have many interactions, the latter being called "hubs".

Hubs

Highly connected nodes (proteins) are called hubs. Han et al. have coined the term "party hub" for hubs whose expression is correlated with its interaction partners. Party hubs also connect proteins within functional modules such as protein complexes. In contrast, "date hubs" do not exhibit such a correlation and appear to connect different functional modules. Party hubs are found predominantly in AP/MS data sets, whereas date hubs are found predominantly in binary interactome network maps. Note that the validity of the date hub/party hub distinction was disputed. Party hubs generally consist of multi-interface proteins whereas date hubs are more frequently single-interaction interface proteins. Consistent with a role for date-hubs in connecting different processes, in yeast the number of binary interactions of a given protein is correlated to the number of phenotypes observed for the corresponding mutant gene in different physiological conditions.

Modules

Nodes involved in the same biochemical process are highly interconnected.

Interactome Evolution

The evolution of interactome complexity is delineated in a study published in Nature. In this study it is first noted that the boundaries between prokaryotes, unicellular eukaryotes and multicellular eukaryotes are accompanied by orders-of-magnitude reductions in effective population size, with concurrent amplifications of the effects of random genetic drift. The resultant decline in the efficiency of selection seems to be sufficient to influence a wide range of attributes at the genomic level in a nonadaptive manner. The Nature study shows that the variation in the power of random genetic drift is also capable of influencing phylogenetic diversity at the subcellular and cellular levels. Thus, population size would have to be considered as a potential determinant of the mechanistic pathways underlying long-term phenotypic evolution. In the study it is further shown that a phylogenetically broad inverse relation exists between the power of drift and the structural integrity of protein subunits. Thus, the accumulation of mildly deleterious mutations in populations of small size induces secondary selection for protein–protein interactions that stabilize key gene functions, mitigating the structural degradation promoted by inefficient selection. By this means, the complex protein architectures and interactions essential to the genesis of phenotypic diversity may initially emerge by non-adaptive mechanisms.

Criticisms, Challenges, and Responses

Kiemer and Cesareni raise the following concerns with the state (circa 2007) of the field especially with the comparative interactomic: The experimental procedures associated with the field are error prone leading to "noisy results". This leads to 30% of all reported interactions being artifacts. In fact, two groups using the same techniques on the same organism found less than 30% interactions in common. However, some authors have argued that such non-reproducibility results from the extraordinary sensitivity of various methods to small experimental variation. For instance, identical conditions in Y2H assays result in very different interactions when different Y2H vectors are used.

Techniques may be biased, i.e. the technique determines which interactions are found. In fact, any method has built in biases, especially protein methods. Because every protein is different no method can capture the properties of each protein. For instance, most analytical methods that work fine with soluble proteins deal poorly with membrane proteins. This is also true for Y2H and AP/MS technologies.

Interactomes are not nearly complete with perhaps the exception of *S. cerevisiae*. This is not really a criticism as any scientific area is "incomplete" initially until the methodologies have been improved. Interactomics in 2015 is where genome sequencing was in the late 1990s, given that only a few interactome datasets are available.

While genomes are stable, interactomes may vary between tissues, cell types, and developmental stages. Again, this is not a criticism, but rather a description of the challenges in the field.

It is difficult to match evolutionarily related proteins in distantly related species. While homologous DNA sequences can be found relatively easily, it is much more difficult to predict homologous interactions ("interologs") because the homologs of two interacting proteins do not need to interact. For instance, even within a proteome two proteins may interact but their paralogs may not.

Each protein–protein interactome may represent only a partial sample of potential interactions, even when a supposedly definitive version is published in a scientific journal. Additional factors may have roles in protein interactions that have yet to be incorporated in interactomes. The binding strength of the various protein interactors, microenvironmental factors, sensitivity to various procedures, and the physiological state of the cell all impact protein–protein interactions, yet are usually not accounted for in interactome studies.

Gene Regulatory Network

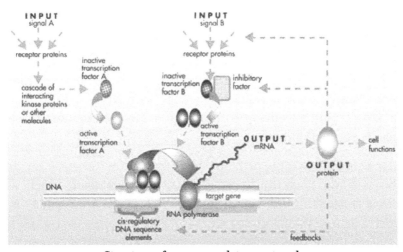

Structure of a gene regulatory network

A gene (or genetic) regulatory network (GRN) is a collection of molecular regulators that interact with each other and with other substances in the cell to govern the gene expression levels of mRNA and proteins. These play a central role in morphogenesis, the creation of body structures, which in turn is central to evolutionary developmental biology (evo-devo).

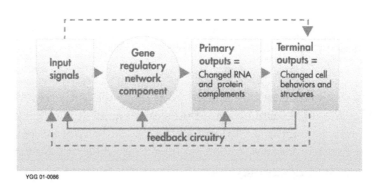

YGG 01-0086

Control process of a gene regulatory network

The regulator can be DNA, RNA, protein and complexes of these. The interaction can be direct or indirect (through transcribed RNA or translated protein). In general, each mRNA molecule goes on to make a specific protein (or set of proteins). In some cases this protein will be structural, and will accumulate at the cell membrane or within the cell to give it particular structural properties. In other cases the protein will be an enzyme, i.e., a micro-machine that catalyses a certain reaction, such as the breakdown of a food source or toxin. Some proteins though serve only to activate other genes, and these are the transcription factors that are the main players in regulatory networks or cascades. By binding to the promoter region at the start of other genes they turn them on, initiating the production of another protein, and so on. Some transcription factors are inhibitory.

In single-celled organisms, regulatory networks respond to the external environment, optimising the cell at a given time for survival in this environment. Thus a yeast cell, finding itself in a sugar solution, will turn on genes to make enzymes that process the sugar to alcohol. This process, which we associate with wine-making, is how the yeast cell makes its living, gaining energy to multiply, which under normal circumstances would enhance its survival prospects.

In multicellular animals the same principle has been put in the service of gene cascades that control body-shape. Each time a cell divides, two cells result which, although they contain the same genome in full, can differ in which genes are turned on and making proteins. Sometimes a 'self-sustaining feedback loop' ensures that a cell maintains its identity and passes it on. Less understood is the mechanism of epigenetics by which chromatin modification may provide cellular memory by blocking or allowing transcription. A major feature of multicellular animals is the use of morphogen gradients, which in effect provide a positioning system that tells a cell where in the body it is, and hence what sort of cell to become. A gene that is turned on in one cell may make a product that leaves the cell and diffuses through adjacent cells, entering them and turning on genes only when it is present above a certain threshold level. These cells are thus induced into a new fate, and may even generate other morphogens that signal back to the original cell. Over longer distances morphogens may use the active process of signal transduction. Such signalling controls embryogenesis, the building of a body plan from scratch through a series of sequential steps. They also control and maintain adult bodies through feedback processes, and the loss of such feedback because of a mutation can be responsible for the cell proliferation that is seen in cancer. In parallel with this process of building structure, the gene cascade turns on genes that make structural proteins that give each cell the physical properties it needs.

Overview

At one level, biological cells can be thought of as "partially mixed bags" of biological chemicals – in the discussion of gene regulatory networks, these chemicals are mostly the messenger RNAs (mRNAs) and proteins that arise from gene expression. These mRNA and proteins interact with each other with various degrees of specificity. Some diffuse around the cell. Others are bound to cell membranes, interacting with molecules in the environment. Still others pass through cell membranes and mediate long range signals to other cells in a multi-cellular organism. These molecules and their interactions comprise a *gene regulatory network*. A typical gene regulatory network looks something like this:

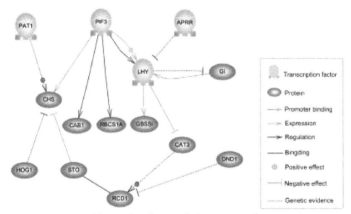

Example of a regulatory network

The nodes of this network are proteins, their corresponding mRNAs, and protein/protein complexes. Nodes that are depicted as lying along vertical lines are associated with the cell/environment interfaces, while the others are free-floating and can diffuse. Implied are genes, the DNA sequences which are transcribed into the mRNAs that translate into proteins. Edges between nodes represent individual molecular reactions, the protein/protein and protein/mRNA interactions through which the products of one gene affect those of another, though the lack of experimentally obtained information often implies that some reactions are not modeled at such a fine level of detail. These interactions can be inductive (the arrowheads), with an increase in the concentration of one leading to an increase in the other, or inhibitory (the filled circles), with an increase in one leading to a decrease in the other. A series of edges indicates a chain of such dependencoes, with cycles corresponding to feedback loops. The network structure is an abstraction of the system's chemical dynamics, describing the manifold ways in which one substance affects all the others to which it is connected. In practice, such GRNs are inferred from the biological literature on a given system and represent a distillation of the collective knowledge about a set of related biochemical reactions. To speed up the manual curation of GRNs, some recent efforts try to use text mining and information extraction technologies for this purpose.

Genes can be viewed as nodes in the network, with input being proteins such as transcription factors, and outputs being the level of gene expression. The node itself can also be viewed as a function which can be obtained by combining basic functions upon the inputs (in the Boolean network described below these are Boolean functions, typically AND, OR, and NOT). These functions have been interpreted as performing a kind of information processing within the cell, which determines cellular behavior. The basic drivers within cells are concentrations of some proteins, which determine both spatial (location within the cell or tissue) and temporal (cell cycle or developmental stage) coordinates of the cell, as a kind of "cellular memory". The gene networks are only beginning to be understood, and it is a next step for biology to attempt to deduce the functions for each gene "node", to help understand the behavior of the system in increasing levels of complexity, from gene to signaling pathway, cell or tissue level.

Mathematical models of GRNs have been developed to capture the behavior of the system being modeled, and in some cases generate predictions corresponding with experimental observations. In some other cases, models have proven to make accurate novel predictions, which can be tested experimentally, thus suggesting new approaches to explore in an experiment that sometimes wouldn't be considered in the design of the protocol of an experimental laboratory. The most common modeling technique involves the use of coupled ordinary differential equations (ODEs). Several other promising modeling techniques have been used, including Boolean networks, Petri nets, Bayesian networks, graphical Gaussian models, Stochastic, and Process Calculi. Conversely, techniques have been proposed for generating models of GRNs that best explain a set of time series observations.Recently it has been shown that ChIP-seq signal of Histone modification are more correlated with transcription factor motifs at promoters in comparison to RNA level. Hence it is proposed that time-series histone modification ChIP-seq could provide more reliable inference of gene-regulatory networks in comparison to methods based on expression levels.

Structure and Evolution

Global Feature

Gene regulatory networks are generally thought to be made up of a few highly connected nodes (hubs) and many poorly connected nodes nested within a hierarchical regulatory regime. Thus gene regulatory networks approximate a hierarchical scale free network topology. This is consistent with the view that most genes have limited pleiotropy and operate within regulatory modules. This structure is thought to evolve due to the preferential attachment of duplicated genes to more highly connected genes. Recent work has also shown that natural selection tends to favor networks with sparse connectivity.

There are primarily two ways that networks can evolve, both of which can occur simultaneously. The first is that network topology can be changed by the addition or subtraction of nodes (genes) or parts of the network (modules) may be expressed in different contexts. The *Drosophila* Hippo signaling pathway provides a good example. The Hippo signaling pathway controls both mitotic growth and post-mitotic cellular differentiation. Recently it was found that the network the Hippo signaling pathway operates in differs between these two functions which in turn changes the behavior of the Hippo signaling pathway. This suggests that the Hippo signaling pathway operates as a conserved regulatory module that can be used for multiple functions depending on context. Thus, changing network topology can allow a conserved module to serve multiple functions and alter the final output of the network. The second way networks can evolve is by changing the strength of interactions between nodes, such as how strongly a transcription factor may bind to a cis-regulatory element. Such variation in strength of network edges has been shown to underlie between species variation in vulva cell fate patterning of *Caenorhabditis* worms.

Local Feature

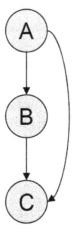

Feed-forward loop

Another widely cited characteristic of gene regulatory network is their abundance of certain repetitive sub-networks known as network motifs. Network motifs can be regarded as repetitive topological patterns when dividing a big network into small blocks. Previous analysis found several types of motifs that appeared more often in gene regulatory networks than in randomly generated networks. As an example, one such motif is called feed-forward loops, which consist three nodes. This motif is the most abundant among all possible motifs made up of three nodes, as is shown in the gene regulatory networks of fly, nematode, and human.

The enriched motifs have been proposed to follow convergent evolution, suggesting they are "optimal designs" for certain regulatory purposes. For example, modeling shows that feed-forward loops are able to coordinate the change in node A (in terms of concentration and activity) and the expression dynamics of node C, creating different input-output behaviors. The galactose utilization system of *E. coli* contains a feed-forward loop which accelerates the activation of galactose utilization operon *galETK*, potentially facilitating the metabolic transition to galactose when glucose is depleted. The feed-forward loop in the arabinose utilization systems of *E.coli* delays the activation of arabinose catabolism operon and transporters, potentially avoiding unnecessary metabolic transition due to temporary fluctuations in upstream signaling pathways. Similarly in the Wnt signaling pathway of *Xenopus*, the feed-forward loop acts as a fold-change detector that responses to the fold change, rather than the absolute change, in the level of β-catenin, potentially increasing the resistance to fluctuations in β-catenin levels. Following the convergent evolution hypothesis, the enrichment of feed-forward loops would be an adaptation for fast response and noise resistance. A recent research found that yeast grown in an environment of constant glucose developed mutations in glucose signaling pathways and growth regulation pathway, suggesting regulatory components responding to environmental changes are dispensable under constant environment.

On the other hand, there are also researchers who hypothesize that the enrichment of network motifs are non-adaptive. In other words, gene regulatory networks can evolve to a similar structure without the specific selection on the proposed input-output behavior. Support for this hypothesis often comes from computational simulations. For example, fluctuations in the abundance of feed-forward loops in a model that simulates the evolution of gene regulatory networks by randomly rewiring nodes may suggest that the enrichment of feed-forward loops is a side-effect of evolution. In another model of gene regulator networks evolution, the ratio of the frequencies of gene duplication and gene deletion show great influence on network topology: certain ratios lead to the enrichment of feed-forward loops and create networks that show features of hierarchical scale free networks.

Bacterial Regulatory Networks

Regulatory networks allow bacteria to adapt to almost every environmental niche on earth. A network of interactions among diverse types of molecules including DNA, RNA, proteins and metabolites, is utilised by the bacteria to achieve regulation of gene expression. In bacteria, the principal function of regulatory networks is to control the response to environmental changes, for example nutritional status and environmental stress. A complex organization of networks permits the microorganism to coordinate and integrate multiple environmental signals.

Modelling

Coupled Ordinary Differential Equations

It is common to model such a network with a set of coupled ordinary differential equations (ODEs) or stochastic ODEs, describing the reaction kinetics of the constituent parts. Suppose that our regulatory network has N nodes, and let $S_1(t), S_2(t), \ldots, S_N(t)$ represent the concentrations of the N corresponding substances at time t. Then the temporal evolution of the system can be described approximately by

$$\frac{dS_j}{dt} = f_j\left(S_1, S_2, \ldots, S_N\right)$$

where the functions f_j express the dependence of S_j on the concentrations of other substances present in the cell. The functions f_j are ultimately derived from basic principles of chemical kinetics or simple expressions derived from these e.g. Michaelis-Menten enzymatic kinetics. Hence, the functional forms of the f_j are usually chosen as low-order polynomials or Hill functions that serve as an ansatz for the real molecular dynamics. Such models are then studied using the mathematics of nonlinear dynamics. System-specific information, like reaction rate constants and sensitivities, are encoded as constant parameters.

By solving for the fixed point of the system:

$$\frac{dS_j}{dt} = 0$$

for all j, one obtains (possibly several) concentration profiles of proteins and mRNAs that are theoretically sustainable (though not necessarily stable). Steady states of kinetic equations thus correspond to potential cell types, and oscillatory solutions to the above equation to naturally cyclic cell types. Mathematical stability of these attractors can usually be characterized by the sign of higher derivatives at critical points, and then correspond to biochemical stability of the concentration profile. Critical points and bifurcations in the equations correspond to critical cell states in which small state or parameter perturbations could switch the system between one of several stable differentiation fates. Trajectories correspond to the unfolding of biological pathways and transients of the equations to short-term biological events.

Boolean Network

The following example illustrates how a Boolean network can model a GRN together with its gene products (the outputs) and the substances from the environment that affect it (the inputs). Stuart Kauffman was amongst the first biologists to use the metaphor of Boolean networks to model genetic regulatory networks.

1. Each gene, each input, and each output is represented by a node in a directed graph in which there is an arrow from one node to another if and only if there is a causal link between the two nodes.

2. Each node in the graph can be in one of two states: on or off.

3. For a gene, "on" corresponds to the gene being expressed; for inputs and outputs, "off" corresponds to the substance being present.

4. Time is viewed as proceeding in discrete steps. At each step, the new state of a node is a Boolean function of the prior states of the nodes with arrows pointing towards it.

The validity of the model can be tested by comparing simulation results with time series observations. A partial validation of a Boolean network model can also come from testing the predicted existence of a yet unknown regulatory connection between two particular transcription factors that each are nodes of the model.

Continuous Networks

Continuous network models of GRNs are an extension of the boolean networks described above. Nodes still represent genes and connections between them regulatory influences on gene expression. Genes in biological systems display a continuous range of activity levels and it has been argued that using a continuous representation captures several properties of gene regulatory networks not present in the Boolean model. Formally most of these approaches are similar to an artificial neural network, as inputs to a node are summed up and the result serves as input to a sigmoid function, e.g., but proteins do often control gene expression in a synergistic, i.e. non-linear, way. However, there is now a continuous network model that allows grouping of inputs to a node thus realizing another level of regulation. This model is formally closer to a higher order recurrent neural network. The same model has also been used to mimic the evolution of cellular differentiation and even multicellular morphogenesis.

Stochastic Gene Networks

Recent experimental results have demonstrated that gene expression is a stochastic process. Thus, many authors are now using the stochastic formalism, after the work by. Works on single gene expression and small synthetic genetic networks, such as the genetic toggle switch of Tim Gardner and Jim Collins, provided additional experimental data on the phenotypic variability and the stochastic nature of gene expression. The first versions of stochastic models of gene expression involved only instantaneous reactions and were driven by the Gillespie algorithm.

Since some processes, such as gene transcription, involve many reactions and could not be correctly modeled as an instantaneous reaction in a single step, it was proposed to model these reactions as single step multiple delayed reactions in order to account for the time it takes for the entire process to be complete.

From here, a set of reactions were proposed that allow generating GRNs. These are then simulated using a modified version of the Gillespie algorithm, that can simulate multiple time delayed reactions (chemical reactions where each of the products is provided a time delay that determines when will it be released in the system as a "finished product").

For example, basic transcription of a gene can be represented by the following single-step reaction (RNAP is the RNA polymerase, RBS is the RNA ribosome binding site, and Pro_i is the promoter region of gene i):

$$\text{RNAP} + \text{Pro}_i \xrightarrow{k_{i,bas}} \text{Pro}_i(\tau_i^1) + \text{RBS}_i(\tau_i^1) + \text{RNAP}(\tau_i^2)$$

Furthermore, there seems to be a trade-off between the noise in gene expression, the speed with which genes can switch, and the metabolic cost associated their functioning. More specifically, for any given level of metabolic cost, there is an optimal trade-off between noise and processing speed and increasing the metabolic cost leads to better speed-noise trade-offs.

A recent work proposed a simulator (SGNSim, *Stochastic Gene Networks Simulator*), that can model GRNs where transcription and translation are modeled as multiple time delayed events and its dynamics is driven by a stochastic simulation algorithm (SSA) able to deal with multiple time delayed events. The time delays can be drawn from several distributions and the reaction rates from complex functions or from physical parameters. SGNSim can generate ensembles of GRNs within a set of user-defined parameters, such as topology. It can also be used to model specific GRNs and systems of chemical reactions. Genetic perturbations such as gene deletions, gene over-expression, insertions, frame shift mutations can also be modeled as well.

The GRN is created from a graph with the desired topology, imposing in-degree and out-degree distributions. Gene promoter activities are affected by other genes expression products that act as inputs, in the form of monomers or combined into multimers and set as direct or indirect. Next, each direct input is assigned to an operator site and different transcription factors can be allowed, or not, to compete for the same operator site, while indirect inputs are given a target. Finally, a function is assigned to each gene, defining the gene's response to a combination of transcription factors (promoter state). The transfer functions (that is, how genes respond to a combination of inputs) can be assigned to each combination of promoter states as desired.

In other recent work, multiscale models of gene regulatory networks have been developed that focus on synthetic biology applications. Simulations have been used that model all biomolecular interactions in transcription, translation, regulation, and induction of gene regulatory networks, guiding the design of synthetic systems.

Prediction

Other work has focused on predicting the gene expression levels in a gene regulatory network. The approaches used to model gene regulatory networks have been constrained to be interpretable and, as a result, are generally simplified versions of the network. For example, Boolean networks have been used due to their simplicity and ability to handle noisy data but lose data information by having a binary representation of the genes. Also, artificial neural networks omit using a hidden layer so that they can be interpreted, losing the ability to model higher order correlations in the data. Using a model that is not constrained to be interpretable, a more accurate model can be produced. Being able to predict gene expressions more accurately provides a way to explore how drugs affect a system of genes as well as for finding which genes are interrelated in a process. This has been encouraged by the DREAM competition which promotes a competition for the best prediction algorithms. Some other recent work has used artificial neural networks with a hidden layer.

Gene Co-expression Network

A gene co-expression network constructed from a microarray dataset containing gene expression profiles of 7221 genes for 18 gastric cancer patients

A gene co-expression network (GCN) is an undirected graph, where each node corresponds to a gene, and a pair of nodes is connected with an edge if there is a significant co-expresson relationship between them. Having gene expression profiles of a number of genes for several samples or experimental conditions, a gene co-expression network can be constructed by looking for pairs of genes which show a similar expression pattern across samples, since the transcript levels of two co-expressed genes rise and fall together across samples. Gene co-expression networks are of biological interest since co-expressed genes are controlled by the same transcriptional regulatory program, functionally related, or members of the same pathway or protein complex.

The direction and type of co-expression relationships are not determined in gene co-expression networks; whereas in a gene regulatory network (GRN) a directed edge connects two genes, representing a biochemical process such as a reaction, transformation, interaction, activation or inhibition. Compared to a GRN, a GCN does not attempt to infer the causality relationships between genes and in a GCN the edges represent only a correlation or dependency relationship among genes. Modules or the highly connected subgraphs in gene co-expression networks correspond to clusters of genes that have a similar function or involve in a common biological process which causes many interactions among themselves.

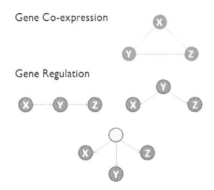

The direction of edges is overlooked in gene co-expression networks. While three genes X, Y and Z are found to be co-expressed, it is not determined whether X activates Y and Y activates Z, or Y activates X and Z, or another gene activates three of them.

Gene co-expression networks are usually constructed using datasets generated by high-throughput gene expression profiling technologies such as Microarray or RNA-Seq.

History

The concept of gene co-expression networks was first introduced by Butte and Kohane in 1999 as *relevance networks*. They gathered the measurement data of medical laboratory tests (e.g. hemoglobin level) for a number of patients and they calculated the Pearson correlation between the results for each pair of tests and the pairs of tests which showed a correlation higher than a certain level were connected in the network (e.g. insulin level with blood sugar). Bute and Kohane used this approach later with mutual information as the co-expression measure and using gene expression data for constructing the first gene co-expression network.

Constructing Gene Co-expression Networks

A good number of methods have been developed for constructing gene co-expression networks. In principle, they all follow a two step approach: calculating co-expression measure, and selecting significance threshold. In first step, a co-expression measure is selected and a similarity score is calculated for each pair of genes using this measure.

Then, a threshold is determined and gene pairs which have a similarity score higher than the selected threshold are considered to have significant co-expression relationship and are connected by an edge in the network.

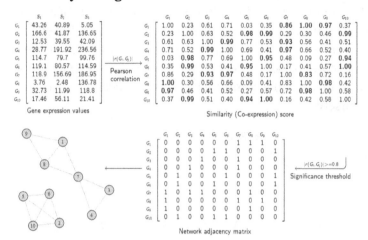

The two general steps for constructing a gene co-expression network: calculating co-expression score (e.g. the absolute value of Pearson correlation coefficient) for each pair of genes, and selecting a significance threshold (e.g. correlation > 0.8).

The input data for constructing a gene co-expression network is often represented as a matrix. If we have the gene expression values of m genes for n samples (conditions), the input data would be an $m{\times}n$ matrix, called expression matrix. For instance, in a microarray experiment the expression values of thousands of genes are measured for several samples. In first step, a similarity score (co-expression measure) is calculated between each pair of rows in expression matrix. The resulting matrix would be an $m{\times}m$ matrix, called similarity matrix. Each element in this matrix shows how similar the expression level of two genes change together. In second step, the elements in similarity matrix which are above a certain threshold (i.e. significant co-expressions) are replaced by 1 and the remaining elements are replaced by 0. The resulting matrix, called adjacency matrix, represents the graph of the constructed gene co-expression network. In this matrix, each element shows whether two genes are connected in the network (the 1 elements) or not (the 0 elements).

Co-expression Measure

The expression values of a gene for different samples can be represented as a vector, thus calculating the co-expression measure between a pair of genes is the same as calculating the selected measure for two vectors of numbers.

Pearson's correlation coefficient, Mutual Information, Spearman's rank correlation coefficient and Euclidean distance are the four mostly used co-expression measures for constructing gene co-expression networks. Euclidean distance measures the geometric distance between two vectors, and so considers both the direction and the magnitude of the vectors of gene expression values. Mutual information measures how much knowing the expression levels of one gene reduces the uncertainty about the expression levels of another. Pearson's correlation coefficient measures the tendency of two vectors to increase or decrease together, giving a measure of their overall correspondence. Spearman's rank correlation is the Pearson's correlation calculated for the ranks of gene expression values in a gene expression vector. Several other measures such as partial correlation, regression, and combination of partial correlation and mutual information have also been used.

Each of these measures have their own advantages and disadvantages. The Euclidean distance is not appropriate when the absolute levels of functionally related genes are highly different. Furthermore, if two genes have consistently low expression levels but are otherwise randomly correlated, they might still appear close in Euclidean space. One advantage to mutual information is that it can detect non-linear relationships; however this can turn into a disadvantage because of detecting sophisticated non-linear relationships which does not look biologically meaningful. In addition, for calculating mutual information one should estimate the distribution of the data which needs a large number of samples for a good estimate. Spearman's rank correlation coefficient is more robust to outliers, but on the other hand it is less sensitive to expression values and in datasets with small number of samples may detect many false positives.

Pearson's correlation coefficient is the most popular co-expression measure used in constructing gene co-expression networks. The Pearson's correlation coefficient takes a value between -1 and 1 where absolute values close to 1 show strong correlation. The positive values correspond to an activation mechanism where the expression of one gene increases with the increase in the expression of its co-expressed gene and vice versa. When the expression value of one gene decreases with the increase in the expression of its co-expressed gene, it corresponds to an underlying suppression mechanism and would have a negative correlation.

There are two disadvantages for Pearson correlation measure: it can only detect linear relationships and it is sensitive to outliers. Moreover, Pearson correlation assumes that the gene expression data follow a normal distribution. Song et al. have suggested *biweight midcorrelation (bicor)* as a good alternative for Pearson's correlation. "Bicor is a median based correlation measure, and is more robust than the Pearson correlation but often more powerful than the Spearman's correlation". Furthermore, it has been shown that "most gene pairs satisfy linear or monotonic relationships" which indicates that "mutual information networks can safely be replaced by correlation networks when it comes to measuring co-expression relationships in stationary data".

Threshold Selection

Several methods have been used for selecting a threshold in constructing gene co-expression networks. A simple thresholding method is to choose a co-expression cutoff and select relationships which their co-expression exceeds this cutoff. Another approach is to use Fisher's Z-transformation which calculates a z-score for each correlation based on the number of samples. This z-score is then converted into a p-value for each correlation and a cutoff is set on the p-value. Some methods permute the data and calculate a z-score using the distribution of correlations found between genes in permuted dataset. Some other approaches have also been used such as threshold selection based on clustering coefficient or random matrix theory.

The problem with p-value based methods is that the final cutoff on the p-value is chosen based on statistical routines(e.g. a p-value of 0.01 or 0.05 is considered significant), not based on a biological insight.

WGCNA is a framework for constructing and analyzing weighted gene co-expression networks. The WGCNA method selects the threshold for constructing the network based on the scale-free topology of gene co-expression networks. This method constructs the network for several thresholds and selects the threshold which leads to a network with scale-free topology. Moreover, the WGCNA method constructs a weighted network which means all possible edges appear in the network, but each edge has a weight which shows how significant is the co-expression relationship corresponding to that edge.

Metabolic Network

A metabolic network is the complete set of metabolic and physical processes that determine the physiological and biochemical properties of a cell. As such, these networks comprise the chemical reactions of metabolism, the metabolic pathways, as well as the regulatory interactions that guide these reactions.

With the sequencing of complete genomes, it is now possible to reconstruct the network of biochemical reactions in many organisms, from bacteria to human. Several of these networks are available online: Kyoto Encyclopedia of Genes and Genomes (KEGG), EcoCyc , BioCyc and metaTIGER . Metabolic networks are powerful tools for studying and modelling metabolism.

Cell Signaling

Cell signaling (cell signalling in British English) is part of a complex system of communication that governs basic activities of cells and coordinates cell actions. The ability of cells to perceive and correctly respond to their microenvironment is the basis of development, tissue repair, and immunity as well as normal tissue homeostasis. Errors in cellular information processing are responsible for diseases such as cancer, autoimmunity, and diabetes. By understanding cell signaling, diseases may be treated more effectively and, theoretically, artificial tissues may be created.

Traditional work in biology has focused on studying individual parts of cell signaling pathways. Systems biology research helps us to understand the underlying structure of cell signaling networks and how changes in these networks may affect the transmission and flow of information (signal transduction). Such networks are complex systems in their organization and may exhibit a number of emergent properties including bistability and ultrasensitivity. Analysis of cell signaling networks requires a combination of experimental and theoretical approaches including the development and analysis of simulations and modeling. Long-range allostery is often a significant component of cell signaling events.

Signaling between Cells of One Organism and Multiple Organisms

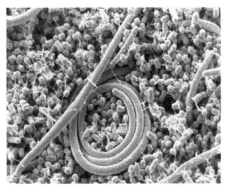

Example of signaling between bacteria. *Salmonella enteritidis* uses
N-Acyl homoserine lactone for Quorum sensing

Cell signaling has been most extensively studied in the context of human diseases and signaling between cells of a single organism. However, cell signaling may also occur between the cells of two different organisms. In many mammals, early embryo cells exchange signals with cells of the uterus. In the human gastrointestinal tract, bacteria exchange signals with each other and with human epithelial and immune system cells. For the yeast *Saccharomyces cerevisiae* during mating, some cells send a peptide signal (mating factor pheromones) into their environment. The mating factor peptide may bind to a cell surface receptor on other yeast cells and induce them to prepare for mating.

Classification

Cell signaling can be classified to be mechanical and biochemical based on the type of the signal. Mechanical signals are the forces exerted on the cell and the forces produced by the cell. These forces can both be sensed and responded by the cells. Biochemical signals are the biochemical molecules such as proteins, lipids, ions and gases. These signals can be categorized based on the distance between signaling and responder cells.

Signaling within, between, and among cells is subdivided into the following classifications:

- *Intracrine* signals are produced by the target cell that stay within the target cell.

- *Autocrine* signals are produced by the target cell, are secreted, and affect the target cell itself via receptors. Sometimes autocrine cells can target cells close by if they are the same type of cell as the emitting cell. An example of this are immune cells.

- *Juxtacrine* signals target adjacent (touching) cells. These signals are transmitted along cell membranes via protein or lipid components integral to the membrane and are capable of affecting either the emitting cell or cells immediately adjacent.

- *Paracrine* signals target cells in the vicinity of the emitting cell. Neurotransmitters represent an example.

- *Endocrine* signals target distant cells. Endocrine cells produce hormones that travel through the blood to reach all parts of the body.

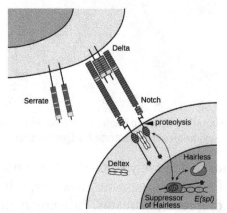

Notch-mediated juxtacrine signal between adjacent cells.

Cells communicate with each other via direct contact (juxtacrine signaling), over short distances (paracrine signaling), or over large distances and/or scales (endocrine signaling).

Some cell–cell communication requires direct cell–cell contact. Some cells can form gap junctions that connect their cytoplasm to the cytoplasm of adjacent cells. In cardiac muscle, gap junctions between adjacent cells allows for action potential propagation from the cardiac pacemaker region of the heart to spread and coordinately cause contraction of the heart.

The notch signaling mechanism is an example of juxtacrine signaling (also known as contact-dependent signaling) in which two adjacent cells must make physical contact in order to communicate. This requirement for direct contact allows for very precise control of cell differentiation during embryonic development. In the worm *Caenorhab-ditis elegans*, two cells of the developing gonad each have an equal chance of terminally differentiating or becoming a uterine precursor cell that continues to divide. The choice of which cell continues to divide is controlled by competition of cell surface signals. One cell will happen to produce more of a cell surface protein that activates the Notch receptor on the adjacent cell. This activates a feedback loop or system that reduces Notch expression in the cell that will differentiate and that increases Notch on the surface of the cell that continues as a stem cell.

Many cell signals are carried by molecules that are released by one cell and move to make contact with another cell. *Endocrine* signals are called hormones. Hormones are produced by endocrine cells and they travel through the blood to reach all parts of the body. Specificity of signaling can be controlled if only some cells can respond to a particular hormone. *Paracrine* signals such as retinoic acid target only cells in the vicinity of the emitting cell. Neurotransmitters represent another example of a paracrine signal. Some signaling molecules can function as both a hormone and a neurotransmitter. For example, epinephrine and norepinephrine can function as hormones when released from the adrenal gland and are transported to the heart by way of the blood stream. Norepinephrine can also be produced by neurons to function as a neurotransmitter within the brain. Estrogen can be released by the ovary and function as a hormone or act locally via paracrine or autocrine signaling. Active species of oxygen and nitric oxide can also act as cellular messengers. This process is dubbed redox signaling.

Cell Signaling in Multicellular Organisms

In a multicellular organism, signaling between cells occurs either through release into the extracellular space, divided in paracrine signaling (over short distances) and endocrine signaling (over long distances), or by direct contact, known as juxtacrine signaling. Autocrine signaling is a special case of paracrine signaling where the secreting cell has the ability to respond to the secreted signaling molecule. Synaptic signaling is a special case of paracrine signaling (for chemical synapses) or juxtacrine signaling (for electrical synapses) between neurons and target cells. Signaling molecules interact with a target cell as a ligand to cell surface receptors, and/or by entering into the cell through its membrane or endocytosis for intracrine signaling. This generally results in the activation of second messengers, leading to various physiological effects.

A particular molecule is generally used in diverse modes of signaling, and therefore a classification by mode of signaling is not possible. At least three important classes of signaling molecules are widely recognized, although non-exhaustive and with imprecise boundaries, as such membership is non-exclusive and depends on the context:

- Hormones are the major signaling molecules of the endocrine system, though they often regulate each other's secretion via local signaling (e.g. islet of Langerhans cells), and most are also expressed in tissues for local purposes (e.g.

angiotensin) or failing that, structurally related molecules are (e.g. PTHrP).

- Neurotransmitters are signaling molecules of the nervous system, also including neuropeptides and neuromodulators. Neurotransmitters like the catechol-
  amines are also secreted by the endocrine system into the systemic circulation.

- Cytokines are signaling molecules of the immune system, with a primary paracrine or juxtacrine role, though they can during significant immune responses
  have a strong presence in the circulation, with systemic effect (altering iron metabolism or body temperature). Growth factors can be considered as cytokines
  or a different class.

Signaling molecules can belong to several chemical classes: lipids, phospholipids, amino acids, monoamines, proteins, glycoproteins, or gases. Signaling molecules binding
surface receptors are generally large and hydrophilic (e.g. TRH, Vasopressin, Acetylcholine), while those entering the cell are generally small and hydrophobic (e.g. gluco-
corticoids, thyroid hormones, cholecalciferol, retinoic acid), but important exceptions
to both are numerous, and a same molecule can act both via surface receptor or in an
intracrine manner to different effects. In intracrine signaling, once inside the cell, a
signaling molecule can bind to intracellular receptors, other elements, or stimulate enzyme activity (e.g. gasses). The intracrine action of peptide hormones remains a subject
of debate.

Hydrogen sulfide is produced in small amounts by some cells of the human body and
has a number of biological signaling functions. Only two other such gases are currently
known to act as signaling molecules in the human body: nitric oxide and carbon mon-
oxide.

Receptors for Cell Motility and Differentiation

Cells receive information from their neighbors through a class of proteins known as
receptors. Notch is a cell surface protein that functions as a receptor. Animals have a
small set of genes that code for signaling proteins that interact specifically with Notch
receptors and stimulate a response in cells that express Notch on their surface. Molecules that activate (or, in some cases, inhibit) receptors can be classified as hormones,
neurotransmitters, cytokines, and growth factors, in general called receptor ligands.
Ligand receptor interactions such as that of the Notch receptor interaction, are known
to be main interactions responsible for cell signaling mechanisms and communication.

As shown in Figure (above; left), notch acts as a receptor for ligands that are expressed
on adjacent cells. While some receptors are cell surface proteins, others are found inside cells. For example, estrogen is a hydrophobic molecule that can pass through the
lipid bilayer of the membranes. As part of the endocrine system, intracellular estrogen
receptors from a variety of cell types can be activated by estrogen produced in the ova-
ries.

A number of transmembrane receptors for small molecules and peptide hormones as well as intracellular receptors for steroid hormones exist, giving cells the ability to respond to a great number of hormonal and pharmacological stimuli. In diseases, often, proteins that interact with receptors are aberrantly activated, resulting in constitutively activated downstream signals.

For several types of intercellular signaling molecules that are unable to permeate the hydrophobic cell membrane due to their hydrophilic nature, the target receptor is expressed on the membrane. When such signaling molecule activates its receptor, the signal is carried into the cell usually by means of a second messenger such as cAMP.

Signaling pathways

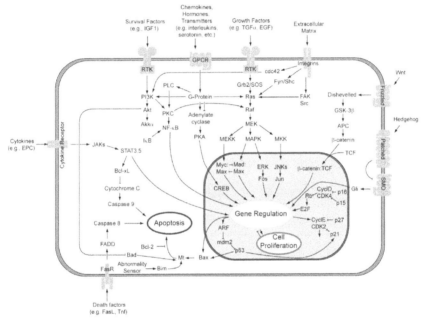

Overview of signal transduction pathways.

In some cases, receptor activation caused by ligand binding to a receptor is directly coupled to the cell's response to the ligand. For example, the neurotransmitter GABA can activate a cell surface receptor that is part of an ion channel. GABA binding to a $GABA_A$ receptor on a neuron opens a chloride-selective ion channel that is part of the receptor. $GABA_A$ receptor activation allows negatively charged chloride ions to move into the neuron, which inhibits the ability of the neuron to produce action potentials. However, for many cell surface receptors, ligand-receptor interactions are not directly linked to the cell's response. The activated receptor must first interact with other proteins inside the cell before the ultimate physiological effect of the ligand on the cell's behavior is produced. Often, the behavior of a chain of several interacting cell proteins is altered following receptor activation. The entire set of cell changes induced by receptor activation is called a signal transduction mechanism or pathway.

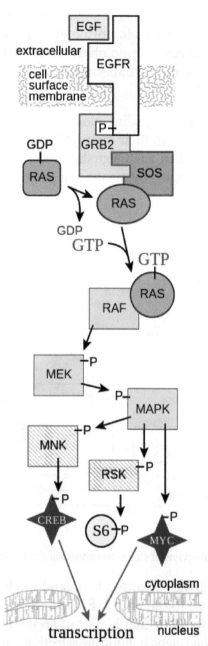

Diagram showing key components of a signal transduction pathway.

In the case of Notch-mediated signaling, the signal transduction mechanism can be relatively simple. As shown in Figure (above), activation of Notch can cause the Notch protein to be altered by a protease. Part of the Notch protein is released from the cell surface membrane and takes part in gene regulation. Cell signaling research involves studying the spatial and temporal dynamics of both receptors and the components of signaling pathways that are activated by receptors in various cell types.

A more complex signal transduction pathway is shown in Figure 3. This pathway involves changes of protein–protein interactions inside the cell, induced by an external signal. Many growth factors bind to receptors at the cell surface and stimulate cells to progress through the cell cycle and divide. Several of these receptors are kinases that start to phosphorylate themselves and other proteins when binding to a ligand. This phosphorylation can generate a binding site for a different protein and thus induce protein–protein interaction. In Figure 3, the ligand (called epidermal growth factor (EGF)) binds to the receptor (called EGFR). This activates the receptor to phosphorylate itself. The phosphorylated receptor binds to an adaptor protein (GRB2), which couples the signal to further downstream signaling processes. For example, one of the signal transduction pathways that are activated is called the mitogen-activated protein kinase (MAPK) pathway. The signal transduction component labeled as "MAPK" in the pathway was originally called "ERK," so the pathway is called the MAPK/ERK pathway. The MAPK protein is an enzyme, a protein kinase that can attach phosphate to target proteins such as the transcription factor MYC and, thus, alter gene transcription and, ultimately, cell cycle progression. Many cellular proteins are activated downstream of the growth factor receptors (such as EGFR) that initiate this signal transduction pathway.

Some signaling transduction pathways respond differently, depending on the amount of signaling received by the cell. For instance, the hedgehog protein activates different genes, depending on the amount of hedgehog protein present.

Complex multi-component signal transduction pathways provide opportunities for feedback, signal amplification, and interactions inside one cell between multiple signals and signaling pathways.

Intraspecies and Interspecies Signaling

Molecular signaling can occur between different organisms, whether unicellular or multicellular, the emitting organism produces the signaling molecule, secrete it into the environment, where it diffuses, and it is sensed or internalized by the receiving organism. In some cases of interspecies signaling, the emitting organism can actually be a host of the receiving organism, or vice versa.

Intraspecies signaling occurs especially in bacteria, yeast, social insects, but also many vertebrates. The signaling molecules used by multicellular organisms are often called pheromones, they can have such purposes as alerting against danger, indicating food supply, or assisting in reproduction. In unicellular organisms such as bacteria, signaling can be used to 'activate' peers from a dormant state, enhance virulence, defend against bacteriophages, etc. In quorum sensing, which is also found in social insects, the multiplicity of individual signals has the potentiality to create a positive feedback loop, generating coordinated response, in this context the signaling molecules are called autoinducers. This signaling mechanism may have been involved in evolution from unicellular to multicellular organisms. Bacteria also use contact-dependent signaling, notably to limit their growth.

Molecular signaling can also occur between individuals of different species, this has been particularly studied in bacteria. Different bacterial species can coordinate to colonize a host and participate in common quorum sensing. Therapeutic strategies to disrupt this phenomenon are being investigated. Interactions mediated through signaling molecules are also thought to occur between the gut flora and their host, as part of their commensal or symbiotic relationship. Gram negative microbes deploy bacterial outer membrane vesicles for intra- and inter-species signaling in natural environments and at the host-pathogen interface.

Additionally, interspecies signaling occurs between multicellular organisms. In *Vespa mandarinia*, individuals release a scent that directs the colony to a food source.

Biological Neural Network

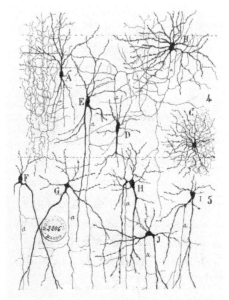

From "Texture of the Nervous System of Man and the Vertebrates" by Santiago Ramón y Cajal. The figure illustrates the diversity of neuronal morphologies in the auditory cortex.

In neuroscience, a biological neural network (sometimes called a neural pathway) is a series of interconnected neurons whose activation defines a recognizable linear pathway. The interface through which neurons interact with their neighbors usually consists of several axon terminals connected via synapses to dendrites on other neurons. If the sum of the input signals into one neuron surpasses a certain threshold, the neuron sends an action potential (AP) at the axon hillock and transmits this electrical signal along the axon.

In contrast, a neural circuit is a functional entity of interconnected neurons that is able to regulate its own activity using a feedback loop (similar to a control loop in cybernetics).

Biological neural networks have inspired the design of artificial neural networks.

Early Study

Early treatments of neural networks can be found in Herbert Spencer's *Principles of Psychology*, 3rd edition (1872), Theodor Meynert's *Psychiatry* (1884), William James' *Principles of Psychology* (1890), and Sigmund Freud's Project for a Scientific Psychology (composed 1895). The first rule of neuronal learning was described by Hebb in 1949, Hebbian learning. Thus, Hebbian pairing of pre-synaptic and post-synaptic activity can substantially alter the dynamic characteristics of the synaptic connection and therefore facilitate or inhibit signal transmission. The neuroscientists Warren Sturgis McCulloch and Walter Pitts published the first works on the processing of neural networks. They showed theoretically that networks of artificial neurons could implement logical, arithmetic, and symbolic functions. Simplified models of biological neurons were set up, now usually called perceptrons or artificial neurons. These simple models accounted for neural summation (i.e., potentials at the post-synaptic membrane will summate in the cell body). Later models also provided for excitatory and inhibitory synaptic transmission.

Connections Between Neurons

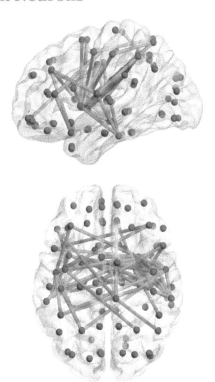

An example of a neural network in a human brain

The connections between neurons are much more complex than those implemented in neural computing architectures. The basic kinds of connections between neurons are chemical synapses and electrical gap junctions. One principle by which neurons work is neural summation, i.e. potentials at the post synaptic membrane will sum up in the cell body. If the depolarization of the neuron at the axon goes above threshold an action potential will occur that travels down the axon to the terminal endings to transmit a signal to other neurons. Excitatory and inhibitory synaptic transmission is realized mostly by inhibitory postsynaptic potentials and excitatory postsynaptic potentials.

On the electrophysiological level, there are various phenomena which alter the response characteristics of individual synapses (called synaptic plasticity) and individual neurons (intrinsic plasticity). These are often divided into short-term plasticity and long-term plasticity. Long-term synaptic plasticity is often contended to be the most likely memory substrate. Usually the term "neuroplasticity" refers to changes in the brain that are caused by activity or experience.

Connections display temporal and spatial characteristics. Temporal characteristics refer to the continuously modified activity-dependent efficacy of synaptic transmission, called spike-dependent synaptic plasticity. It has been observed in several studies that the synaptic efficacy of this transmission can undergo short-term increase (called facilitation) or decrease (depression) according to the activity of the presynaptic neuron. The induction of long-term changes in synaptic efficacy, by long-term potentiation (LTP) or depression (LTD), depends strongly on the relative timing of the onset of the excitatory postsynaptic potential and the postsynaptic action potential. LTP is induced by a series of action potentials which cause a variety of biochemical responses. Eventually, the reactions cause the expression of new receptors on the cellular membranes of the postsynaptic neurons or increase the efficacy of the existing receptors through phosphorylation.

Backpropagating action potentials cannot occur because after an action potential travels down a given segment of the axon, the voltage gated sodium channels' (Na+ channels) m gate becomes closed, thus blocking any transient opening of the h gate from causing a change in the intracellular [Na+], and preventing the generation of an action potential back towards the cell body. In some cells, however, neural backpropagation does occur through the dendritic arbor and may have important effects on synaptic plasticity and computation.

A neuron in the brain requires a single signal to a neuromuscular junction to stimulate contraction of the postsynaptic muscle cell. In the spinal cord, however, at least 75 afferent neurons are required to produce firing. This picture is further complicated by variation in time constant between neurons, as some cells can experience their EPSPs over a wider period of time than others.

While in synapses in the developing brain synaptic depression has been particularly widely observed it has been speculated that it changes to facilitation in adult brains.

Representations in Neural Networks

A receptive field is a small region within the entire visual field. Any given neuron only responds to a subset of stimuli within its receptive field. This property is called tuning. As for vision, in the earlier visual areas, neurons have simpler tuning. For example, a neuron in V1 may fire to any vertical stimulus in its receptive field. In the higher visual areas, neurons have complex tuning. For example, in the fusiform gyrus, a neuron may only fire when a certain face appears in its receptive field. It is also known that many parts of the brain generate spatiotemporal patterns of electrical activity that spatially correspond closely to the layout of the retinal image (this is known as retinotopy). It seems further that imagery that originates from the senses and internally generated imagery may have a shared ontology at higher levels of cortical processing. About many parts of the brain some characterization has been made as to what tasks are correlated with its activity.

In the brain, memories are very likely represented by patterns of activation amongst networks of neurons. However, how these representations are formed, retrieved and reach conscious awareness is not completely understood. Cognitive processes that characterize human intelligence are mainly ascribed to the emergent properties of complex dynamic characteristics in the complex systems that constitute neural networks. Therefore, the study and modeling of these networks have attracted broad interest under different paradigms and many different theories have been formulated to explain various aspects of their behavior. One of these—and the subject of several theories—is considered a special property of a neural network: the ability to learn complex patterns.

Philosophical Issues

Today most researchers believe in mental representations of some kind (representationalism) or, more general, in particular mental states (cognitivism). For instance, perception can be viewed as information processing through transfer information from the world into the brain/mind where it is further processed and related to other information (cognitive processes). Few others envisage a direct path back into the external world in the form of action (radical behaviorism).

Another issue, called the binding problem, relates to the question of how the activity of more or less distinct populations of neurons dealing with different aspects of perception are combined to form a unified perceptual experience and have qualia.

Neuronal networks are not full reconstructions of any cognitive system found in the human brain, and are therefore unlikely to form a complete representation of human perception. Some researchers argue that human perception must be studied as a whole; hence, the system cannot be taken apart and studied without destroying its original functionality. Furthermore, there is evidence that cognition is gained through a well-orchestrated barrage of sub-threshold synaptic activity throughout the network.

Study Methods

Different neuroimaging techniques have been developed to investigate the activity of neural networks. The use of "brain scanners" or functional neuroimaging to investigate the structure or function of the brain is common, either as simply a way of better assessing brain injury with high resolution pictures, or by examining the relative activations of different brain areas. Such technologies may include fMRI (functional magnetic resonance imaging), PET (positron emission tomography) and CAT (computed axial tomography). Functional neuroimaging uses specific brain imaging technologies to take scans from the brain, usually when a person is doing a particular task, in an attempt to understand how the activation of particular brain areas is related to the task. In functional neuroimaging, especially fMRI, which measures hemodynamic activity that is closely linked to neural activity, PET, and electroencephalography (EEG) is used.

Connectionist models serve as a test platform for different hypotheses of representation, information processing, and signal transmission. Lesioning studies in such models, e.g. artificial neural networks, where parts of the nodes are deliberately destroyed to see how the network performs, can also yield important insights in the working of several cell assemblies. Similarly, simulations of dysfunctional neurotransmitters in neurological conditions (e.g., dopamine in the basal ganglia of Parkinson's patients) can yield insights into the underlying mechanisms for patterns of cognitive deficits observed in the particular patient group. Predictions from these models can be tested in patients or via pharmacological manipulations, and these studies can in turn be used to inform the models, making the process iterative.

References

- Hausman, Geoffrey M. Cooper, Robert E. (2000). "Signaling Molecules and Their Receptors". In NCBI bookshelf. The cell : a molecular approach (2nd ed.). Washington, D.C.: ASM Press. ISBN 087893300X.

- Gilbert, Scott F. (2000). "Juxtacrine Signaling". In NCBI bookshelf. Developmental biology (6. ed.). Sunderland, Mass.: Sinauer Assoc. ISBN 0878932437.

- Bruce Alberts; et al. (2002). "General Principles of Cell Communication". In NCBI bookshelf. Molecular biology of the cell (4th ed.). New York: Garland Science. ISBN 0815332181.

- Bolouri, Hamid; Bower, James M. (2001). Computational modeling of genetic and biochemical networks. Cambridge, Mass: MIT Press. ISBN 0-262-02481-0

- Han, Y.-C. et al. Prediction and characterization of protein–protein interaction network in Bacillus licheniformis WX-02. Sci. Rep. 6, 19486; doi: 10.1038/srep19486 (2016).

- Han Y, Niu J, Wang D, Li Y (2016) Hepatitis C Virus Protein Interaction Network Analysis Based on Hepatocellular Carcinoma. PLoS ONE 11(4): e0153882. doi:10.1371/journal.pone.0153882

- Osterman A, Stellberger T, Gebhardt A, Kurz M, Friedel CC, Uetz P, Nitschko H, Baiker A, Vizoso-Pinto MG (2015). "The Hepatitis E virus intraviral interactome". Sci Rep. 5: 13872. doi:10.1038/srep13872. PMC 4604457. PMID 26463011.

- Vo, T.V.; et al. (2016). "A Proteome-wide Fission Yeast Interactome Reveals Network Evolution

Principles from Yeasts to Human". Cell. 164 (1–2): 310–323. doi:10.1016/j.cell.2015.11.037. PMC 4715267. PMID 26771498.

- "Dynamic aberrant NF-κB spurs tumorigenesis: A new model encompassing the microenvironment". Cytokine Growth Factor Rev. 26: 389–403. Aug 2015. doi:10.1016/j.cytogfr.2015.06.001. PMID 26119834.

- Hagen, N; Bayer, K; Roesch, K; Schindler, M (2014). "The intra viral protein interaction network of hepatitis C virus". Molecular & Cellular Proteomics. 13 (7): 1676–89. doi:10.1074/mcp.M113.036301. PMID 24797426.

- Wang, K; Grivennikov, SI; Karin, M (2013). "Implications of anti-cytokine therapy in colorectal cancer and autoimmune diseases". Ann. Rheum. Dis. 72 Suppl 2: ii100–3. doi:10.1136/annrheumdis-2012-202201. PMID 23253923.

Permissions

All chapters in this book are published with permission under the Creative Commons Attribution Share Alike License or equivalent. Every chapter published in this book has been scrutinized by our experts. Their significance has been extensively debated. The topics covered herein carry significant information for a comprehensive understanding. They may even be implemented as practical applications or may be referred to as a beginning point for further studies.

We would like to thank the editorial team for lending their expertise to make the book truly unique. They have played a crucial role in the development of this book. Without their invaluable contributions this book wouldn't have been possible. They have made vital efforts to compile up to date information on the varied aspects of this subject to make this book a valuable addition to the collection of many professionals and students.

This book was conceptualized with the vision of imparting up-to-date and integrated information in this field. To ensure the same, a matchless editorial board was set up. Every individual on the board went through rigorous rounds of assessment to prove their worth. After which they invested a large part of their time researching and compiling the most relevant data for our readers.

The editorial board has been involved in producing this book since its inception. They have spent rigorous hours researching and exploring the diverse topics which have resulted in the successful publishing of this book. They have passed on their knowledge of decades through this book. To expedite this challenging task, the publisher supported the team at every step. A small team of assistant editors was also appointed to further simplify the editing procedure and attain best results for the readers.

Apart from the editorial board, the designing team has also invested a significant amount of their time in understanding the subject and creating the most relevant covers. They scrutinized every image to scout for the most suitable representation of the subject and create an appropriate cover for the book.

The publishing team has been an ardent support to the editorial, designing and production team. Their endless efforts to recruit the best for this project, has resulted in the accomplishment of this book. They are a veteran in the field of academics and their pool of knowledge is as vast as their experience in printing. Their expertise and guidance has proved useful at every step. Their uncompromising quality standards have made this book an exceptional effort. Their encouragement from time to time has been an inspiration for everyone.

The publisher and the editorial board hope that this book will prove to be a valuable piece of knowledge for students, practitioners and scholars across the globe.

Index

www.ingramcontent.com/pod-product-compliance
Lightning Source LLC
Jackson TN
JSHW052152130125
77033JS00004B/174